SLOVENIA AND THE SLOVENES

JAMES GOW
CATHIE CARMICHAEL

Slovenia
and the
Slovenes

*A Small State and
the New Europe*

HURST & COMPANY, LONDON

First published in the United Kingdom by
C. Hurst & Co. (Publishers) Ltd.,
38 King Street, London WC2E 8JZ
© James Gow and Cathie Carmichael, 2000
All rights reserved.
Printed in England

ISBNs
1-85065-387-9 (casebound)
1-85065-428-X (paperback)

CONTENTS

PREFACE AND ACKNOWLEDGEMENTS

This book had a long gestation. We first met somewhere in 1987, or 1988. Our paths crossed in two directions. One was through John Allcock at the University of Bradford who introduced us to each other. The other was mutual inquisitiveness to discover who, if not we, had received the British Council Scholarship to study at the University of Ljubljana, in 1988 for which we had both applied, but neither was successful. If we knew, that information has now turned to dust. Our different interests in south-eastern Europe and, especially, our somewhat peculiar interest in matters Slovenian, including our courage in attempting to come to terms with the Slovene language, led us to maintain common ground. It was not until some point after the break-up of the old Yugoslav federation and Slovenia's independence that the possibility of writing a book on what was then completely virgin territory was raised. It then became an idea that, at various stages, one or the other of us was less inclined to pursue. Although there were moments when the point of writing a book on Slovenia was clear, our winding route to the present manuscript was peppered with significant other activity and considerable fluctuation over what the book should be. Like the weather people, it seemed that when one of us favoured a straightforward thread, the other preferred something more thematic — and then vice versa, more than once. The manuscript was completed in the spring of 1999, in Washington DC, where James was a Public Policy Scholar at the Woodrow Wilson Center for International Scholars in Washington DC, beginning a period of sabbatical. The exceptional facilities and kindness of the Wilson Center facilitated this work and also provided the chance for Cathie to spend one crucial week of very long hours working together with James on the manuscript.

The book's long genesis was concluded with an eventual commitment in 1998 to complete the book in the present format. This clearly represents the more thematic approach to our topic. But, it is a thematic approach that goes beyond those we had contemplated previously. The problem was always to find a way that would introduce a small people and their new place in the world through a broad analysis of that which was Slovenian, without appearing either to diminish history and culture, or falsely to present it as though things had ever been the way they are and Slovenia had not only gained independent international status in the 1990s. In a sense, this was a reflection of the problem that Slovenia and the Slovenes faced in blending tradition and culture with modernity and prosperity. We firmly hope that we have met this challenge in our treatment. Certainly, this was a most satisfying approach, forcing us to explore some aspects of our subject that we might have otherwise ignored.

Along the way, we have not only endured each other, our whims, alternative engagements and perspectives, and personal difficulties, but have met and benefited from the time, help, knowledge, wisdom, assistance – and more – of a multitude of friends, colleagues and contacts. It seems as though almost everyone with whom we have had contact since our interest in Slovenia was born has contributed in some way to this volume, although responsibility for its content, especially for any failings, rests with us. It is sad, but almost certain, that in the long list below of those to whom our gratitude is owed, we might well have forgotten someone. To whomever this might be, we extend humble apologies and thank you for your part in our finally achieving this book. Regarding the others, it is almost invidious to single out individuals for special mention, but in two cases it would be even more heinous not to do so. One of us has been supported through friendship, intellectual engagement and a frontierman spirit by Janez Damjan over this whole period. The other one has constantly benefited from the scholarship, guidance and encouragement of Peter Vodopivec, whose work on Slovenia is unmatchable.

To have indentified these two individuals is in no way to reduce our gratitude to others. For the record, we acknowledge our various debts of various kinds to the following, in no designated order: Metka Čuk, Glenda Sluga, Ljuba Črnivec, Miha Bregant, John Allcock, John Horton, Martyn Rady, Marko Milivojević, Peter, Maja, Barbara and Nina Vodopivec, Janez Šumrada, Rajko Muršič, Bojan Baskar, Borut Brumen, Mojca Ramšak, Zmago Šmitek, Patrick Carmichael, Gerry Stone, Dunja Rihtman-Auguštin, Mark Thompson, Sanja Malbaša, Nebojša Čagorović, M.A Nationalism students at Middlesex, Andy Wood, Norah Carlin,

Mary Trimble, Stephen Barbour, Irena Watton, Rada Lečić, Chris
Szejnmann, Božo Jezernik, Mark Wheeler, Wendy Bracewell,
Celia Hawkesworth, Nick Oliver, Deryn Verity, Sara Sežun, Saša
Pajević, Rada Stojanović, Chiara Cuneo, the late Ernest Gellner,
Pam Ballinger, Elke Kappus, Aleks Zobec, Cathy Derow, Linda
Wild, Trevor Shaw, Karl Stühlpfarrer, Aleks Kalc, Ženja Leiler,
Irena Hlede, Alenka Jensterle, Tatjana Ličen, Radivoj Podbršek,
Stane Mačgon, Marjan Malešič, Anton Grizold, Anton Bebler,
Jelko Kacin, Janez Janša, Chris Cviić, Dora and Karl Lavrenčič,
Božo Cerar, Mirko Cigler, Matjaž Šinkovec, Jože Pirjevec, Renata
Salecl, Alexei Monroe, George Schöpflin, Keith Miles, Joanna
Hanson, Cornelia Sorabji, Matthew Rycroft, Carole Birch, Vicky
Abel, Blaž Zgaga, Jurij Rifelj, Bob Ponichtera, Marty Sletzinger,
John Lampe, Sam Wells, Denny and Mary Rusinow, all at GRAL,
and the late Duška Primožič.

Work of this kind requires opportunity and opportunity requires
funding. We are therefore glad to ackowledge the benefit to this
work of financial support from our respective institutions, King's
College London and Middlesex University, including the provision
of sabbatical leave, the Woodrow Wilson Center for International
Scholars in Washington, DC, the PHARE Democracy Programme
of the EC, the Republic of Slovenia Ministry of Defence and the
Defence Research Centre at the University of Ljubljana, the British
Council, the Republic of Slovenia Ministry of Science and Technology and the Philosophy Faculty of the University of Ljubljana,
and the Central Research Fund of the University of London.

Finally, we owe personal thanks. From James these go to Janez,
Duška, Peter, Dušica, June and Donald. From Cathie they go
to Win, David, Una, John, Christina and Igor for putting up
with her, as well as to her late grandmother, Vera, for giving
her a home while carrying out research at the John Rylands
Library, Manchester. At the very end of this very long list there
remains one more person for both of us to thank — Milena, who
not only manages to cope with James on a permanent basis, but
was a mainstay of support, encouragement and mediation as she
put up with both of us at various stages througout and in DC,
especially, at the end.

Summer 2000 J. G.
C. C.

NOTE ON LANGUAGE

The Slovenian regions of Koroška and Štajerska have accepted English versions as Carinthia and Styria. In this volume we have used both English and Slovene versions, depending on context. For example, in contemporary security policy use of the English versions would seem anachronistic. Conversely, in some of the historical and cultural parts of the book, where there is a body of literature that conventionally uses the English versions, it would seem unhelpful to insist on the original Slovene usage. We therefore alert the reader to this practice and to the fact that Koroška and Carinthia are the same place, and that the same applies to Štajerska and Styria. We have also adopted an English-language standard for the use of capitals, so that some words which might be written purely in lower-case in Slovene have been presented as they would be in English.

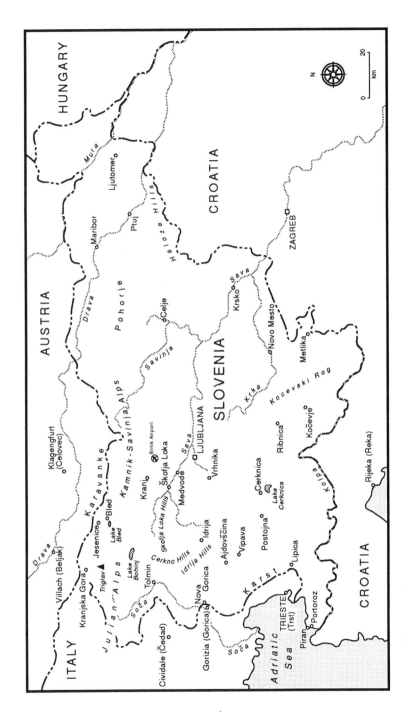

1

INTRODUCTION

Slovenia is a small, new state that has to adapt itself to meet the challenges of the 'New Europe' at the close of the 1990s. In the space of ten years it came from being part of a federal communist state, Yugoslavia, that fostered its statehood before dissolving, to the brink of joining the European Union. While it has had an easier time than others escaping the crumbling of communism and Yugoslavia, it has not been without difficulties: it has risked its progress with the European Union and, after much promise, failed to be part of the enlargement of the North Atlantic alliance.

That Slovenia has been subject to the decisions of outsiders in both cases is beyond doubt, but there were ways in which the Slovenes themselves were responsible for their own fate. Yet it was almost inevitable that these problems would arise, even with Slovenia's seemingly model transition, because newly-found independent statehood was not only an expression of modern values, such as democracy and the market, but also the hub of cultural expression. For Slovenia becoming part of the 'New Europe' through integration in bodies such as the EU, and if it could recover its way, NATO, means harmonising the forces of internationalisation and openness with conservation of a small people and its specific character.

The challenge of reconciling identity with integration is not unique to Slovenia and the Slovenes – all countries embracing 'Europe' have to face some of these problems. Yet, however far these problems can be seen as part of a general trend, the newness of Slovenian statehood and the importance of cultural peculiarity to the Slovenes mean that there are aspects entirely specific to them. From this we can understand how Slovenia missed its early chances with NATO, and the problems it faces if it is to prosper with the European Union.

The image and the interest of Slovenia

There are many images of Slovenia and the Slovenes. Historically, this small people, fiercely protective of its language-based identity, has been seen in many different ways by those outsiders who have taken an interest in them and their land. As one of the novelist Vitomil Zupan's characters notes, 'The Italians call us Schiavi, the Austrians Windisch swine, the rest of Europe thinks we belong to the Balkans, Balkan peoples think that we're part of the old Austrian empire, while for the rest of the world we're just somewhere tucked away between Turkey and Czechoslovakia.'[1] Had Zupan been writing in the 1990s, he might have noted the confusion of many outsiders between Slovenia and Slovakia, each emerging from its own communist federation. This caused some irritation to the Slovenes.

Most images of Slovenia and the Slovenes are attractive. Where the people are concerned, some have ironic negative tinges, such as their famed miserliness.[2] However, the reactions of visitors tend to be positive. The Slovenes organised their country well, both before and after the end of communism. Those who came from the West were pleasantly surprised to find a land that in wealth and quality of living looked like neighbouring Italy or Austria, and not at all like even the most prosperous of the other communist and, later, former communist countries (which is not to say that Slovenes themselves were happy with the relative benefits they experienced). Those coming from the communist side of the divide were amazed at the relative variety and tone of life in what bore little resemblance on the surface to their own countries.

[1] This remarkably insightful official's analysis was uncovered by Jože Pirjevec who notes that the official 'predicted the collapse of the Kingdom of Serbs, Croats and Slovenes in the event of a Serb-Slovene conflict'. *Jugoslavija, 1918-1992. Nastanek, Razvoj ter Razpad Karadjorjevićeve in Titove Jugoslavije*, Ljubljana: Založba Lipa, 1995, p. 380.

[2] This was captured in the stereotype offered by Serbian President Slobodan Milošević in the film interview 'Death of Yugoslavia: the Milošević Interview', London: Brian Lapping Associates for the BBC, 1995. He humourously alleged that the Slovene delegation to what ended as the final congress of the Yugoslav Communist party had already packed its bags and checked out of its hotel to save on the bill the morning that it walked out of the congress after persistent baiting by Serbian delegates.

For, Westerners here was a country which shared the picturesque Alpine scenery of Switzerland and Austria with the Mediterranean climate of Italy. Crucially, enough of the comforts of those countries were available, including well-surfaced roads that did not change abruptly on crossing the border. But there were also Slavonic and Balkan traits that made Slovenia interesting to discover. It could be an adventure yet without the discomforts that might be found by going further south and east into the imagined lands of surly waiters, unmodernised water-closets, or worse. These were reactions on which Slovenes were able to capitalise in marketing the country whether for tourism, business or politics.

In the early 1990s Slovenia was on the 'Sunny Side of the Alps'; this was the image being conveyed in all arenas. It supported tourism, pleased domestic audiences and, crucially, transmitted the notion internationally that this was a pleasant land on the edge of the Julian Alps, linked through the Alpine region with Switzerland, France, Germany and Austria. In short, Slovenia was a country which belonged in this company. For Western tourists it was not only 'somewhere you've never been – to a new state',[3] but also somewhere reassuringly comfortable and familiar. In other words, it was just different enough but otherwise 'so bloody normal'.[4]

While in later branding the element of sentimental playfulness that the evocative 'Sunny Side of the Alps' label captured was ceased out, the messages about natural beauty remained. Parts of Slovenia were the 'Jewel in the Wilderness', while British Airways, announcing its new service to Ljubljana in the late 1990s, stressed that the country was prosperous, clean and contented, 'and it's in the former Yugoslavia'. This eulogy of the country's qualities was juxtaposed with pictures of romantic Alpine peaks, pastures, and lakes and what one of Slovenia's smart pieces of tourist propaganda from the early 1990s described as the 'immeasurably picturesque ancient town of Piran'. This reflected 'Europe in miniature' with 'a pinch of everything that is typical

---

[3] Rudi Tavčar, 'I've Been Somewhere You've Never Been Before – To a New State', *MM – Marketing Magazine*, no. 2, yr. 12 (May 1992), p. 42.

[4] Marko Crnkovič, 'Heaven and Television', *MM – Marketing Magazine*, no. 2, yr. 12 (May 1992), p. 11.

of the continent'.[5] Such topographical variety, compressed into a land in which no border is more than two hours by car from the capital, is both pleasant and remarkable: it brings together the Alps and the feel of the Mediterranean blended with the most fully wooded surface of any country in the world and limestone scrubland, to say nothing of the caves at Postojna and the geographically unique Karst nearby. Equally, Slovenia is home to the world-famous Lippizaner horses, from Lipica (as Slovenia pointed out in 1999 when Italy dropped a six-year claim against Austria to secure copyright over the term: it was Slovenian). All this and a capital city described by a well-known writer as the most desirable of all in which to live.[6] In the words of an in-flight magazine, there were few nations 'so neat, varied and good-looking'.

These elements of Slovenia were linked to its outlook. As the headline to one of the *Financial Times*'s occasional country surveys put it, Slovenia was 'small, scenic and flexible'.[7] Flexibility was one of the hallmarks of its transition, which enabled Slovenes to feel comfortable with their assertions of being a 'part of the New Europe'.[8] This was supported by a wealth of empirical material – statistical pamphlets, brochures and booklets – which appeared before and after independence attesting Slovenia's prowess and performance.[9] Once the shadow of armed conflict began to pass (and no thanks to clumsy actions, such as the letter sent to whoever would read it by Foreign Minister Dimitrij Rupel[10]), Slovenia's

---

[5] 'Slovenija', *Regions of Europe*, 3/1991, p. 135.

[6] John Ardagh, *A Tale of Five Cities: Life in Provincial Europe Today*, London: Secker and Warburg, 1979, pp. 375-437.

[7] *Financial Times*, 12 Apr. 1994.

[8] 'Slovenija. A Part of the New Europe', Ljubljana: Ministry of Information, October 1992.

[9] Among these were 'Discover the Sunny Side of the Alps: Slovenia in Numbers 1991', Ljubljana: Secretariat of Information of the Republic of Slovenia, 1991; 'Slovenia in Numbers', Ljubljana: Institute of the Republic of Slovenia for Statistics, no date; 'Republic of Slovenia: Basic Development Indicators', Ljubljana: Statistical Office of the Republic of Slovenia, February 1991; 'Facts about Slovenia: Useful Data', Ljubljana: LIST, 1996.

[10] In a letter dated 21 February 1992 and addressed to 'Your Excellency' (accompanied by another letter from the foreign ministry spokesman addressed 'To Whom it May Concern'), Rupel pleaded for 'valued assistance and meditation' (*sic*) to get governments to rescind travel restrictions to the country and recognise

status began to speak for itself. The only thing that could possibly stand in the way of this was the behaviour of the Slovenes themselves, either through awkward attempts to push their case, or at later stages, as some concerned observers noted, complacency.[11] This last concern, as it turned out, was partly justified (as will be seen in Chapter 6).

Slovenia's geographical location lends much to its peculiar blend of elements. When the image-makers played with the idea of the country's being at the heart of Europe, or at its crossroads,[12] they were playing with something real. All parts of Europe – north, south, east, west and central – met in Slovenia. Two straight line drawn across Europe 'from Gibraltar to Moscow and from Scotland to Crete' would intersect in Slovenia.[13] At that intersection lie the country's different symbols. These include the greenness of the land, the mix of Austrian and Mediterranean architecture, the accordion-dominated Central European folk music tinged on occasion with Balkan tones and, above all else, 'Triglav', the '*lipa*' and 'Janez'. The last of these is the Slovene equivalent of John –close to 'Jan' in Czech and Polish, but unique as a name with the telltale '-*ez*' on the end. It is a common Slovene male name and has both a well-established traditional stereotype and a more superficial new connotation. The first captures the small farmer with a feather in his hat from the valleys and hills of the Gorenjska region who may never have travelled as far as Ljubljana, while the second reflects the Slovenia of modernity: computers and Western cars.

The *lipa* is an even more archetypally Slovenian symbol, the lime tree leaf which dots the 'i' on promotional material or is worn as a gold-plated brooch. It is the stuff of love songs and poems, as well as of all forms of marketing. If anything captured the sense of spring among young Slovenes as they challenged

---

that it was not part of a war zone. This is unlikely to have been the most persuasive instrument in improving the country's image.

[11] '*Financial Times* Survey: Slovenia', *Financial Times*, 28 Apr. 1997.

[12] Sandi Sitar, 'Slovenia at the Crossroads' in *Slovenija*, vol. I, no. 1 (spring 1992), pp. 29-34; Gorazd Bohte, 'Slovenia at the Crossroads of Europe', *MM – Marketing Magazine*, no. 2, yr. 12 (May 1992), p. 15.

[13] Alenka Puhar, quoted in Tony Barber, 'Welcome to Slovenia', *Independent on Sunday*, 31 Mar. 1991.

authority in the late 1980s, it was the *lipa* – the fictional currency invented by the editors of *Mladina*, (officially the weekly magazine of the Slovenian communist youth movement), who put it on the cover to make the price appear constant when inflation was debilitating the Yugoslav dinar. *Mladina* was the dynamo of icono-clastic youth rebellion and the voice of liberalism, making it the most important publication in communist Yugoslavia in the 1980s and perhaps unintentionally one of the sharpest, yet least violent, swords that cut the Yugoslav federation apart. The other Yugoslav states had nothing so liberal, subversive, shocking, or funny.[14]

Of all Slovenian symbols, however, Triglav (Three Peaks) is the country's hallmark. Close to the Austrian border, Triglav was the highest mountain in the old Yugoslavia and by definition in Slovenia. In this stylised representation, with the central peak flanked on each side by a lesser one, it is the quintessential image of Slovenia's blend of old and new. While central to traditional Slovenian identity, it is in its contemporary form that Triglav, crossed by water and covered by three stars, appears on the shield that crosses the border between the white and blue horizontal strands of the Slovenian national flag (to the left of centre), which is completed by a red strand at the bottom. This rendering of an old symbol is repeated in numerous contexts, such as banknotes. The mountain itself serves as a link with the past, but the clear lines and sharp geometerical features convey modernity and youth-fulness, the essence of Slovenia's transition.

Slovenia initially considered adopting anachronistic 'historic' symbols to mark its new found independence at the beginning of the 1990s, as was the case in every other 'newly independent' state, following the collapse of communism in Europe. One of these 'traditional' symbols was the Knežni Kamen, the ancient investiture stone, (the actual stone happened to lie in contemporary Austria). There was a possibility that Slovenia's use of this symbol could have led to the same kind of problem as affected relations between Greece and another former Yugoslav republic, Mace-donia.[15] However, demonstrating its commitment to modern life

---

[14] For more on *Mladina* and its impact, see Chapters 3 and 5.

[15] See James Gow, *Triumph of the Lack of Will: International Diplomacy and the Yugoslav War*, London: Hurst/New York: Columbia University Press, 1997, n. 32, pp. 78-9.

rather than invented traditions, Slovenia opted for the sharply modern representation of Triglav, the least questionable symbol of the Slovenes.

However, there remains a tension between the modern and traditional approaches taken by the Slovenes to images of themselves and the country. Central to this is Slovenian culture, to which in turn the Slovene language is central. While Slovenes are a highly literate and multilingual people, it is Slovene itself that lies at the heart of their sense of identity. The language preserves unique and peculiar features, one of which is the multi-purpose non-verb '*lahko*' (with the syncopated emphasis on the '*o*' with a rising voice). The word can mean 'easy' or 'light' as a qualifier. However, it is the word in Slovene that almost renders others unnecessary at times, since it is used as a verb – even though in a language with six cases it is a form that does not decline. Two speakers might communicate using this word alone: the first simply says '*lahko?*' as a question, meaning something like 'May I?'; then the second replies '*lahko*', meaning roughly 'You may'. The conjunction of this form with any other set of words creates the one truly foreigner-friendly element in Slovene.

However, '*lahko*' is by no means the most striking facet of Slovene's uniqueness. Whereas other languages vary between singular and plural, Slovene maintains the dual – the grammatical concept between the two.[16] Thus not only does Slovene have its equivalents to 'I am' and 'we are' (*jaz sem* and *mi smo*), it also has 'we-two are-two' (*midva sva*). Similarly, the dual carries versions for 'you-two' and 'they-two' in masculine, feminine and neuter. This is linked to an idiosyncratic musicality in the language which, philologically, seems to lie somewhere closer to a Latin-script derivative of Russian than it does to the dominant versions of the neighbouring language group, Serbo-Croat. It is thus a language almost impossible for outsiders to command.

The difficulty faced by outsiders is manifest in the cartoons in magazines and newspapers showing émigré Slovenes and their descendants returning to the 'motherland' but unable to impress those living there with their use of the language. It could also be detected during the late 1980s in the column in *Mladina* mocking

[16] Sorbian, a Slavonic language now spoken by only around 1,000 people in eastern Germany, is the only other language to maintain the dual form.

the linguistic competence of the migrant workers from Bosnia and Hercegovina who lived predominantly in the Fužine area of Ljubljana. Whereas the Bosnian community would struggle to escape the Serbo–Croat '*u Fužine*', Slovenes would emphasise the grammatically correct '*na Fužinah*'.

This attachment to the precision and peculiarity of the language also translated into a sometimes schizophrenic approach to those unfortunates who had no connection either through a common federal country or by emigration and family, but still attempted to use some Slovene. On the one hand, there was a sense of gratitude, bewilderment and warmth that any foreigner should attempt to learn this strange language. On the other, there was constant correction, little tolerance and even sometimes apparent contempt for the fools who had taken up this challenge. The language was precious, and it was therefore flattering – yet at the same time sacrilege – that an outsider should try to speak it.

The focus on their own small, peculiar language goes far towards explaining Slovenes' self-obsession and vanity over what is Slovene. Above all this translates into overwhelming commitment to litera-ture and poetry and the sense that those things which Slovenes consider the pearls of the language are not accessible to the outside world. Such is this commitment to Slovene literature and poetry that the remark of one commentator that, for Slovenes, the reason 'Slovenia didn't get into NATO, on to the dream piste of Europe' was because those making decisions in NATO 'didn't know this stuff' – i.e. Slovenian poetry has to be seen as only ironic.[17] For Slovenes the essence of this problem is that they form a small people with a language which outsiders not only find difficult to learn but generally have no reason to learn either.

The relative smallness of Slovenia and of the number of the Slovenes means that they not only have problems with transmitting their experience to the world and testing it against international standards,[18] but also face questions regarding plurality, variety and, possibly, quality. This point was rammed home when the newspaper *Jutrajnik* collapsed after only twenty-two editions in the summer of 1998. It thus followed *Slovenec*, which published its last edition

---

[17] Tom Ložar at the 1997 Annual Convention of the American Association for the Advancement of Slavic Studies, Seattle, WA, 22 Nov. 1997.

[18] On this issue, see Chapter 3 regarding literature.

on 15 November 1996 after five years of operation, and *Republika* on 6 February 1997. All three had tried but failed to compete with *Delo*, the broadsheet newspaper founded as the organ of the Slovenian Communist party. There were a number of reasons for this outcome – among them the strength and depth of *Delo*'s operation: in existence for over forty years, even under communism, it had been a high-quality newspaper despite the need to take account of party requirements. Under communism and then during and after its demise it commanded the loyalty of its readers because of the excellence of its reporting and writing. Slovenia was indeed fortunate that *Delo* was a newspaper of merit; had it not been, as the collapse of the three pretenders to its crown showed, neither the country nor the area inhabited by Slovene-speakers was big enough to sustain more than one serious daily newspaper.

Slovenia's size and the linguistic and cultural specificity of the Slovenes lie at the heart of the challenges of the end of the twentieth century. After almost a decade of independence, while the survival of Slovenia as a country is assured, the essence of being Slovene is facing new demands. For the Slovenes this is ironic: they had adapted and protected their identity through language and culture over the centuries; yet it was at the point where a state had come into being as titular repository of this identity that these faced their biggest test as Slovenia sought to balance its modern and conservative characteristics in order to deal with European, international and global demands of openness and integration. It is this theme that permeates later chapters. The remainder of this introductory chapter considers the survival of the Slovenes and their culture through eras of empire and collective statehood.

People and land through the centuries

The survival of '*Slovenstvo*' is a remarkable phenomenon.[19] Slavs first arrived in south-eastern Europe in the great migration between

[19] '*Slovenstvo*' is a difficult term to render into good English, but means something like 'Sloveneness' or 'the essence of being Slovene'. It is commonplace to marvel at the survival of Slovene culture through the ages. Fred Singleton writes: 'With remarkable tenacity, the mass of Slovene peasants retained their Slav culture and language'. in his *Short History of the Yugoslav Peoples*, Cambridge: Cambridge University Press, 1985, p. 51. In a similar vein, in his *National Question*

the sixth and eighth centuries. They left far behind them the old habits and practices developed in the mists of the Pripet marshes and soon developed individual cultures which evolved slowly and separately. As long ago as the sixth century one of these groups, which would call itself *Slovenci*, 'the people of the word', settled in the Eastern Alps. Until their incorporation into the feudal system of the Habsburg monarchy, these people lived in extended families in common with other Slavs. This gave the Slovenes their 'archaic' national character, according to Gregor Tomc. The other main elements of the modern Slovene national character are the 'traditional', stemming from the experience of living within multinational Empires, and the 'contemporary' which developed during the Yugoslav period.[20]

The initial extent of Slavonic settlement was far greater than the area now covered by the Republic of Slovenia, stretching across much of what is now Austria and north-eastern Italy. However a process of gradual contraction took place over the ensuing centuries and clues to earlier Slavonic settlement can now only be found in place-names, such as the Austrian toponym Toplitz (*toplice* – warm springs) and some popular customs.[21] By the modern period, dialects of the Slovene language were spoken in the hills of Friuli-Venezia Giulia from the coastal town of Monfalcone to the Tarvisio in the Alps. It was also found in the southern parts of Carinthia from Hermagoras through to villages near Graz in Styria, although again the pressure to assimilate linguistically exerted by the German-speaking towns, especially Klagenfurt, was strong.

---

in Yugoslavia: Origins, History, Politics, Cornell University Press, 1994, Ivo Banac remarks: 'In the light of...obstacles, the 19th century Slovene national awakening appears as an achievement of seemingly supernatural scale', p. 45.

[20] Gregor Tomc, 'Slovenski Etnički Značaj', *Nova Revija,* let.XII, st.134-5 (1993), pp. 203-26. Perhaps one of these archaic characteristics to have survived is the Slavonic love for mushroom picking. The Slovene language has more than forty words for types of mushrooms and many varieties are readily available at the Ljubljana market.

[21] Early toponymic evidence is reproduced in Andrej Pleterski, 'Arheologija in Nastanek Brižinskih Spomenikov' in Janko Kos *et al., Zbornik Brižinski spomeniki,* Ljubljana: Inštitut za Slovensko Literaturo in Literarne Vedi – SAZU, 1996, pp. 32ff.

The coastal villages around Trieste and northern Istria used a Slovene vernacular.

For centuries the Slovenes cohabited with other linguistic neighbours, and the differences between the Italian-speaking coast and the Slovene hinterland were often noted, as by Archibald Andrew Paton in the mid-nineteenth century:

Down at the port [Trieste] the strong contrasts of glaring sunshine and the deep shadow, athwart which one sees, at the end of the streets, the intense azure of the Adriatic; the current of air, redolent of Bologna sausage and garlic, or strange spices and the almost universal use of the language of 'si' proclaim our vicinity to Italy. At the back of the town, just under the green uplands dotted with white villas, the dress and appearance of the people remind one of the vicinity to the lands broad and wide that stretch from the Alps to the Baltic. Those Carniolan peasants...that throng the market place and people all the villages on those hills are Slaavs [sic] or Winds and speak the same dialect as is heard in Istria, Carinthia and Styria, which is different from Illyrian, although resembling it. Their temperament is melancholy, compared with the German and Italian, but they are rather shy and diffident.[22]

The heartland of Slovene territory was the hinterland of the city of Ljubljana – and has remained so to this day. Ljubljana was the intellectual and economic heart of Slovenia by 1848, when ideas to unite the people into a common state first emerged. The southern and eastern borders of Slovene ethnic territory (with modern Croatia and Hungary) have been far more stable. The Croatian dialects which border on Slovene bear some resemblance to it, and something like a dialect continuum exists between the states, although the codified languages are quite distinct.[23]

[22] A.A. Paton, *Researches on the Danube and the Adriatic*, Leipzig: Brockhaus, 1861, p. 41. The 'shyness' of the Slovenes was often noted by travellers. See, for example, Josiah Gilbert and Joseph Churchill, *The Dolomite Mountains: Excursions through Tyrol, Carinthia, Carniola and Friuli in 1861, 1862 and 1863*, London: Longman, Roberts and Green, 1864, p. 202.

[23] Jernej Kopitar and certain contemporaries doubted the existence of Croat linguistic distinctiveness, which influenced other scholars before 1914. Kajkavian folk poems are included in Karol Štrekelj's *Slovenske Narodne Pesmi*, Ljubljana: Slovenska Matica, 1900-11, 4 vols. (Kajkavian is the label used for the variant of Croatian close to Slovene, based around the use of the word *kaj* to mean 'what', whereas Serbo-Croat is marked by the use of *što*, hence 'stokavian.') On the extension of Slovene into Istria, see for example Franz Raffelsberger, 'Karte der Herzogthuemer Steiermark, Kaernten, Krain, der Grafschaften Goerz,

Despite the fact that the Slovene people lived in ethnically contiguous areas (and were not, like the Magyars or the Germans, divided by other peoples), the Slovenes did not form an independent state until the twentieth century, although Slovene customs, including the ritual of investiture by peasant voting, were found in Karantanija in the seventh century.[24] For nineteenth-century Marxist writers the Slovenes (and likewise other political latecomers such the Slovaks and the Ukrainians) were a 'non-historic people' who had no state (and therefore no culture, no laws, no traditions etc.).[25] In 1991, having almost passed the point when any new good nations could be made having singularly failed Bismarck's 'blood and iron' test, the Slovenes created a state with the minimum of fuss and violence and with a supreme democratic mandate.

In many ways the Slovenes created a state at the best possible time in history, when Vaclav Havel's vision of a peaceful transition to the participation of civil society was successfully realised. In addition, having studied the mistakes of older countries, Slovenia had a clean slate when it created the Constitution of 1991. Slovenia's emergence seemed to concur with the ancient Greeks and Jean-Jacques Rousseau that only small polities could be truly democratic.[26]

Gradisca, Istrien und der Reichstadt Triest' (c. 1860), reproduced in Milos Mikeln, *Malo Zgodovinsko Berilo*, Ljubljana: Založnistvo Slovenske Knjige, 1991, pp. 10-11.

[24] The ducal stone (*Knežni Kamen*) was the centre of a ceremony, known as *ustoličevanje* that took place in Gospa Sveta in Carinthia, Austria. In the 1960s Joseph Felicjan developed the (infamous) thesis that both Jean Bodin and Thomas Jefferson had been influenced by this proto-democratic ceremony, giving as it did the (Slovene) peasants the right to choose their duke. See, Joseph Felicjan, *The Genesis of the Contractual Theory and the Installation of the Dukes of Carinthia*, Klagenfurt: Družba Svetega Mohorja, 1967. More recently, Andrej Pleterski has traced the origins of this ceremony back to the 2nd millennium BC, identifying similar ceremonies among the Irish and the Hittites. See Pleterski, *Mitska Stvarnost Koroških Knežnjih Kamnov*, Ljubljana: Zveza Zgodovinskih Društev Slovenije –SAZU, 1997.

[25] On the concept of 'Geschichtslosigkeit' see Roman Rosdolsky, *Zur Nationalen Frage: Friedrich Engels und das Problem der 'Geschichtslosen Völker'*, Berlin: Olle and Wolter, 1979.

[26] Edvard Kovač, 'Slovenija kot izziv Evropi', *Nova Revija*, let.XII, st.134-5 (1993), pp. 142-51.

Given these somewhat lofty considerations, there is a curious opposing issue to consider. This concerns the question of how the Slovene people could have got as far as the twentieth century without having a state of their own. An examination of events before the twentieth century also demonstrates that the Slovenes have never been, as Slavoj Žižek has pointed out, 'a sub-species of Serb'.[27] Nor, despite centuries of relentless foreign domination, have they ever become German, Italian or some variety of Illyrian.[28] There are tangible reasons why the Slovenes formed a state in the twentieth rather than in the mid-nineteenth century.[29]

Several factors impeded earlier state formation. These are complicated and intertwined but can be broadly seen as political, cultural, geographical, linguistic and economic. The Slovene lands never formed the centre of a significant Slavonic state. Before the sixth century, the area was populated by Thracians, Illyrians, Celts and Romans. The ancestors of the modern Slovenes in turn became vassals of the Avars and then were incorporated into the Frankish empire, experiencing only brief periods of autonomy under the rule of Samo in the seventh century and Kocelj in the ninth. By 1382 most of the Slovene lands were ruled from Vienna by the Habsburg dynasty and were to remain so until 1918, and although the Slovenes were divided between the historic provinces of Carniola, Gorizia, Istria, Carinthia and Styria, the lands of 'Inner Austria' (as it was known administratively) had a singular character.[30] During the fifteenth century, the Dukes of Celje ruled with relative autonomy and patronised the arts in a manner reminiscent of a Renaissance court. Only a small geographical area, governed by the Venetians and now part of Italy, was to be beyond this Habsburg world, politically at least if not linguistically. In addition the Hungarian crownlands (part of the Habsburg

---

[27] Slavoj Žižek, 'Eastern Europe's republics of Gilead', *New Left Review*, vol. 30, no. 183 (Sept/Oct 1990), pp. 50-62.

[28] Milko Kos, 'Odnos med Kolonizacijo in Oblikovanjem Narodnostih Meja', *Zgodovinski časopis*, no. 9, 1955, pp. 140-5.

[29] This, of course, does not mean that there is an argument for seeing Slovenes as a 'lesser people' – something about which Slovenes are sensitive and that outsiders might sometimes presume.

[30] Victor Thiel, 'Die innerösterreichischen Zentralverwaltung, 1564-1749', *Archiv für Österreichische Geschichte*, no. 105, 1917, pp. 1-120.

Monarchy until 1918) contained a small Slovene population that was separated from the mainstream.

Despite the geographically small area that the Slovenes inhabited, these lands were remarkably diverse in climate, soil and agriculture. Nova Gorica and its hinterland form fruit-growing country with gentle hills and the turquoise blue of the Soča river, famed for its trout. The limestone Karst in northern Istria and the Triestine hinterland have a harsh climate, with the 'Burja' wind threatening to blow away whatever is growing, in addition to deep karstic holes, into which cattle occasionally fall. The Karst is also home to *Proteus Anguinus*, the 'human fish' which was brought as a curiosity to Trieste by local peasants. The coastal towns of Istria are typically Mediterranean and have for centuries produced salt to sell to the neighbouring areas.

Further inland, in Notranjsko, the land is riddled with sub-terranean limestone caves and the landscape is characterised by gentler hills and fertile valleys. This region also developed the practice of skiing several hundred years ago, in isolation from other Alpine areas. Around Ljubljana the marsh brings a very stagnant air which in winter hangs over the city in the form of mists. The locals refer to this as their 'bad air'. South of Ljubljana are Bela Krajina and the fertile hills of Dolenjska. Towards Hungary, southern Styria (or Štajerska) has a flatter Pannonian landscape, although the hills south of Ptuj are steep and suitable for vineyards. North of Ljubljana are the Eastern Alps, the massive Julian and Karawanken ranges. For most of the year they are topped by a light dusting of snow and their villages are typically Alpine in culture and economy.

Economically Slovenia did not exist as a single entity before the eighteenth century.[31] The only exception to this is arguably the peasant uprising, led by Matija Gubec in 1573[32] under the

---

[31] For details of Slovenia's economic integration see, Joze Šorn, *Začetki Industrije na Slovenskem*, Maribor: Založba Obzorja, 1984.

[32] In common with peasants across Europe, the rebels' imagined that when they demanded 'ancient rights' there was an immemorial time before feudalism when peasants had been free from feudal obligations. Gubec was finally executed in the manner of all premodern challengers to state authority, that is as cruelly as possible – by being crowned *rex rusticorum* in Zagreb Cathedral with a red-hot metal rod. He and his comrades were immortalised in the Kajkavian prose of Miroslav Krleža in his *Balade Petrice Kerempuha*, Zagreb: Nakladni Zavod Hrvatske,

universal slogan 'For the old rights', which spread chaos in its wake. This period saw a series of uprisings, but a level of 'class' solidarity did not emerge due to frequent Turkish incursions and the necessity to mobilise against a foreign threat. For most of the time, the economy remained at the level of what Lenin would have referred to as a 'natural economy', with serfdom and local agricultural practices predominant. There were small pockets of proto-industrialisation (for instance, the villagers at Kropa had produced nails since the Middle Ages). Any further industry that existed was almost accidental. For example, the imperial mercury mines at Idrija had been opened only after the chance discovery of quicksilver in the local stream by a barrel-maker in 1497 (according to the early encyclopedist J. W. von Valvasor (1641-93).[33]

Karst peasants brought bread, crayfish, ice and other necessities to the port of Trieste, and their lands were almost denuded of deciduous trees for Venetian shipbuilding in the early modern period, making the impact of the 'Burja' wind when it blew even stronger. Peasants in the Alpine districts were drawn into the economies of the local towns of Villach, Kranj or Klagenfurt. Ljubljana had close economic links with Dolenjska, and peasants from Styria inevitably brought their produce to Ptuj and Maribor.

Simon Clements, an English wine merchant who travelled through Slovenia in 1715, described a rural landscape which would be recognisable in the late twentieth century, but certainly also captured the pre-modern economy. Travelling from Metlika, he described:

[...] the pretty large tract of a country between the mountains, composed of thousands of hillocks and bottoms, wonderfully cultivated and in many places vineyards, little churches and poor dorfs shewing themselves at small distances from one another, so that tis very remarkable to see how much the industry of the inhabitants exceeds that of the lazy Hungarians in their fertil plains. Passing a high woody mountain and very strong steepy ways we open another scene of a well-inhabited hillocky country, of a large circumference between distant high moun-

---

1946. The last recorded peasant uprising, at Tolmin in 1713, is documented in Branko Marušič, *Veliki Tolminski Punt leta 1713*, Trieste: Založništvo Tržaškega Tiska, 1973.

[33] Helfried Valentinitsch, *Das landesfuerstiliche Quecksilberbergwerk Idria 1575-1659*, Graz: Historische Landeskommission für Steiermar, 1981.

tains, and we could see several castels, and otherwise pretty fair buildings on the tops and sides of the hills and still a better face of wealth and improvement, till we came to Rudolfswert...called...by the country people No-mesty.[34]

In their cultural life the Slovenes were dominated, at least where the written word was concerned by the Austrian authorities. Although not entirely a peasant culture, the chance of a literary version of Slovene was severely curtailed before the national awakening of the late eighteenth century. The Slovene language was both a unifying and a dividing factor in the history of the nation, but the status of the language is the single most important *leitmotiv* running through the history of this people and can in some senses be said to define the parameters of Slovene national development.

As a language it varies enormously between regions and has absorbed many foreign influences (neighbouring languages, particularly Friulian, have also absorbed elements of Slovene).[35] Colloquial Slovene spoken in Ljubljana at the turn of the twentieth century was littered with Germanisms, and peasants in the hinterland of Trieste swear in Italian. The Windisch dialects of Carinthia, rather like the *Küchelböhmisch* of the Czechs, have lost almost all resemblance to Slovene. In the remote Alpine valley of Resia, the local inhabitants, numbering a few thousand, speak a language which is so distant from modern Slovene that it might even be classified as a separate Slavonic tongue.[36] Modern Slovene is almost unique among the Slavonic languages in that it has preserved the

---

[34] Simon Clements, *A Journal of my travels into Lower Hungary, Sclavonia, Croatia, Friuli, Carniola and Styria in the year 1715*, British Library, Egerton Mss., 2167.

[35] One example of this regional variety, as Professor Miha Bregant pointed out to one of the authors, is that there are at least twelve different words (including slang) for the million or so Slovene 'girls' now alive: *dekle, deklica, punca, pupa, ceca, deklina, dečva, diklina, frajla, frčafela, fraca* and *mrha*.

[36] This micro-language was recorded by the great Polish linguist Jan Niecislaw Baudouin de Courtenay (1845-1929) during a fieldwork expedition in 1873, although it was already known to Kopitar and his contemporaries. The leading contemporary scholars of the language of Resia are Milko Matičetov and Gian Battista Pellegrini. Their publications are listed in Milko Matičetov, *Resia. Bibliografia ragionata, 1927-79*, Udine: Graphik Studio, 1981. More recently the fieldwork mantle has been taken on by Han Steenwijk, *The Slovene Dialect of Resia San Giorgio*, Atlanta/Amsterdam: Rodopi, 1992.

dual form or *dvojina*, yet this is not found in all dialects (and in the 1990s was generally beginning to be less used). Before the language was codified, simple communication was all that was possible between valleys, especially as the majority of Slovenes remained essentially monolingual before the twentieth century.[37]

After the eighteenth century all the strands that did not by themselves make a single Slovene nation were brought together by different aspects of modernisation: economic growth, a rise in literacy and cultural awareness, and the creation of a Slovene intelligentsia. The modernisation of the economy came with the expansion of the port of Trieste after 1719. After Emperor Joseph II officially ended most of the feudal obligations in the Habsburg Monarchy in the last decades of the eighteenth century, Slovene peasants operated in an increasingly capitalised market economy.[38] The Triestine hinterland became increasingly geared to the wider export market, which was intensified further by expansion of the railway system after 1846.

In the nineteenth century, agricultural improvements (including reforestation of the Karst and Notranjsko) took place under the aegis of the veterinarian Dr Janez Bleiweis (1808-81), president of the Slovenska Matica (Slovene Society, literally 'Slovene queen bee', founded in 1864) and editor of the journal *Novice*. He founded an economic society in 1843, which evolved to become the confessional Slovene People's Party (Slovenska Ljudska Stranka) by 1905. An important cooperative movement developed in the second half of the nineteenth century, inspired by the writing of the Christian socialist Janez Evangelist Krek (1865-1917), which also furthered Slovene national consciousness.[39]

---

[37] Travellers from Edward Browne in 1660s onwards have continually remarked on the problems of communicating with Slovene peasants. They usually had to rely on local dignitaries, or the school-educated, as guides. As a coda to the issue of the identity of Lippizaner horses, it should be noted that two German scientists in Lipica in the early nineteenth century found that the local peasants knew no German. See David H. Hoppe and Friedrich Hornschuh, *Tagebuch einer Reise nach den Küsten des Adriatischen Meers*, Regensberg: J.B. Rotermundt, 1818, pp. 189-90.

[38] Marta Verginella, *Družina v Dolini pri Trstu v 19 stoletju*, Ljubljana: SAZU, 1990, pp. 3-5.

[39] Vincenc Rajšp, 'Prispevek katoliške duhovščine k promociji slovenskega jezika in slovenske narodnosti' in Stane Granda and Barbar Satej (eds), *Slovenija 1848-*

Economic modernisation opened up the Slovene lands to the rest of the world, creating the prospect of emigration and a new life in the Americas.[40] Because the new nationalism was accompanied by an increase in literacy and social mobility, it also drastically altered political discourse, and as it spread from Western and Central Europe it gradually threw the anachronistic traits of the Habsburg Monarchy into bold relief. When Napoleon's troops carved up the Habsburg dominions, creating to replace it a quasi-ethnic state stretching fron Graz to Dubrovnik, the so-called Illyrian Provinces (1809-13), linguistic nationalism received a short term boost through the publication of the *Telegraph Officiel*.[41]

Although Habsburg domination was reaffirmed by the Treaty of Vienna in 1815, Slovene national consciousness had been given enough encouragement for expression to flourish during the rest of the nineteenth century. The Imperial librarian Jernej Kopitar (1780-1844) built up a huge empirical knowledge of the languages of the Balkans, which led him to sponsor the promising Serb Vuk Karadžić and to produce his own Slovene grammar in 1808.[42] Slovene as a literary medium received another boost from the work of the man who was subsequently to become Slovenia's national poet, the melancholic France Prešeren (1800-49), and from the pedagogic reforms of Bishop Anton Slomšek (1800-62) which resulted in the use of Slovene in primary schools.

After the shock of the Napoleonic wars, the Habsburg Monarchy was again struck at its roots by a rise in regional tensions that

---

1998. Iskanje Lastne Poti, Ljubljana: Zveza Zgodovinskih Društev Slovenije, 1998, pp. 216-22.

[40] Josip Broz, a half-Slovene village boy from Kumrovec in the Kolpa valley, toyed with the idea of catching the New York ferry from Trieste before turning north to work in Bohemia. While it is possible to imagine Tito as a Texan millionaire (his lavish Adriatic lifestyle displayed a deep affection for wealth), it is hard to contemplate the history of Yugoslavia without him. His contemporary Louis Adamič left his native Alpine village at the age of fourteen before going back and writing his minor classic of rediscovery, *The Native's Return: An American Immigrant visits Yugoslavia and Discovers his Old Country*, New York: Harper, 1934.

[41] Fran Zwitter, 'Illyrisme et sentiment Yugoslave', *Le Monde Slave*, vol. VI, (1933), pp. 363-4.

[42] Sergio Bonazza, 'Austro-Slavism as the motive of Kopitar's work', *Slovene Studies*, vol. 5, no. 2 (1983), pp. 155-64.

led to a series of revolts in 1848. In Ljubljana a small number of radicals even began to call for a united Slovenia *(Zedinjena Slovenija)*. Here undoubtedly, Slovenes were influenced by the increasingly radical language of the Italians and Germans in the Empire – a radicalisation that was eventually to lose them Trieste to Italy and see the partition of multinational Istria between several states.

Early Slovene nationalists did not envisage the loss of ethnic territory that was to occur after 1918. The Society of St Hermagoras, founded in 1853 by Slomšek, aimed to spread national consciousness from Klagenfurt into the remote Alps, and the Slovenska Matica (see above, p.18) did not envisage a 'Slovenia' which was as territorially limited as the Republic which emerged 1991. In 1848 – the so-called springtime of peoples – Slovenes were generally loyal to the Habsburgs, envisaging their future within the Monarchy. Activists of 1848 included one of Europe's pre-eminent linguists, Franc Miklošič (1813-91), who was rector of Vienna University. Like Kopitar, he was led by his patriotic loyalty to the Monarchy to develop Austroslavist leanings, which emphasised the importance of the third great potential power axis in the Habsburg lands, namely the Slavs from Dalmatia to Galicia.

Austroslavism, within the context of Habsburg 'Trialism', the idea that the Slavs would be the third great force within the Monarchy, was one of several ideological trends among the Slovene intelligentsia. These grew in confidence with the publication of journals, such as *Kranjska Čbelica*,[43] from 1830 onwards.[44] The writer Fran Levstik (1831-87), who recorded the folktale 'Martin Krpan', revived the national movement in the 1860s, leading the

---

[43] Written as '*Kraynska Zhbelica*', the orthography of Slovene was not fully standardised until the 1840s with the general acceptance of Ljudevit Gaj's orthography, known as *gajica*.

[44] The years from 1830 to 1914 saw a huge growth in Slovene-language journals, including *Kranjske Novice, Drobtinice, Slovenec, Slovenski gospodar, Slovenski Cerkveni Časopis, Slovenski Narod, Primorec, Enotnost, Ljudski Glas, Domoljub, Rodoljub, Veda, Ljubljanski Zvon, Dom in Svet, Pavliha, Glasnik* and *Napredna Misel*. Even in the 1990s, as Matjaz Kmecl points out, 'Each year five books per head appear in Slovenia, in Austria only 2.5. The 2,000 literary titles produced for the 2 million Slovenes each year would be equivalent to around 56,000 titles in Italy, or in France, where in reality no more than half this number appear.' 'Le Lilliput Slovène au Pied des Alpes', *Gospodarski Vestnik*, May 1991, p. 23.

so-called '*Mladislovenci*' (Young Slovenes) at outdoor rallies to renew calls for a united Slovenia.

From its inception until complete independence came in 1991, Slovene national consciousness was beset by several fundamental problems. First and foremost was what might be termed a size complex. This reflects the belief common among Slovene intellectuals that there were really too few of them to go it alone. This complex led the Slovenes to form alliances with other South Slavs, despite wholly different political traditions (Serbia had gained its independence from the Ottomans, whereas Croatian autonomy was severely curtailed by the Austro-Hungarian *Ausgleich* in 1867).

The second factor was strong loyalty to the Habsburgs, which meant that the student '*Preporodovci*', active from 1912 onwards, were really the first group to abandon the notion of Trialism.[45] The Dualism of the Monarchy after 1867 and the subsequent Germanisation of the Austrian half of the Monarchy altered the position of the Slovenes and led to fears that their language would be eroded. These fears exploded in the 1890s with plans for a Slovene-language gymnasium in Celje, which rocked the Viennese political establishment.[46]

Despite fears about their size, very few Slovene writers of the pre-1914 period were prepared to abandon their language and become absorbed into the numerically dominant Serbo-Croat-speaking areas to the south. At an early stage, Valentin Vodnik (1758-1819) had expressed culturally Illyrianist or Yugoslav sentiments in his poem 'Ilirija oživljena'. A disagreement surfaced between Stanko Vraž and Prešeren, in the 1830s, over whether Slovene should be absorbed into Serbo-Croat, but whereas the former exited to Zagreb, the latter held the fort in Ljubljana. With a tradition of literary intransigence going back to Primož Trubar (1508-86,) and a more bookish culture than their Yugoslav brethren,[47] cultural Yugoslavism involved an element of sacrifice which nagged at the Slovene individualist.

---

[45] Carole Rogel, 'Preporodovci: Slovene students for an independent Yugoslavia', *East European Quarterly*, vol. 4, no. 4 (1971), pp. 408-18.

[46] Janez Cvirn, *Boj za Celje*, Ljubljana: SAZU, 1988.

[47] According to Carole Rogel, in 1921 only 8.8% of Slovenes were illiterate, compared with 49.8% of Croats and 67.8% of Serbs. 'The Slovenes and Cultural Yugoslavism on the Eve of World War I', *Canadian Slavic Studies*, vol. II, no. 1

In common with other parts of Central Europe, a racial nationalist society, *Sokol* (meaning 'The Hawk'), was founded in 1862, which advocated muscularity and the cult of the healthy body, as well as Slavonic brotherhood, but not cultural absorption. Slovene distinctiveness was also preserved by the heavy influence of the Church in secular politics (it favoured absorption within a Croat and Catholic milieu, but distrusted the Orthodox Serbs). The Slovene Social Democrats, who published *Rdeči Prapor* (renamed *Žarja* in 1911), adopted the Austro-Marxist position on nationalism, seeing it as basically progressive and nations as equals, irrespective of size. However, they were divided over their degree of Yugoslavism. Etbin Kristan (1867-1953) foresaw a gradual absorption into a future Yugoslav nation, but was opposed by the *Naši Zapiski* group that favoured Slovene distinctiveness. In 1913 the writer Ivan Cankar (1876-1918) foresaw the creation of a Yugoslav state which would preserve cultural difference, while at the same time uniting the South Slav nations politically and economically.[48] This was indeed what was to happen. He also realised that this state would face problems, since it went so much against regional 'tradition'.

The development of national consciousness in all the centres of the Habsburg monarchy spelt imminent disaster for Slovene territorial integrity. Primary education and increased social mobility gradually Germanised the local peasants in Carinthia during the nineteenth century. The creation of a Karadjordjević 'Kingdom of Serbs, Croats and Slovenes' in 1918 and the Slavonic propaganda that it spewed forth was not enough to entice the Carinthian Slovenes to leave their economic markets, and they therefore rejected the South Slav state in the plebiscite of 1920. In the area designated Voting Zone A, almost 60 per cent of voters stated a preference for Austrian rule, although in areas such as Eisenkappel the pro-Yugoslav vote was predominant.[49] The Austrian authorities successfully stirred up fears over the internal chaos that had beset what they referred to as 'S-H-S' (i.e. the

---

(spring 1968), p. 66.

[48] On Cankar, see Peter Vodopivec, 'The Slovenes and Yugoslavia', *East European Politics and Society*, vol. 6, no. 3 (fall 1992), pp. 220-41.

[49] Valentin Inžko *et al.*, *Zgodovina Koroških Slovencev od Leta 1918 do Danes*, Klagenfurt: Družba sv. Mohorja, 1985, pp. 58-61.

Kingdom of Serbs, Croats and Slovenes) in their propaganda, and less than two months after the vote launched an assimilation programme. This targeted education and religion, which emphasised the historic mission of German culture in its most southerly territory.[50]

The fate of the Slovenes in the coastal regions was somewhat worse than that of the Carinthians – until 1945. In July 1920, as an ominous precursor to subsequent events, the Narodni Dom (National Centre) in Trieste was burned down. Under the terms of the Treaty of Rapallo in 1920, large areas of Slovene ethnic territory with a population of at least 300,000 were included in the new Italian state. The new border ran from just west of Kranjska Gora, skirted past Triglav and Planina, and divided Rijeka. Mussolini's regime, after coming to power in 1922, embarked on an Italianisation programme, which included forcing 'Slavs' to change their surnames and moving intellectuals to other parts of the state.[51] After the collapse of the the Kingdom of Yugoslavia in 1941, the former administrative unit known as 'Dravska', which corresponded to the Slovene areas, was partitioned. The Italians controlled Ljubljana and the lands to the west, while the Germans 'reclaimed' Styria for the Reich. They committed the huge blunder of underestimating Slovene resistance which began in 1941 and became the most significant arena of resistance to the Nazis from within the Third Reich itself.[52]

After managing to drive the occupying forces from Slovene territory, Communist partisans liberated Trieste in May 1945, but only a little over two months later, after an Allied ultimatum to Tito, it was partitioned into Zones A and B, which became the demilitarised 'Territorio Libero di Trieste' after 1947. With the London Memorandum of 1954 (confirmed in the Treaty of Osimo in 1975), the partition of Trieste into two post-war 'zones' became the basis for the Italo-Yugoslav frontier, with Italy gaining the port itself and Yugoslavia the hinterland. Nearby Gorizia was also

[50] Inžko, *Zgodovina*, p. 65.

[51] Fran Barbalič, 'The Jugoslavs of Italy', *Slavonic Review*, vol. 15, no. 43 (July 1936), pp. 177-90.

[52] Resistance included sabotage of the railways and industrial unrest. See Tim Kirk, 'Limits to Germandom: Resistance to the Nazi Annexation of Slovenia', *Slavonic and East European Review*, vol. 69, no. 4 (October 1991), pp. 646-7.

divided, the Slovenes remaining in the suburbs, which they pragmatically renamed 'Nova Gorica'. This frontier remained unchanged when Slovenia broke away from Yugoslavia in 1991.

The first cataclysmic event that divided the Slovene people between states was the creation of the Karadjordjević 'Kingdom of Serbs, Croats and Slovenes' in 1918. The Second World War merely made these divisions irreparable. State formation after 1918 was the consequence of more than a hundred years of ideology-building that emphasised incompatibility between neighbours of different ethnicity, despite centuries of cohabitation.

At the beginning of the modern period, Slovene culture rested on a tripod of cities – Trieste, Ljubljana and Klagenfurt. After 1945, each was confirmed as being in a different country and lost much of its multi-ethnic character. Ethnic singularity prevailed, although it was by no means exclusive, as areas remained mixed. The process of separation ultimately facilitated the issue of Slovenian statehood by removing large mixed border communities, but this also removed the zest of cultural mix, along with two of the three centres of Slovene population.

Within the new border, Piran, built in a characteristically Venetian style, became a predominantly Slovene town as newcomers moved into Italian houses (which in some cases still had warm stoves) since their occupants had fled over the border to become permanent exiles in Trieste.[53] For centuries German had been heard on the streets of Ljubljana, and most official records were written in that language before 1918. But after the war ethnic Germans, including a large minority around Kočevje, were returned 'home', mostly to Styria. Trieste became Italianised, while Austrian Carinthia increasingly became solely German-speaking. Beyond the protective embrace of the Slovenian republic in federal Yugoslavia, Slovene remained a private language spoken at home or in trusted public places, but rarely used for official purposes.[54]

---

[53] On the predominantly Italian character of Piran in the last decade of the nineteenth century, see Darja Mihelič, *Piran*, Koper: Knjižnica Annales, 1996.

[54] As a British writer remarked in 1881, 'The Slavonic speech in [Cividale] is modest and retiring. It does not thrust itself into print or show itself flauntingly on doors or windows. At Cividale if Slavonic was to be heard it was at least not to be seen.' Edward A. Freeman, *Sketches from the Subject and Neighbour Lands of Venice*, London: Macmillan, 1881, p. 43.

After 1991 there were signs that some of the old complexities were returning. Perhaps these could be traced back to the Friulian earthquake disaster of 1976, which prompted cross-border cooperation and the setting up of the Alpe-Adria Organisation in 1978 to foster cultural and economic cooperation between regions of Hungary, Italy, Germany, Austria, Slovenia and Croatia. Citizens of these regions may yet discard national appellations in favour of something more regional, such as the sometimes fashionable notion of '*Mitteleuropa*', but this would go against the grain of over two centuries of history and require big changes in all the governments of the region. For Slovenes and Slovenia there was far more likely to be a question of preserving cultural traits at the same time as harmonising them with elements of regional and European association.

The challenge for Slovenia and the Slovenes is successfully to define themselves as part of the 'New Europe'. The difficulties associated with this are tied up with the political and economic transition from both the communist period and the dissolution of the Yugoslav federation. Those difficulties and the problems of transition affected Slovenia's development and its prospects regarding the key international institutions in Europe – NATO and the European Union. The following chapters will follow the ways in which Slovenia's recent history, economy and society, culture, political life and, lastly, approach to questions of security and European institutions contribute to meeting the challenge the country faces. This is simultaneously to consolidate that which is intrinsic to Slovenia and the Slovenes and to transcend it.

2

CONTEMPORARY HISTORY

Both royal Yugoslavia and communist Yugoslavia were vital in shaping the Slovenian state which emerged with an independent international personality in the early 1990s. Slovene aspirations for statehood became pronounced in the final stages of the Habsburg Empire. Although the inherent weakness of the desire for statehood at the time was evident in the various proposals put forward and alliances formed within the Empire, as will be shown below, this only served to strengthen the desire of Slovenes to gain their own state, even within a larger political framework, such as the Empire, or some form of common state with other South Slavs, notably the Croats and Serbs. This consciousness grew throughout the life of the first Yugoslavia, which the Slovenes joined in 1918. As a result, Slovenes entered the second Yugoslavia, formed under communist rule, with a clear commitment to, and basis for, statehood.

The peculiarities of that communist federation and its historical evolution served to foster Slovenian statehood in circumstances which saw the dissolution of federal Yugoslavia. In many respects Slovenes provided the peg that held the disparate South Slavs together. As a perspicacious British official noted at an early stage, if the Slovenes were ever to leave the South Slav state it would collapse completely.[1] Slovene self-governance within that South Slav framework was therefore vital to the existence of the common state. Ironically, the Yugoslav framework was also vital for the growth of Slovene statehood and ultimate self-governance. The

---

[1] This remarkably insightful unnamed diplomat's analysis was uncovered by Jože Pirjevec who notes that the official 'predicted the collapse of the Kingdom of Serbs, Croats and Slovenes in the event of a Serb-Slovene conflict'. *Jugoslavija, 1918-1992. Nastanek, Razvoj ter Razpad Karadjordjevićeve in Titove Jugoslavije,* Ljubljana: Založba Lipa, 1995, p.380.

present chapter examines the maturation of Slovenian statehood, through two world wars and two Yugoslavias.

Slovenia's evolution through the first Yugoslavia was defined by three factors: the circumstances at the end of the First World War in which Slovene-populated lands, with two-thirds of the Slovene people, became part of royal Yugoslavia; the experience of a period of autonomous government and divisions within Slovene political life; and, ultimately, Slovenia's position within the unified South Slav state created after the First World War. Stemming from this, *de facto* acceptance that not all Slovene-inhabited lands would be joined in statehood could begin to emerge, although political aspirations for a united Slovenia would be prominent through the Second World War. At the same time, whatever the disillusionment resulting from the actual political arrangements for the common South Slav state, compromises with that Yugoslav state could serve, in practice, as a greenhouse for Slovene social, cultural and political evolution. Taken together, these elements combined to create a situation in which, with hindsight, the conditions were present for the Slovenian proto-state which was to be incubated by communist Yugoslavia after the Second World War (as will be seen below). The starting point for this process was the evolution of Slovene political thought in the course of the First World War.

The First World War and the emergence of a South Slav state

Before the First World War, the options for a Slovenian state were limited. While the notion of united Slovenia – *zedinjena Slovenija* – had been a dominant theme in clerical politics, the chances of achieving this either inside or outside the Habsburg Empire were almost non-existent. This was due to the relatively small size of the population and the pressures of being part of the Austrian half of the Dual Monarchy. Because of the weakness of the Slovene cause, both clerical and, increasingly, liberal politicians came to view Trialism as the framework for what can be termed Slovene self-determination. With this came the politics of alliance with other South Slavs under Habsburg rule, notably the Croats.

The central notion in Trialism was that a third element would be created within the Habsburg Empire. The Dual Monarchy would become a Triple Monarchy, with an additional South Slav component emerging alongside the existing Austrian and Hungarian constituents. Primarily a Croatian idea, this was a prospect favoured in the capital of the Empire, Vienna, by the heir to the imperial throne, Archduke Franz Ferdinand, and political parties such as the Christian Socialists. However, this support was more for Croatian autonomy within the Hungarian part of the Empire, thereby weakening Hungary *vis-à-vis* its imperial partner. Vienna had less enthusiasm for a South Slav crown including the Slovenes because they lived in the Austrian part of the Empire.

Despite likely resistance from Vienna, the Trialist option was the only one open to Slovenes seeking to gain greater self-government. The cause of a Slovene state was tied to alliance with other South Slavs in the Habsburg Empire, the fellow Roman Catholic Croats and the Orthodox Serbs – although the latter were not necessarily embraced by all in Roman Catholic political circles as the First World War began: after the assassination of Archduke Franz Ferdinand by a Serb terrorist the daily *Slovenec*, no doubt reflecting the politics of Vienna as much as the ethnic hostility of Roman Catholic Slovenes, reportedly published the words to a song in which the call was to 'hang the Serbs from the trees'.[2] The idea of a South Slav unit within the Empire became stronger as the First World War progressed.

Perhaps the single most important factor in the course of the First World War affecting the South Slavs was the secret Treaty of London signed between Italy and the Allies on 15 June 1915. This brought Italy over to the Allied side in return for promises of land in the regions of Istria and Dalmatia, part of the Habsburg Empire but populated by Slovenes and Croats as well as an Italian minority. It was the prospect of Italian occupation which above all else galvanised Slovene action in the course of the First World War. Thus Slovene units fought fiercely and suffered heavy losses on the Soča front, officially for Austria but undoubtedly also for the land where they lived. Beyond this, the Italian factor was a key influence for Slovene political leaders in their pursuit of political dominion from Vienna. The considerable contribution of Slovene

---

[2] Georges Castellan and Andrea Bernard, *La Slovénie*, Paris: Presses Universitaires de France (*Que sais-je?* series), 1996, p.42.

troops to the Austrian cause provided ammunition in dealings with the imperial capital.

The key Slovene politicians – Janez Evangelist Krek, leader of a conservative group within the Slovene People's Party (SLS – Slovenska Ljudska Stranka), and his close collaborator Anton Korošec, leader of the South Slav Deputies to the Austrian parliament and also a prominent member of the SLS[3] – used this contribution to the war, as well as a vital alliance with the Croatian Stranka Prava (Party of Right), to pressure Vienna on two counts: opposition to a proposal by German parties in Austria to make the whole state German, thereby Germanising Slovenes and others; and organising a response to the wartime suspension of parliament and provincial assemblies in the form of a body called the Yugoslav Deputies' Club. This helped to persuade Vienna that there was a groundswell of Yugoslavism in the southern lands of the Empire. In the absence of appropriate political forums in which to voice their concerns, all the South Slav deputies from the different parts of the Empire joined the Club to give voice to their aspirations. These were framed in the May Declaration of 1917, made after this united group of deputies, with support from some German counterparts, had forced the new Emperor Karl to recall parliament.

The May Declaration was a strong restatement of Trialism. It demanded the union of all Habsburg territories inhabited by Slovenes, Croats and Serbs into one state, founded on principles of democracy, under the sceptre of the Imperial house. This meant disestablishment of the Dual Monarchy and creation of a third Slavic element. The Declaration did not receive significant support from any part of the Monarchy, or from political circles in Austria or Hungary. However, it was the basis for the mobilisation of Slovene opinion, and a campaign beginning in the autumn succeeded in collecting over 250,000 signatures by the spring of 1918, as well as support from Slovene municipalities. There was a groundswell of opinion in favour of Slovene statehood. This

---

[3] Krek had been leader of the conservative Christian Social Movement in the late nineteenth century and, until 1916, held a position closer to that of the then leader of the SLS, Ivan Šusteršič, whose maximal position was for autonomy in Austria. It has been suggested that it was Krek who provided ideas and Korošec who presented them. After Krek died in October 1917, Korošec became the unchallengeable leader of the clericals. See Janko Prunk, *Slovenski Narodni Vzpon*, Ljubljana: Državna Založba Slovenije, 1992, p.181.

marginalised the conservatives in the SLS who, under the leadership of Ivan Šušteršič, sought to promote loyalty to Austria and autonomy within it rather than statehood, whether in a purely Slovene or a Yugoslav guise. The Slovene position was supported by the Croatian Stranka Prava, but not by other elements in the Zagreb parliament. When Emperor Karl denounced the idea of a united Slovenia on 15 May 1918, it seemed possible that Trialist status might be granted to Croatia alone, where such a move could accommodate Croatian-Serbian moves for a South Slav state, while Slovenia would remain firmly under Austrian dominion. In August the Slovene leaders took the important step of forming a National Council (NS – Narodni Svet) as a vehicle for ensuring a position and influence in the emerging National Committee of Slovenes, Croats and Serbs. By September the NS had begun to assume powers of government as Austrian rule collapsed, including, vitally, the collection of revenues. This helped to fund work on the future constitutional shape of the land.

Plans were devised for the formation of a Yugoslav state which would have three components: Slovenia-Istria; Croatia-Slavonia-Vojvodina; Bosnia and Hercegovina-Dalmatia. Developments outside Slovenia, notably the Corfu Declaration signed by the Serbian government and the émigré Yugoslav Committee on the formation of a common South Slav state meant that Slovene projections could not exclude Serbia's becoming a fourth federal unit – as Korošec pointed out. However, the looming shadow of union with Serbia did not delay political development in the Habsburg territories.

The NS joined the National Council (NV – Narodno Vijeće) of the Habsburg South Slavs formed in Zagreb. On 6 October the NV established a parliament of Slovenes, Croats and Serbs in Zagreb. Emperor Karl, desperately trying to salvage the Empire, proposed a federated Habsburg monarchy on 16 October, despite being warned against attempts to stem the tide of South Slav unity, *inter alia* by Korošec at a meeting on 12 October. The Slovene leader told the moist-eyed Emperor that this would be unacceptable to peoples who wanted a free and joint state – certainly to Slovenes, who would not remain part of Austria.[4] On 18

4 Feliks J. Bišter, *Anton Korošec. Državnozborsko Poslanec na Dunaju*, Ljubljana:

October, the Zagreb parliament rejected the proposals before declaring the formation of the State of Slovenes, Croats and Serbs on 29 October 1918. A gathering of 60,000 people in Congress Square, Ljubljana, made a complementary declaration by acclamation. With this, despite the Trialist origins of these political movements, a relationship was no longer realistic as the Habsburg Empire dissolved under Allied imperative and national pressures in the last weeks of the war. At the same time, the immanence of a Yugoslav union with Serbia was rapidly dawning.

On 7 November Korošec, as President of the NV,[5] made a joint declaration with Nikola Pašić, the Serbian Prime Minister, and Ante Trumbić, representing the Yugoslav Committee, that the State of Slovenes, Croats and Serbs would join with the Kingdom of Serbia to form a unified Kingdom of Serbs, Croats and Slovenes. This new state would provisionally have a collective leadership, with four ministries to be taken by the Kingdom of Serbia and four by the State of Slovenes, Croats and Serbs (even though the Belgrade leadership renounced this equality of representation soon afterwards). The constitution and other arrangements for this union would be worked out later, as Korošec urgently implored: 'First form a state, then discuss everything else.'[6]

There was good reason for this urgency. While Korošec was meeting the representatives of the Serbian government and the Yugoslav Committee in London between 6 and 9 November, Italian troops had begun to advance. Italy moved first towards the demarcation line designated in the secret Treaty of London – the Slovene-populated areas of Primorska and Istria, but then beyond it towards Ljubljana. Beginning on 3 November, Italian forces occupied Trieste on 5 November, Gorizia on 6 November

---

Slovenska Matica, 1992, transl. from the German 'Anton Korošec und die slowenische Politik im wiener Reichsrat', Ph.D. diss., University of Vienna, 1990, p.258.

[5] Although Korošec signed the declaration, the Serb leader of the Croatian-Serbian coalition in the NV in Zagreb, Svetozar Pribićević, argued that he acted without authority because he did not have backing from the whole collective leadership of the NV (although he had the support of Slovenes and the majority Croatian parties) and opposed the Geneva Declaration. See Stane Kos, *Stalinistična Revolucija na Slovenskem, 1941-1945*, Rome: Samozaložba, 1984, p.9.

[6] Kos, *Stalinistična*, p.11.

and Rijeka on 12 November, moving well beyond the London line to Logatec and seeking to move even further towards Vrhnika, 7 km. from Ljubljana. Military units were quickly and spontaneously formed by the NV and deployed to turn back the Italian advance. Primarily composed of Serbian ex-soldiers under the command of a Serbian officer, Lieutenant-Colonel Stevan Švabić, they were reinforced, in the context of forming a common state, by units of the Serbian kingdom, under agreement with the NV, drafted in for the defence of Ljubljana. These units were able to stop the Italian advance and force a retreat from Logatec, but they could not expel Italy from much of the territory it had occupied. When, eventually, the border was settled under the Treaty of Rapallo on 12 November 1920, Italy acquired most of this territory, which was more than the lands promised under the Treaty of London; it also demanded the Postojna Basin, and before long incorporated Rijeka which had been intended to be a free state under the League of Nations.[7] Significant portions of territory were ceded to Italy. It was vital to jump quickly into union with Serbia in order to stop Italian forces as they knocked at the doors of Ljubljana, and to preserve Slovene lands.

Union in a South Slav state provided both the forces and the political cloak of one victorious ally against the claims of another, and it was established as a matter of necessity before constitutional arrangements could be completed. Once proclaimed, on 1 December 1918, the Kingdom of Serbs, Croats and Slovenes was in existence for over two and a half years before the majority of Slovenes, who aspired to a federal arrangement, became disappointed with the unitarist constitutional form adopted under the Vidovdan Constitution of 28 June 1921.[8]

Intra-Slovene politics: cleavage and development

In the period between the proclamation of a common state under the Serbian monarchy and the adoption of a constitution for it,

---

[7] See, for example, Josip Mal, *Zgodovina Slovenskega Naroda*, vol.II, Celje: Mohorjeva Družba, 1993, first published in ten volumes, 1928-39, pp.1128-32.

[8] Vidovdan (St Vitus's Day), 28 June, was a particularly symbolic day, being the anniversary of the legendary Serbian defeat at Kosovo Polje in 1389.

Slovenes experienced their first brief period of self–rule. In all, this lasted formally for less than two months and for a few months in practice, although it was not wholly ended until the adoption of the Vidovdan constitution. The initial period of self–government, however, demonstrated a balanced and co–operative approach to political affairs which was also to mark Slovene politics later in the transitional phases from the advent of the Second World War to the formation of communist Yugoslavia and from the end of communist Yugoslavia to Slovenian independence in the late 1980s and early 1990s.

The NS was renamed the Slovenian National Government on 31 October 1918, a move confirmed the same day by the National Parliament of Slovenes, Croats and Serbs in Zagreb. This began a brief period in which Slovenia was largely self–governing, while taking part in the constitutive deliberations of the new kingdom. Officially the National Government only ruled until it formally resigned on 23 December 1918, to be replaced by a Regional Government appointed by King Aleksandar on 20 January 1919. Throughout the last stages of the First World War and the first stages of the period of autonomy Slovene political life was almost unmarred by the internal divisions which had existed before 1914. It was the relationship with the other South Slavs, however, which was the main issue of differentiation as autonomy dwindled during 1919. This continued to be the case throughout the 1920s and 1930s.

The National Government was notable as a coalition of traditional opponents. The conventional political division in Slovenia was between clericals and liberals (although party names would change).[9] The prime minister was Josip Pogačnik of the SLS, the party which, at the last elections in 1911, had gained over two–thirds

---

[9] For an account of the clerical-liberal development in the second half of the nineteenth century and into the twentieth century, see Bojan Balkovec, *Prva Slovenska Vlada, 1918-1921*, Ljubljana: Znanstveno in Publicistično Središče, 1992, pp.26-31, and *Zgodovina Slovencev*, Ljubljana: Cankarjeva Založba, 1979, pp.560-84. The latter, written during the communist period, also gives what appears to be undue attention to the development of socialist and social democratic forces, at the time. The clerical-liberal divide was to a considerable extent a rural-urban, or agricultural-industrial division, with the clericals having an understanding of and appeal to the former group, in either case, and the liberals to the latter, with Ljubljana having the only liberal mayor.

of the vote. He led a coalition cabinet which did not reflect this balance of support. Of its twelve members six were from his own party, ensuring the prime minister a majority within the cabinet. Of the other six, five were from the newly-formed Yugoslav Democratic Party (JDS –Jugoslovanska Demokratska Stranka),[10] while the remaining representative was from the Yugoslav Social Democratic Party.

The National Government immediately set about implementing changes. Slovene was adopted as the language of all official business and Slovenes were brought in to run the administration, while the Germans who had previously run the Austrian bureaucracy were pushed out. A concomitant measure was the disestablishment of the Austrian regional committee of the Kranjska and Austrian regional administration. Laws were adopted across the full range of economic, social and political life with a view to establishing full Slovenian authority and restoring normal conditions after the war. In the field of defence, the government within its first month facilitated the withdrawal of the Austrian army from the Soča front, while ensuring that whatever weaponry Slovenia needed would be handed over.

In this same period the National Government also formed an army, with a major part of the force mobilised for the defence of territory on the borders with Austria. There the Austrian regional government of Carinthia had responded to the National Government's formation by proclaiming the province indivisible and incorporated in the Republic of Austria. This defence was under the command of a former Habsburg officer, General Rudolf Maister.[11] Maister's troops were able to take Styria, but were too weak to hold Carinthia against larger and better-equipped opponents. The only area in which the National Government did not have authority was foreign policy, where the NV, led by Korošec of the SLS, took responsibility. The key issue was that of uniting all the Habsburg South Slavs with Serbia.

Although the National Government formally ceased to exist

---

[10] The JDS was a pan-Yugoslav party with which the two liberal parties, the National Party, from Styria and the National Progress Party, from Carniola, had amalgamated in June 1918.

[11] Janez Švajncer, *Slovenska Vojska, 1918-1919*, Ljubljana: Prešernova Družba, 1990, pp.34-5.

and was replaced by the regional government, for some months more it retained full authority *de facto* and, until it was disestablished after the adoption of the Vidovdan Constitution in 1921, it retained autonomy in a number of areas.[12] Laws continued to be adopted until the first regional government was agreed upon and announced by the Council of Ministers in Belgrade on 7 March 1919, although King Aleksandar had already named Janko Brejc of the SLS as prime minister on 20 January. In those areas over which the regional government had authority, it continued to adopt laws until 1921, although it can be surmised from a comprehensive review of the activities of the Slovenian governments in this period that the bulk of the legislation was adopted before the end of 1919.[13]

The Ljubljana government was appointed with eight members, including the prime minister, while thirteen offices of ministries in Belgrade were established in Ljubljana. The government had authority over internal affairs, justice, the economy, education and agriculture. Four of its members were from the SLS and two each from the JDS and the Yugoslav Social Democratic Party (JSDS – Jugoslovanska Socialna Demokratska Stranka). Troubled by disagreements, resignations and pressure from the liberals for it to resign – all emanating from strains connected with the common South Slav state being formed – this government lasted until 5 November. It was a somewhat schizophrenic exercise, being on the one hand a manifestation of a will to strike a balance between parties and to forge a national coalition, and on the other a sign of the friction within coalitions and their fragility.

After the fall of this first government, there were four more

---

[12] Throughout this period of full authority, something close to a confederal arrangement of the State of Slovenes, Croats and Serbs was a reality, as well as being the preferred configuration of the joint South Slav state favoured by most of the former Habsburg peoples in negotiations between the NV and the Serbian government about the kingdom's political structure. Balkovec, *Prva*, p.38.

[13] Balkovec, *Prva*, pp.99-183, reviews the activity of the National and Regional governments throughout the period. Most measures were taken by the first half of 1919, while over time fewer and fewer steps were taken. To some extent this can be seen as a function of the removal of Austrian dominion, which created the need for a new legal framework for the new political community. It is surely also linked to developments in the Kingdom of Serbs, Croats and Slovenes.

until the adoption of the Vidovdan Constitution brought an end to political autonomy. The second prime minister nominated was Gregor Žerjav, who had been deputy to Brejc, but unable to unite liberals and social democrats and not receiving co-operation from the SLS, his government lasted less than three months. The third government, formed in February 1920, was affected by events in Belgrade, where the prime minister of the government of the Kingdom of Serbs, Croats and Slovenes, Stojan Protič, formed his second cabinet in which members of the SLS were included. Against this background Brejc again became prime minister of the regional government. Žerjav was nominated as justice minister – a post he did not in practice take up, arguing that it should be seen as a political and not an administrative role, as well as opposing a number of decisions taken by the government. Despite these arguments, rejected by Brejc, it was the outcome of the Carinthian vote which prompted the third government to offer its resignation at the end of the year, as Korošec resigned from the Belgrade government.

The fourth government was formed by Leonid Pitamac, Professor of Law at the recently formed University of Ljubljana. This government was also short-lived, with changes being made in February 1921, again in connection with ones in the Belgrade government. The essentially administrative approach of Pitamac was replaced by a more political one under the liberal Viljem Baltič of the JDS. Apart from welcoming a Belgrade decision to prohibit women from voting in municipal elections, Baltič also reflected party–government developments in Belgrade, where the Farmers' Party had also joined the government. For the first time the Independent Farmers' Party (SKS – Samostojna Kmetska Stranka) formed the government, with four members of the JDS and one non-party member. Because the SKS had been formed originally as a means of prising rural support from the SLS, this was in essence an entirely liberal government. It ceased to function on 9 July 1921, eleven days after the Vidovdan Constitution had been adopted, when centralised administration from Belgrade was introduced and the Slovene part of the kingdom was divided into two districts, Maribor and Ljubljana. This brought to a close the brief period in which Slovenia had for the first time experienced, more or less, a good measure of autonomy.

Slovenian politics and the evolution of Royal Yugoslavia

As much as autonomy from Austria had divided liberals and the SLS under Habsburg dominion, it had come to divide them again in the Kingdom of Serbs, Croats and Slovenes following a period of co-operation during the last years of the war and the brief transitional period. Autonomy was also to be the defining issue in the relationship between Slovenes and the kingdom during the inter-war period. While at various times Slovene politicians of various hues joined the government in Belgrade, their position was always conditioned by questions of autonomy.

The several governments of the Kingdom of Serbs, Croats and Slovenes before the adoption of the Vidovdan Constitution had contained a number of Slovenes, but only one of these, Ivan Pucelj of the SKS, survived to become minister of agriculture under the second government led by Pašić in 1921. However, it was not Pucelj but Korošec, unquestionably the leading Slovene politician, who was the most important figure in Slovene relations with Belgrade. Despite his background as a federal-confederalist, he joined several governments in Belgrade, mostly as deputy prime minister, between 1918 and 1921, but opposed the Vidovdan Constitution. He was to return to the Belgrade government at later stages, including a short, difficult period as prime minister. but he also spent periods outside government arguing for Slovene autonomy. He was a supreme politician who favoured the pragmatic and the possible over the emotional and ideological, but yet retained principle blended with commonsense.[14]

The adoption of the Vidovdan Constitution did not have wide support among Slovenes. In the Constitutive Assembly, out of

[14] Because of this, Korošec has a disputed heritage. He is seen by some as the man who led Slovenes from heroic independence, or confederation in the State of Slovenes, Croats and Serbs, into the prison of union with Serbia. Not only this, but he then joined the government that disestablished autonomous governmental structures in Slovenia. Yet at other times he would make a stand on the question of autonomy. Most of all, his reputation as 'father of the Slovene nation' is supported by those who note that, despite his joining centralist governments much of the time, there were many significant ways in which Slovenia developed during the inter-war period, including the accomplishment of *de facto* autonomy in many areas. See Miroslav Slana-Miros, *Oživitev Dr. Antona Korošca. Oče Domovine na Tehtnici*, Maribor: Založba za Alternativno Teorijo, 1991.

forty deputies only the nine SKS and three JDS representatives voted in favour of it. The majority of Slovene deputies abstained from the vote, led by Korošec's SLS with fourteen deputies, followed by the whole communist complement of five members and three out of the seven Social Democrats.[15] The other four Social Democrats voted against, as did the two National Socialists.[16] From this point onwards, however, all power in the new kingdom would rest in Belgrade.

Having played an important role as leader of the NV in forging the common South Slav state, but having failed to give that form the content preferred by the majority of Slovenes, Korošec went into opposition till 1924. The JDS, on the other hand, having joined the Belgrade government, remained part of it till 1927. This reflected disagreements on autonomy. In February 1921 Korošec had stated the SLS position for autonomy: this involved proposals for a constitutional plan to divide the kingdom into six provinces, one of which would be Slovenia.[17] Each of the provinces would have its own government and parliament, in addition to which it would have authority in all affairs regarding its territory, albeit in accordance with constitutional arrangements for cooperation with the organs of state. This position strengthened support for the SLS in Slovenia.

---

[15] The representation of Slovene parties was based on the outcome of elections to the Constitutive Assembly on 28 November 1918. SLS strength at this point was considerably below what it had been before the war, or was to be later. In 1911 the SLS had garnered around two-thirds of the Slovene vote under the Habsburgs, a level it would reach again in the 1920s, while in the constitutive elections it harvested only a little over a third of the vote (although it still retained the single largest share of the vote). See Janko Pleterski, 'Politika Naroda v Krizi Družbe, Države in Idej' in Peter Vodopivec and Jože Mahnič (eds), *Slovenska Trideseta Leta. Simpozij 1995*, Ljubljana: Slovenska Matica v Ljubljani, 1997, pp.44–7.

[16] Balkovec, *Prva*, p.31.

[17] The other provinces proposed were Croatia with Slavonia and Medjimurje, Bosnia and Hercegovina with Dalmatia, Serbia, Montenegro and, lastly, Vojvodina. To some extent this was clearly an adaptation of earlier positions in the NV on a federative-confederative structure for the Habsburg South Slavs. It is notable that this scheme did not envisage a Macedonian province. According to Prunk, this represented a compromise between the old idea of federalism and the centralisation advocated by Slovene liberals and by Serbs in the new state. See Prunk, *Vzpon*, p.228.

While out of government between 1921 and 1924, the SLS supported an opposition grouping in parliament which included Bosnian Muslim representatives and the Democratic Party from Serbia of Ljubomir Davidović. When this coalition came to power in the summer of 1924, Korošec was again part of the government for several months. However, over time SLS cooperation shifted towards the Serbian Radical Party, resulting in the signing of a pact between Korošec and the Serbian Radical leader Veljo Vukičević at Lake Bled in the summer of 1927. The following September, Vukičević became prime minister and Korošec returned to government. In doing so he (and the SLS) had realised that opposition had to be turned into power if the autonomy sought was to be advanced.

Over the next two years, Korošec succeeded in putting this on the agenda and fostering *de facto* Slovene authority, based on the overwhelming electoral strength of his SLS which, since 1923, had held twenty-one out of twenty-six Slovenian parliamentary seats.[18] However, this was an acutely troubled period for the South Slav state. The Croatian Peasants' Party, led by Stjepan Radić, took a hard line of opposition to Belgrade, demanding an autonomous Croatian area. This led to Radić and two others being killed in parliament by a Montenegrin deputy on 20 June 1928. The Davidović government was replaced by one with Korošec as prime minister, appointed by King Aleksandar on 1 July.

The new prime minister's mission was to promote ways to defuse the increasingly violent nationalist strains on the Kingdom, preferably by returning to a version of the Trialist federative-confederative position with four units: Serbia with Vojvodina; Montenegro with the majority of Bosnia; Croatia with Slavonia, Dalmatia and a part of northern Bosnia; and finally a unified Slovene territory, incorporating the Ljubljana and Maribor districts together. Korošec's government included both Serbian Radicals and Davidović's Democratic Party. However, some of the former and all of the latter resigned at the end of 1928, finding the Slovene's anti-centralist approach too much. Korošec was removed as prime minister, but remained part of the government of General Petar Živković until the autumn of 1930,[19] when King Aleksandar

---

[18] Mal, *Zgodovina*, p.1140.

[19] The SLS, without Korošec, remained involved in government into 1931.

moved to proclaim a Royal Dictatorship in the country, renamed as the Kingdom of Yugoslavia.

Under the Royal Dictatorship political parties were banned, although in 1931 a pro-government pan-state party was formed. It was called the Yugoslav National Party (JNS – Jugoslovanska Narodna Stranka), and its composition included the Slovene liberals. At this moment Korošec and the SLS were once more in opposition (and technically an illegal organisation following the ban on political parties) and returned to a more radical autonomist position in December 1932 when Korošec issued the Slovene Declaration, also known as the 'Korošec Points'. These were: that the Slovenes were divided between four countries but should be united in one political community; that it was the role of the greater part of the Slovenes, i.e. those who lived in Yugoslavia, to fight to accomplish this; that Slovenes in Yugoslavia should have an independent status which would be a beacon to Slovenes in neighbouring countries; and that recognition of peculiar national status should be acknowledged by, *inter alia*, the use of their collective name, a flag, ethnic solidarity, financial independence, political and cultural freedom, and radical social legislation which would satisfy the living needs of those engaged in production, particularly in agriculture and industry.[20] Essentially this was a demand for a self-governing Slovene political community, as the Declaration made clear: 'To achieve this, it is necessary for Slovenes, Croats and Serbs to create by free agreement and on a democratic basis a state of self-ruling units, of which one would be Slovenia.'[21]

Although strongly rejected by the Slovene liberals and the Belgrade government with which they were associated, the points in the Declaration were a rallying cry and coincided with, and acted as a catalyst, for a process of social and political transformation throughout the 1930s. The points were to be tempered when with opposition permitted again, Korošec and the SLS agreed to join the new pan-Yugoslav, pro-government political movement, the Yugoslav Radical Community (JRZ – Jugoslovanska Radikalna Zajednica), and to form part of the government of Milan Stojadinović,

---

See Prunk, *Kratka Zgodovina Slovenije*, Ljubljana: Založba Grad, 1998, p.99.

[20] Prunk, *Kratka*, p.100.

[21] Prunk, *Vzpon*, p.262.

appointed by the Regent Prince Paul in 1935 following the assassination of King Aleksandar in Marseilles the previous year by
a Macedonian-Croatian terrorist joint-venture. This was the beginning of the last phase of royal Yugoslavia. Korošec now kept the
Slovenes ever more closely part of a united Yugoslavia, which,
by preserving neutrality towards Hitler's Germany (about which
he had no illusions and for which he had no sympathy), he
judged would be in the best interest of all.[22]

While the cooperation of Korošec (who was to die in 1940),
and the SLS with Belgrade left an opening for criticism from a
nationalist-autonomist perspective, it was also undeniable that,
one way or another, a degree of *de facto* autonomy had been
established and maintained. The most important and notable of
these achievements, from the point of view of strengthening
Slovenia culturally and politically, was the creation of the University
of Ljubljana during the national government period in 1919. Something long demanded from the Habsburgs, this was the precursor
of other academic and cultural institutions. These included the
establishment in 1928 of Radio Ljubljana broadcasting in Slovene,
a national museum and a national gallery, the Slovenian National
Theatre and, in 1938, of the Slovenian Academy of Sciences and
Arts.[23] However, these accomplishments, spread over two decades,
were not enough.

By the mid-1930s, even attempts to revive the points of the
Slovene Declaration could not appease criticism from a breakaway
movement from the SLS. Throughout the 1920s and especially
the 1930s, there was a modernisation and transformation of the
structure of Slovene society and politics.[24] This was manifest with

---

[22] See Kos, *Stalinistična*, p.47.

[23] See Castellan and Bernard, *Slovénie*, p.46, and Slana-Miros, *Oživitev*, p.23.

[24] This is argued interestingly by Pleterski, who uses *inter alia* analysis of electoral
results to show that the strength of the SLS in the 1920s and 1930s was not a
return, or continuation, of the same clerical dominance in Slovene politics but part
of a process of political and social restructuring, including secularisation, which led
to the split in the clerical movement in the 1930s. This split was important in two
ways. First because the division among clericals led to a situation, unlike that elsewhere
in Central and Eastern Europe, where clerical forces were not united in opposition
to communism. Secondly, the division actually paved the way for a new secular
bloc which would see the KSG cooperating with, among others, communists,
as the Second World War began. 'Politika Naroda', *passim*.

the division of both the clerical and liberal movements in the early 1930s. On the clerical side an element of the SLS, which represented its links with the working classes, left under the influence of the Christian Socialist Movement (KSG – Krščansko Socialistično Gibanje), which had a strong trade union operation and thought that the SLS ignored working-class voters; also because of theological divisions regarding the Papal encyclical *Quadragesimo Anno*. It also strongly criticised the SLS decision in 1935 to join the JRZ and the government as an abdication of Slovene interests. However significantly the KSG represented divisions within the Roman Catholic community, it was only one important strand in the evolution of Slovene politics in the 1930s.

This division on the clerical side of the political spectrum was mirrored by one on the liberal side and supplemented by the emergence of a stronger social-democratic and communist movement. Among the liberals a breakaway group of intellectuals founded a new publication, *Sodobnost*, early in 1933. This group rejected the unitarist stand of the liberals, following the line of one of its leading lights, Josip Vidmar, who had produced a book on the cultural position of the Slovenes, *Kulturne Probleme Slovenstva*. In it he pointed to language as the core of authentic culture and national identity, and charged that attempts to forge a unitary Yugoslav identity were 'unnatural, uncultured and immoral'.[25] As the majority of the more adept intellectuals followed this lead towards a more Slovene-focused approach, the liberals were critically damaged. Equally, the *Sodobnost* group and, to a lesser extent, those around the newspaper *Slovenija* were providing a discourse which had parallels with that of the SKG and, notably, the emerging communist movement.

The outlawed communists in Slovenia, a branch of the Communist Party of Yugoslavia (KPJ – Komunistična Partija Jugoslavije), had taken up the Slovene cause, as well as that of other peoples, as far back as 1923. At that time they had demanded a broad federation on the lines of the Soviet Union, in which Slovenia, as well as Croatia, Bosnia and Hercegovina, Macedonia and Montenegro, would join Serbia in a federal state. This had been identified as the best way of mobilising the masses in the non-Serbian parts of Yugoslavia. From 1935 onwards the com-

[25] Prunk, *Vzpon*, p.258.

munists were moving to form a common Popular Front with the breakaway liberals and with the KSG. The young ideologue Edvard Kardelj was in the forefront of this move.

Kardelj, who was to be a figure of great importance in communist Yugoslavia, was prompted to begin his work on the Slovene national question in 1932-3 after reading Vidmar's work. This was to result in the publication in 1939 of his own vitally important book on the development of the Slovene national question.[26] He criticised Vidmar for failing to recognise the complex social questions involved, and applied a Marxist critique, based on Stalin's works, which affirmed that every people had the right to self-determination and that therefore the Slovene national question was one not only of culture but also of politics. This position was not dissimilar in many ways to that of the Slovene Declaration.

This orientation to the national question was confirmed by the decision to form a separate Communist Party of Slovenia (KPS – Komunistična Partija Slovenije) in 1937. Its creation added to the efforts, under Kardelj's aegis, to form a Popular Front. These efforts were making progress until, following the Nazi–Soviet Pact in August 1939, the Popular Front policy was abandoned on instructions from the Comintern, the international organisation of communist parties through which Soviet control of communism in the rest of the world was assured. This created muddle and disarray in Slovene politics as the Second World War approached. However, it also meant that a foundation had been provided for cooperation once that war had begun.

The Second World War and the formation of communist Yugoslavia

After the Second World War, the emergence of communist rule brought formal statehood and sovereignty to Slovenia in the context of a Yugoslav federation and in line with communist thinking on the Yugoslav national question.[27] To some extent, on a formal level, this brought the type of arrangement that Slovenes had

---

[26] Edvard Kardelj, *Razvoj Slovenskega Narodnega Vprašanja*, Ljubljana: Državna Založba Slovenije, 4th edn, 1977.

[27] See Aleksa Djilas, *The Contested Country: Yugoslav Unity and Communist Revolution, 1919-1953*, Cambridge, MA: Harvard University Press, 1991.

sought in the NV and in royal Yugoslavia. In practice this constitutional position was conditioned by communist rule. While this initially served to limit the functioning of the Slovene republic, one of the by-products of communist political control over time was to strengthen the institutions of the state and eventually create *de facto* autonomy. The roots of that autonomy lie in the Second World War, and the advent of communist rule in Slovenia lies in a Yugoslav setting.

The outcome of the Second World War in Slovenia and the arrival of communist rule in Yugoslavia were part of the advent of communist rule across the Yugoslav lands.[28] However, just as the outcome cannot be entirely divorced from the overall Yugoslav war, which combined revolution and civil war with liberation from occupation by the Axis powers, it cannot be understood without consideration of the peculiarities of the war in Slovenia, which was largely a separate affair from that across the rest of Yugoslavia. While the Slovene communists and their partisan army were linked with the communist partisan army (under the command of Josip Broz Tito) in the other Yugoslav lands, they did not become part of it until relatively late in the war. In the mean time, the autonomy of Slovene activity – often criticised by Tito and his command – meant that there was an entirely different character to resistance in Slovenia, where the communists led a coalition of parties. This was formed by the communists, on the lines of the Popular Front they had dissolved in 1939, as early as 27 April 1941. It was formed to oppose the Axis invasion of Yugoslavia – but, against the wishes of the Yugoslav party, under Tito.

Established initially as the Anti-imperialist Front, this movement was renamed the Liberation Front (OF – Osvobodilna Fronta) following the Nazi invasion of the Soviet Union on 22 June 1941

---

[28] For an excellent short account of the Second World War in Yugoslavia, see Jožo Tomashevich 'The Second World War' in Wayne S. Vucinich (ed.), *Contemporary Yugoslavia: Twenty Years of Socialist Experiment*, Berkeley: University of California Press, 1969; for personal accounts which touch on Slovenia, see F.W.D. Deakin, *Embattled Mountain*, Oxford University Press, 1971, and Franklin Lindsay, *Beacons In the Night: With the OSS and Tito's Partisan's in Wartime Yugoslavia*, Stanford University Press, 1993; for the evolution of the communist partisan army, see James Gow, *Legitimacy and the Military: the Yugoslav Crisis*, London: Pinter, 1992, pp.32-9.

– at which point the KPJ, which had previously criticised the Slovene communists' early opposition to the Axis invasion, now sought to help Moscow by organising resistance throughout Yugoslavia.[29] The OF was led by the communists under Kardelj and Boris Kidrič, but included the KSG and the Sokols (a national youth movement), as well as members of the church and individuals from other organisations. It did not, however, have the support of most of those who had been in the SLS, or of the liberal old guard. Despite this, it was a broad-based organisation which involved large parts of society and drew a good deal of popular support, especially in areas which had been under Italian or German control before the war.[30]

Only in Štajerska (Styria) and parts of Gorenjska was there any initial welcome for the occupation – and that was mostly limited to the ethnic communities. Because the Nazis felt that these were Germanic areas, they were incorporated in the Reich. Indeed, rather than treating the Slovene lands as a whole, the occupiers divided Slovenia among themselves, with parts being annexed by Italy, Hungary and the Reich while most of it was organised into provinces. Following an invasion in which the Yugoslav army offered no real resistance, the Nazis took responsibility for the area north of a demarcation line, marked by the Sava river, divided into the regions of Oberkrain and Untersteiermark.[31] Italy took control of the Ljubljana Province south of the Sava.[32]

Unlike many other countries in occupied central Europe, Slovenia did not have a native pro-Nazi movement which could have immediately stepped in to run the country; hence division made sense. Indeed, it would take time before significant collaboration with the occupiers emerged. In the mean time, although

[29] See Metod Mikuž, *Pregled Zgodovine NOV v Sloveniji*, vol.I, Ljubljana: Cankarjeva Založba, 1960, p.154.

[30] Mikuž, *Pregled*, vol.I, pp.96ff. It should be noted that, following the *Anschluss* uniting Germany and Austria in 1938, Slovenia and Yugoslavia had bordered the Nazi Third Reich.

[31] The Slovenian lands incorporated by the Nazis were the biggest point of resistance within the Third Reich itself. See Tim Kirk, 'The Limits of Germandom: Resistance to the Nazi Annexation of Slovenia', *Slavonic and East Euroepan Review*, vol.69, no.4 (October 1991).

[32] See Kos, *Stalinistična* pp.92ff. and *Zgodovina Slovencev*, pp.734–43.

there was always some collaboration, the bulk of the population, while opposed to the occupation, did not actively engage with resistance movements. Instead they found a *modus vivendi*, especially in the areas under Italian control where it was possible to get on with life to a large extent without confronting the occupier and being forced into either collaboration or open hostility. Where there was non-communist resistance, as with some other cases in Yugoslavia at that time, it became collaboration. Neither the communists nor their Slovene opponents were particularly active militarily in the early stages of the war, although the OF was always strongly engaged in political-ideological and information campaigns.[33]

The OF, with its communist core, was the more active, but was still criticised by Tito and the Yugoslav communist leadership for its lack of activity and failure to turn strong popular support into membership of the Partisan forces.[34] However, the distinctive situation in Slovenia meant that until the latter stages of the war events there were largely separated from those in the rest of Yugoslavia. Because of this, no Slovene delegation attended the first session of the Anti-Fascist Council of National Liberation of Yugoslavia (AVNOJ – Antifašističko Veće Narodnog Oslobodjenja Jugoslavije, in Serbo-Croat) at Bihać in Bosnia and Hercegovina in November 1942. This was the meeting at which the political programme for post-war government, as well as for interim government on territory liberated from Axis occupation, was agreed by the communist-led Partisan movement. While there had been contacts with the Slovene communists and messages of support, the fact was that the Slovenes were not part of the first meeting.

Slovenia's semi-detached status from the Partisan movement could be seen in other ways. One of these was the initial use of the slogan 'brotherhood and peace' rather than the Partisans' 'brotherhood and unity'.[35] Moreover, while there was agreement with the overall concept of a federal Yugoslavia, aired at the

---

[33] See Djuro Šmicberger, *Partizanska Sedma Sila. Tisk in Novinarstvo v NOB*, Ljubljana: Knjižnica OF, 1988.

[34] 'Consultation of HQ Representatives and Commanders of the National Liberation Partisan Detachments of Yugoslavia' in Tito, *Military Thought and Works: Selected Writings, 1936-1979*, Belgrade: VIZ, 1982.

[35] Mikuž, *Pregled*, vol.I, p.154.

second meeting of AVNOJ at Jajce on 29 November 1943, Slovene partisan units were still outside the Yugoslav movement.[36] This, nonetheless, was the meeting at which the new federal Yugoslavia was born. It embraced much that suited Slovenia in terms of territorial aspiration (including Primorska, for example, in the new state) and political organisation (republics, based on the equality of nations). Indeed, the outcome of the second AVNOJ meeting satisfied a large part of the Slovene agenda; this was established when a convention of 572 OF delegates had met at Kočevje, which had become the headquarters of the OF,[37] to elect the 120 representatives of the Slovene National Liberation Committee. At this time it was decided that Slovenia, incorporating Primorska, would voluntarily join the federal Yugoslavia announced at the first meeting of AVNOJ and that the Committee would send a delegation to Jajce.[38]

The collapse of Italy in September 1943 significantly strengthened the position of the OF, as it did for the Partisans elsewhere in Yugoslavia. The movement had been principally organised in Ljubljana up to May 1942, when its leadership had been able to move into 'free territory' outside. Still, the movement continued not to be as strong as it might have been. Although Tito's deputy, Milovan Djilas, could write that 'not only was the entire population on the side of the Liberation Front, but participated in the resistance',[39] the latter was certainly not true, whatever the extent to which the former might have been. The numbers engaged with the OF remained relatively small till the latter stages of the war.[40] The OF itself was subject to internal

---

[36] Prunk, *Vzpon*, p.359, notes that Tito recognised the importance of a separate Slovene army, using the Slovene language. See also Zdravko Klanšček, *Oris Narodnoosvobodilne Vojne na Slovenskem, 1941-1945*, Ljubljana: Partisanska Knjiga, 1982, pp. 74 and 81.

[37] See Miha Mihevc, *Poguna Zvesta Četa*, Ljubljana: Knjižnica NOV in POS, 1990, pp.27ff. Kočevje was to play an important role from this point onwards as a largely secret area under the control of the Slovenian security service after 1945.

[38] Prunk, *Kratka*, pp.139-40.

[39] Milovan Djilas, *Wartime*, London: Secker and Warburg, 1980, p.338.

[40] Throughout 1941 the total number in OF units was no more that 800, while at the time of the Italian capitulation in 1943 figures vary from 3-5,000;

tensions and splits[41] as communist domination grew,[42] and crucially there were other Slovene groups fighting the OF. Opposition to the OF (that is, opposition to the communists) was divided into legal and illegal forms. The legal form was overtly collaborationist, and a part of it was formed under Italian authority – the Milizia Volontaria Anticommunista (MVAC). In other ways collaboration was not necessarily straightforward. Some groups veered from illegal to legal status, depending on circumstances. However, large elements in both of these groups collaborated with the occupiers.

The anti-revolutionary forces were divided into two main strands before the collapse of Italy in 1942. These covered a variety of small groups and 'legions'. The first of these was a very small element of the Yugoslav Army in the Homeland, the 'Chetniks', loyal to the Yugoslav government-in-exile and its commander in Yugoslavia, Colonel Draža Mihailović. Under the leadership of Mihailović's representative, Major Karel Novak, this force, known as the Plavo Garde (Blue Guard), grew to no more than 300 strong and co-operated with Partisan units in Styria, before the Partisans attacked it.[43] After this, Novak, aware that Chetniks in other parts of Yugoslavia were collaborating with the Italians against the communists, did the same. This force became the Legija Smrti (Legion of the Dead), following agreement with the Italians. Novak later took control of the Vaške Straže (Village Sentries), a set of forces which had initially emerged in villages spontaneously to oppose the communists (in some cases with success, in others being completely destroyed); these were known as the Belo Garde (White Guard). In 1943, as the collapse of

---

domestic opponents were perhaps 8,000 strong. See Gow, *Legitimacy*, p.35. See also Stanko Petelin, *Enaintrideseta Divizija*, Ljubljana: Založba Borec, 1985, pp.264-83.

[41] See Ljubo Sirc, *Between Hitler and Tito*, London: André Deutsch, 1989, pp.26-7.

[42] The benchmark of this was the Dolomite Declaration of 1 March 1943, in which the non-communist parties in the OF renounced independent political activity and accepted communist leadership. This paved the way for the Kočevje convention in the autumn.

[43] Kos, *Stalinistična*, pp.204-5.

Italy approached, Novak vacated leadership of these forces to create once again a new illegal force, as the Yugoslav Army in the Homeland. This force moved towards the sea to join up with Chetnik forces from Croatia and wait for what was anticipated to be an Allied landing across the Adriatic, following Italy's surrender. This was unrealistic and, long before it could have happened anyway, the force was annihilated by the Partisans.

The second anti-communist grouping was formed around elements from the main pre-war political parties – the SLS and the JNS. As the Axis invasion began, these parties with others had formed a new version of the NS. At the end of April 1942 this political association became the illegal Slovenska Zaveza (Slovene Covenant), which adopted a political programme that strongly echoed the political positions of the OF. Finally, following the Tito-Šubašić agreement in September 1944 between the leaders of the Yugoslav Partisans and of the government-in-exile in London, this grouping formed a new illegal body. This was the Narodni Odbor (NO – National Committee), comprising seven members of the SLS and six liberals (one of whom was later replaced by a social democrat). It was formed as an alternative to accepting the decision of the government-in-exile to co-operate with the communists.

In military terms there were links with Novak and his groups up to 1943, albeit mostly of a more formal character, since all accepted the authority of the government-in-exile. The parties involved also formed paramilitary groups which attempted to join together, early in the war but were not very active. One of them, the Slovenska Legija, organised by the SLS, was the most significant. However, since the SLS could count on the support of Roman Catholics in peacetime politics, it was for the most part the Belo Garde, or Vaške Straže, which was able to count on them once the communist security service had begun a programme to 'liquidate' those regarded as 'class enemies.' This movement assisted the Slovenska Zaveza, effectively contributing to its cause and, significantly, to its strength.

When the anti-communist forces came to face the partisans in armed hostilities in 1943, it was the partisans who completely routed their opponents despite having significantly smaller forces. The real difference lay in the leadership and organisation of the forces, with the communists easily outstripping the anti-revolutionaries.[44] The Slovenska Zaveza and other anti-communist groups were so badly defeated that, with the Italians out of the war, Germany had to take control of the situation. Therefore, on 15 September 1943 the German command took the decision to form the Domobranci – the Home Defence (or Home Guard, as it is often called). This was done from the remnants of the Vaške Straže, the MVAC and other anti-communist forces, and was placed under direct German command. The leader of this movement was a former general, Leon Rupnik, who had been mayor of Ljubljana under the Italian occupation. Rupnik, through the pro-clerical newspaper *Slovenec*, urged Slovenes that there were only two enemies: 'bolshevism, which with its Jewish leadership wants to turn us into dull robots without soul and God, as well as plutocracy'.[45] However, this unusually virulent approach, for Slovenia, would only damage those associated with it.

The organisation of the Domobranci brought most elements of the anti-communist movements together, although some groups from the Slovenska Zaveza refused to support Rupnik because of his collaboration with the Nazis, and remained illegal 'defenders of the homeland' even after the government in London, on 27 September 1944, had instructed all forces loyal to the monarchy to place themselves under the command of Tito.[46] This principled group was insignificant in practice while the Domobranci were headed for oblivion. With defeat and the end of the war, not only would the communists triumph, through the OF and the Partisans, but those who joined the Domobranci would find that Rupnik had 'summoned them to catastrophe'.[47] Around 8,000 of the Domobranci and other anti-communists were liquidated close to the heart of the wartime OF at Kočevski Rog in October 1945. They were among those who initially thought that they

---

[44] Prunk, *Vzpon*, pp.346-7.

[45] Quoted by Prunk, *Vzpon*, p.348.

[46] However, these illegal groups were wiped out before the end of Nazi occupation. Their leaders were rounded up by the Gestapo and sent to the Dachau concentration camp. By the time there had been a chance for those in hiding to regroup, the war had finished and the communists were in power. See Ciril Žebot, *Neminljiva Slovenija* (Celovec: Ciril Žebot and Založba Sv. Mohorja, 1988, p.381.

[47] Prunk, *Vzpon*, p.349.

had escaped the well-known merciless retribution of their communist foes by escaping into Austria.[48] Returned to an ally by
British forces in Austria, their bones were only revealed in the
cave where they were shot, three years after Slovenia had gained
full international status.

The communists won the war in Slovenia and in the rest
of Yugoslavia. They did so with a considerable degree of popular
support, maintained through much of the war, codified in the
AVNOJ political programme. This offered the Slovenes what
they had sought on joining the common South Slav state in
1918 – sovereignty, self-determination and statehood, albeit in the
context of communist rule. Moreover, in achieving this position
the Slovene communist forces had succeeded in taking control
of territories which had become part of Italy and Austria, not
Slovenia and Yugoslavia, after the First World War – including,
crucially, Trieste. However, as was seen in Chapter 1, while
large parts of that territory were retained, Trieste was lost again
in the post-war settlement. The borders resulting from the Second
World War would in effect become the borders of the first independent Slovene state.

As Slovene communists, supporting Slovenia's sovereignty, prepared to enter the new federation, there were already signs that
the forces of centralism would create problems and try to limit
real freedom. During May and June 1944, with the Slovene Partisans
becoming an integrated part of the Yugoslav Partisan movement,
the Slovene intelligence and security service, VOS (Varnostno-
obveščalna Služba), was closed down and replaced by a federal
service. At the same time Kidrič was temporarily suspended from
all functions by Tito – on the basis of an English-language report
that he had remarked that all the commitments entered into by
AVNOJ were no more than empty words. While these were

---

[48] Despite a general order to the Eighth Army to return all Yugoslav nationals
in the British Sector in Austria to Tito's control, not all were sent back. A
successful campaign by the refugees themselves and civilian humanitarian workers
prevented the deportation of 6,000 Slovenes from the Vitkring camp. An account
of this was given by one of those civilian workers, John Corsellis in a talk at
King's College London, 22 February 1995. The deportations and massacres are
the subject of Count Nikolai Tolstoi's, *The Minister and the Massacres* (London:
Century Hutchinson, 1986; subsequently withdrawn from circulation after legal
proceedings).

matters which could be survived and overcome, they were portents for the future.

Slovenia in communist Yugoslavia

The dynamic of autonomy and centralism, which had been the main strand of Slovenia's relationship with royal Yugoslavia was repeated through the course of communist Yugoslavia – even to the point of having one individual with a family name whose initial letter was K (for Korošec, read Kardelj) somewhat ambiguously dominating relations with Belgrade[49] – always favouring Yugoslavia while increasingly securing Slovenia's effective autonomy. But there were two important differences. The first was that by the end of communist rule the discourse on autonomy had become an agenda for independence, taking Slovene arguments for self-determination to the ultimate conclusion. The second was that pressures for centralism were reinforced by the nature

[49] It is curious that each of the other dominant Slovene political figures during the communist period, also had surnames beginning with K: Boris Kidrič, the wartime leader, prominent in the early post-war years, who died in 1953; Stane Kavčič, the doyen of reform thinking in the 1960s; and Milan Kučan, who, following in the footsteps of Kavčič, led Slovenia through reform in the 1980s, to independence. One of these figures, Kavčič, provides interesting assessments of the other three Ks – Kardelj and Kidrič explicitly, and Kučan in passing, while adding a fourth, Boris Kraigher, and suggesting that they were all victims of misfortune (a curious assessment, given Kardelj's success and prominence, even if he suffered ill-health later in life).

He suggests that the first knew that he was a theoretician and did not want anything more, although he became leader of the Slovene communists after the death of Kidrič. The second was the 'most gifted' and provided the most balanced blend of theory and practice of all the Yugoslav communists. While Kavčič approves of the 'extraordinary' Kidrič in all respects, but especially economic policy, he points critically at Kardelj, with whom he had serious disputes, arguing that the great theoretician was too utopian and intellectual over economic policy, while too prone to compromise on the national question. Kučan is seen as the best hope for the 1980s, although in the mid-1980s his biggest weakness was the degree to which he was still 'under the influence of Kardelj's economic and systemic inheritance', because of which he was a better tactician than strategist, and better at analysis and interpretation than leadership and judgement. Kavčič also notes the resemblance between the careers of Korošec and Kardelj, suggesting that substantial research could be carried out on this. See Stane Kavčič, Dnevnik in Spomini, 1872-87, Ljubljana: Časopis za Kritiko Znanosti, 1988, pp.223, 321, 536-40 and 576.

of communist rule, as were those for a Slovene way whether autonomous or independent. Party control served to make both positions stronger. In a sense, the argument remained the same, but it was made more intense over the course of time by the peculiar characteristics of communist rule.

The essence of the argument at the end of the communist period was the meaning of sovereignty and self-determination in the context of the Yugoslav federation, notably whether the provisions for the exercise of the rights pertaining to these qualities gave the individual republics (that is, Slovenia) the right to separate from the federation. This argument, which finally broke the Yugoslav federation and prompted Slovenia's independence had also been a divisive issue at the time of federation, conducted principally between Slovenia and Serbia as the first federal constitution was being drafted in 1945.

For the Slovenes the meaning of sovereignty and self-determination was quite clear. Both involved the complete set of rights and powers to decide the collective future of the land and the people. The right to self-determination was 'that right, according to which a nation as a whole can decide on the form of its state community, of its connections or contacts with neighbouring peoples, of association with other nations in whatever internationally recognised state configuration, of disassociation and therefore separation from that community, on internal order, etc.'[50] Sovereignty and self-determination were continuing and irrevocable, and moreover, inasmuch as they incorporated the possibility of union with others, the right of separation at some stage in the future was also inherent in them. While Slovenes envisaged the continuing right to separation, the Serbian view was that the decision on union was irrevocable.

This was the basis of disputes about the draft constitution. The constitutional position taken at AVNOJ in 1943 explicitly wrote the right to separation into the document. However, when this provisional arrangement was being transposed to become the con-

---

[50] Josip Rus, one of the Slovenes contributing to the formulation and discussion of the AVNOJ Declaration, in an unpublished handwritten note discovered by Tone Ferenc, 'Vprašanje Samoodločbe in Suverenosti Slovenskega Naroda po Drugem Zasedanji AVNOJ-a', *Zgodovinski Časopis*, vol.44, 1990, p.97; quoted in Prunk, *Vzpon*, p.367.

stitution of the post-war Federal Peoples's Republic of Yugoslavia (FNRJ – Federativna Narodna Republika Jugoslavije), provision for the right to separation had been dropped. On the Serbian side, however, the view was that the right to self-determination was only to be exercised once; thereafter, the matter would be settled and there would be no future right to separation. However, as Kardelj was one of the most prominent thinkers on the matter as well as one of the architects of the AVNOJ position, he was able successfully to argue that, because this had been one of the fundamental conditions for the Slovenes' entry into the federation, it had to be in the new constitution. As a result, the new constitution explicitly addressed the issue in Article 1. The new state was a 'community of equal nations, which, on the basis of the right to self-determination, including the right to separation, have expressed their will to live together in a common federal state'.[51] These terms satisfied the Slovenes.[52]

Despite the inclusion of these provisions, however, life in federal communist Yugoslavia initially provided anything but the self-governance the terms of the constitution suggested. Although there was some scope for autonomy in cultural spheres, the communist federation was 'politically, socially and economically' more centralised than the centralist royal Yugoslavia had been.[53] In Slovenia power was consolidated with Kidrič, who had hitherto been leader of the government, also becoming secretary-general of the Slovene Communist Party in place of the older, less decisive and organisationally less able Franc Leskošec. When Kidrič became a federal minister in Belgrade in 1946, his replacement Miha Marinko also took on the leadership of both party and government. Under this tightly centralised regime, many anti-communists in Slovenia were harassed and arrested by the powerful police and security services, and were convicted of political crimes by the courts.

However, all of this began to change after 1948 when Josef Stalin's Soviet Union expelled Yugoslavia from the world com-

---

[51] Jera Vodušek Starič, *Prevzem Oblasti, 1944-1946*, Ljubljana: Cankarjeva Založba, 1992, p.399.

[52] Castellan and Bernard, *Slovénie*, p.52, make the point that the will expressed was not in fact that of the whole people but only that of the 'progressive' elements in society, under the guidance of the communists.

[53] Prunk, *Kratka*, p.148.

munist family and in response the Yugoslav communists developed an alternative model to justify themselves.[54] Throughout Yugoslavia those suspected of being unreliable and agents of the Soviet Union were arrested and sent to concentration and labour camps such as the notorious Goli Otok. In Slovenia the number treated in this way was relatively low: only 731 individuals were arrested, of whom 334 were 'administratively' convicted while a further 173 were convicted in the courts.[55]

The Yugoslav reaction to expulsion from the Soviet camp was of vital importance for the subsequent development of the communist federation and for Slovenia's position within the federation. It brought ideology to the forefront of concerns and, with it, the national question in Yugoslavia. A key figure in developing the Yugoslav position was Kardelj, who with Tito's most trusted deputies, Milovan Djilas and Vladimir Bakarić, elaborated the doctrine of 'workers' self-management'. The essence of this idea, intended to have more form than substance, was the transfer of decision-making in the workplace to the workers themselves – a form of decentralisation. This opened the possibility of dissent, which occurred in a variety of forms throughout the 1950s in Slovenia, – through strikes by the workers, literary output or direct political criticism.[56] Although this was only intended to apply to the economic sphere, increasingly there were pressures not only to give the measure effect economically but also to extend it to other areas.

As a result, although party rule was maintained, power was more diffuse than in other communist countries. Moreover, pressures led to a series of constitutional changes, whether as amendments (1958, 1968, 1969, 1971 and 1976) or through the adoption of new constitutions (1953, 1963 and 1974). At every stage, ar-

---

[54] See A. Ross Johnson, *The Transformation of Communist Ideology*, Cambridge, MA: MIT Press, 1972.

[55] Prunk, *Kratka*, p.151. The issue of Slovenes and Goli Otok has been treated by Božidar Jezernik, 'Non Cogito Ergo Sum. Arheologija Neke Šale', *Borec: Revija za Zgodovino, Literaturo in Antropologija*, vol.46, 1994, pp.655-856.

[56] Among those falling foul of the regime on the literary front was Edvard Kocbek, a popular and prominent figure in the wartime and early post-war OF from a Christian Socialist background. Among political opponents was Jože Pučnik, who was sentenced to nine years in jail but who returned to the political scene in the late 1980s as leader of one of the first parties to emerge after the acceptance of pluralism (see Chapter 5).

guments for decentralisation and greater autonomy in decision-making emphasised the national question and issues concerning the rights and powers of the republics in relation to each other and to the federation. Slovenia was always in the forefront of arguments for greater freedom for the republics, for example at the 7th Congress of the League of Communists of Yugoslavia in 1958 where a platform for economic and political decentralisation was advanced, criticising the hegemonic tendencies of centralisation as stifling economic development.

As these debates were carried through the 1960s, the tide increasingly appeared to favour Slovene positions, particularly after the fall in 1966 of the arch-Serb centraliser Aleksandar Ranković, interior minister and head of the federal security service.[57] At that time Ranković was widely thought to be the heir-apparent to the man who dismissed him, Tito. After his departure a wave of decentralising and liberal processes evolved rapidly, significantly building on measures adopted by the federation, and particularly by Slovenia, in the first half of the decade. The steps taken in the early 1960s which had particular impact on Slovenia were relative financial and economic liberalisation, improvement in relations with the countries of Western Europe and, concomitantly, the opening of borders – in terms not only of goods but also of travel. The impact of this was completely different in Slovenia from that in the other parts of the federation.[58] Bordering on Italy and Austria, ordinary Slovenes and political leaders alike could visit their neighbours easily and frequently. At the same time, ideas and publications circulated freely. As a consequence, the desire to achieve similar standards of living and ways of working and governing developed.

In Slovenia this quickly became part of the political agenda, albeit implicitly. At the forefront of it was Stane Kavčič, who led a coalition of administrators, technocrats and liberals in the political elite and became Slovene prime minister in May 1967. This group sought economic modernisation, with emphasis on investment in high technology and service industries such as electronics, as well as market reforms and political liberalisation

---

[57] See Dennison Rusinow, *The Yugoslav Experiment, 1948-1974*, London: Hurst for the RIIA, 1977, pp.184-91.

[58] This is discussed in Chapter 4.

– including giving consideration to the notion of ending one-party rule in favour of pluralism.

In the early 1960s, younger Slovene communists began to produce a critique of self-management and party-rule in a new periodical, *Perspektive*. This appraisal became a crusade which was met with some sympathy by liberals in the party leadership, notably Kavčič (then, in charge of ideological affairs), who gave serious consideration to the ideas emerging – even to the notion of ending communist party monopoly in favour of a two-party system, although in the end this was rejected.[59] By openly advocating a two-party system the 'Young Turks' of *Perspektive* caused their own demise, and the journal was closed down. However, much of their critique and the ideas which emerged from it were remembered – in particular by Kavčič when he became prime minister.

As Kavčič tried to implement a radical programme, he ran into opposition both from the Slovene old guard and especially from federal leaders. There were three key moments in this period. The first was the 'Road Affair' in 1969: Slovenia, as part of its vision for economic development and increased and improved links with its immediate neighbours and Western Europe generally, sought to improve its road network significantly, better to facilitate trade with Western Europe and tourist access to Slovenia and, further south, to the Dalmatian coast in Croatia. The funding for this project was solicited from the World Bank, but when it arrived, rather than allocating it as intended to the development of the road network in Slovenia, the federal authorities decided to redistribute these funds for road projects in other republics. This generated significant problems in Slovenia where its relations with the federation were concerned, since most ordinary people and the bulk of its political leadership saw this as a federal abuse and a slight. The Slovenian outcry, however, was met with charges of nationalism from Belgrade as well as from Kardelj. Tito pushed other Slovenes in the federal government, as well as Franc Popit, the Slovenian party leader, and Sergej Kraigher, leader of the republic's parliament, to criticise Kavčič and his sympathisers as a measure of party discipline. This was formally applied at the plenum of the Slovene party's central committee in October. Kavčič was upbraided but not dismissed.

[59] See Rusinow, *Experiment*, p.215.

Following the outcome of the 'Road Affair', the issue of relations with the federation and old-guard opposition to Kavčič became a prominent theme. In 1971 twenty-five members of the Slovenian parliament, supporting liberal positions, decided to nominate Ernest Petrič as a candidate for membership of the federal presidency in opposition to the official party candidate, the conservative Mitja Ribičič. However, this move was blocked by conservatives in the party who successfully applied pressure on Petrič not to stand. This left the 'twenty-five' in the political wilderness. Moreover, it placed additional strain on the liberal-conservative political dynamic in Slovenia, as well as on relations between Slovenia and the federation.

By 1972 this process had come to its culminating point. Kavčič, having compounded his liberal errors by rejecting the chance to hold a federal post,[60] was judged to be a nationalist. In the context of the federal clampdown on national and liberal movements in the other republics, Kavčič and his government were forced out of office. In mid-October Tito had sent a letter of condemnation and criticism to the Central Committee of the Slovene party, the League of Communists of Slovenia (ZKS – Zveza Komunistov Slovenije) and the other party central committees. In consequence, having considered his position deeply as well as the danger of fighting on for himself and his family as well as for Slovenia, Kavčič offered his resignation on 30 October 1972.[61] Only two members of his government survived to become members of its conservative successor, formed by Miha Marinko.[62] However, although Kavčič had been removed from office, the impact on ordinary people of his ideas and of the man himself remained in the background – as indeed did he.[63]

[60] Kavčič himself had no regrets about taking the unusual step of remaining in republican politics, once the chance of a federal job had been offered. To have taken a job with the federal government would only have made sense if there had been a reform-minded federal government. 'If there had been the team' he wished, he 'would have gone'. Kavčič, *Dnevnik*, p.19.

[61] *Ibid.*, pp.31-78, esp. pp.43-50.

[62] *Ibid.*, p.24, n.10.

[63] By the day after his resignation Kavčič had received an enormous number of letters of support, many recognising that he had been afraid to do more. See Kavčič, *Dnevnik*, p.31, n.2. In 1989 a young Slovene, who at most would only just have been born in 1972, told one of the authors how fond she was

By 1975 the ZKS was ready to rehabilitate Kavčič if he were prepared to renounce his ways, but he refused. Marinko dubbed him a Slovene 'Djilas'.[64] The party and the government meanwhile produced 'nothing' of interest and was 'shortsighted'.[65] Indeed, the most significant development for Slovenia, throughout the 1970s was reform of federal relations at both state and party levels. Alongside the purges of nationalist and liberal politicians, in the early 1970s, a new constitution was drafted. It was significant that with those supporting republican positions having been ousted, the new constitution, which was adopted in 1974, considerably consolidated existing republican responsibilities and even extended them.

Relations between the republics had formally become quasi-confederal. Only the presence of party control – itself devolved to the republican level – served as a controlling mechanism.[66] What Tito and the federal leadership did not appear to recognise was that this would become a formula for the consolidation of republican positions. Even though they were communists, leaders in the republics would adopt the focus of their constituencies – which self-management made almost inevitable. As Mark Thompson deftly remarks, rather than 'communizing the republics on Yugoslav lines, the communists were republicanised on national lines'.[67] Because of the nature of communist power in the state, this meant in effect that the 1974 constitution created the embryonic structure of independent states.[68]

Developments throughout the 1970s and early '80s offered no

---

of Kavčič and how much she admired him and his ideas.

[64] Kavčič, *Dnevnik*, p.285. The epithet 'Djilas' referred to the situation of Milovan Djilas, who had been Tito's deputy until 1953 when, having elaborated a sophisticated critique of communism and advocated complete liberalisation, he was expelled from the party and, for periods, imprisoned. See Djilas, *The New Class*, London: Thames and Hudson, 1957, and Rusinow, *Experiment*, pp.81-7.

[65] This is the judgement of Kavčič, *Dnevnik*, pp. 351 and 431. It would be hard to challenge this assessment.

[66] See Rusinow, *Experiment*, pp.326-42.

[67] Mark Thompson, *A Paper House: The Ending of Yugoslavia*, London: Vintage, 1992, p.38.

[68] For a summary of this process see James Gow, 'Deconstructing Yugoslavia', *Survival*, vol. XXXIII, no.4, 1991, pp.291-311.

indications of the moves towards Slovenian independence which would occur at the end of the 1980s and the beginning of the '90s. However, at the end of the 1970s, even though there were no great changes in the ZKS, circumstances began to change. A key dimension to this was the departure from the scene of a number of senior Slovene political figures – Kardelj had died, and others were pushed out or, in the case of General Ivan Dolničar, retired. Added to this, Marinko died, ironically at the same time as Ranković, in August 1983. This was at the very point when federal Yugoslavia was entering a grave compound crisis – simultaneously economic, social, political and constitutional.

In the mean time Slovene voices at the federal level had begun to criticise the federal government and to seek change. Slovenia and Croatia had jointly proposed changes to the hard currency law, the aim being that these two states which earned the greater part of Yugoslavia's hard currency income, should keep the earnings they were responsible for. Before this, in December 1981, Mitja Ribičič, one of the most conservative Slovene communists, had harshly criticised the bureaucratic federal government. Although he withdrew his comments, the fact that they were made by one of the most conservative figures on the Slovene scene was an indication that, although Slovene politicians dealing with the federation were, in Kavčič's term, still 'in puberty',[69] something was stirring.

It was with the advent of Milan Kučan as leader of the ZKS in the mid-1980s that those stirrings began to mature. While initially Kučan and the new party and government leaders who came with him were regarded as younger technocrats, nothing radical was expected from them – least of all by Kavčič, on whose ideas, in a few years' time, they would clearly be building.[70] That initial assessment proved wrong; already before the end of 1986, Kučan had opened up discussion on the question of legalising strikes. While this was a positive step towards reform, openness and democracy, it was potentially a very dangerous move for him to make – strikes could easily bring down his leadership, if major action were taken. However, while Kučan had the tactical

[69] Kavčič, *Dnevnik*, p.322.

[70] *Ibid.*, p.576.

mastery of a technocrat,[71] he also proved to have a strategic instinct over the next decade. Under his leadership through the late 1980s, Slovenia would transcend itself. Against the background of federal dissolution, communist Slovenia under party leader Kučan in 1986 swiftly evolved a system of political pluralism to become independent Slovenia under the democratically elected President Kučan a decade later.[72] A new kind of political life had begun.

Slovenia's new political life had been shaped in the Yugoslav crucible. Entry into the first Yugoslavia contributed significantly to the evolution of the Slovenia which emerged with a full independent international personality in the 1990s. This inescapable fact will always challenge those who might believe that the Slovenes were denied their preferred option for statehood within the Austrian realm and forced by international diplomats to join something akin to a Yugoslav prison. At the time there was no real alternative for Slovene politicians to take: it was they who shaped and managed entry into Yugoslavia as the demise of the Habsburg Empire and the advance of Italian forces created pressures for survival. Not only did a place in Yugoslavia provide survival, however disappointing constitutional arrangements were to prove, but it also contributed notably to Slovene development.

The unique nature of communist party control served to consolidate authority and self-governance in Slovenia during the communist period. Emerging from the Second World War under harsh central rule, the historical contingency of the Soviet-Yugoslav rift and the consequent imperative for change created conditions in which ever greater autonomy would develop. However, given the totalising nature of communist rule, even in the decentralising context of Tito's Yugoslavia, there was no reason to suppose that this would produce out of communist party monopoly the conditions for pluralist politics. However, this is what happened. Perhaps reflecting a tradition of co-operation and coalition, especially in critical times – such as the First World War, the National Government and the OF – Slovenia's communist leaders, notably Kavčič and Kučan, pushed the boundaries of communism to its limits. They brought Slovenia to the verge of pluralism and independent statehood.

---

[71] See n. 46, above.

[72] See Chapter 5.

3

CULTURE

Slovenian political developments through two Yugoslavias were predicated on the preservation of national distinctiveness. This was in line with the persistence of the Slovenes through the centuries. Language was the key element in culture, providing the primary focal point for identity, and so it remained. As a result, development was concentrated in literature, although there were notable accomplishments in other fields. The principal defensive role played by language often ran alongside contradictory openness to international influences and those influences presented a vital challenge as well as sparking creativity. The relative insignificance of Slovenian culture in global terms, as well as the hindrance to global recognition of some kind inherent in the language itself, disguised work of potential general interest. However, elements of contemporary cultural activity at odds with traditional Slovenian symbols changed this situation to some extent. Whatever the appreciation of that activity, it crossed national boundaries to find a wider audience. As we will show, this represented the crux of the Slovenian cultural dilemma: further development, as well as recognition in global eyes, depended on embracing internationalisation while finding a way to maintain tradition.

Roots and shoots of culture

Bogumil Vošnjak, one of the authors of the Corfu Declaration and subsequent diplomat for royal Yugoslavia, described Slovenian culture through the ages as a 'bulwark' against Germanisation.[1]

[1] Bogumil Vošnjak *A Bulwark against Germany: the Fight of the Slovenes, the Western Branch of the Yugoslavs, for National Existence*, London: Geo. Allen and Unwin, 1917.

Like many of his contemporaries, he imagined European history as a series of epic struggles between 'races', which were in some way immutable and implacably opposed to each other.[2] In reality Slovenian culture is not a bulwark but a crossroads: it has absorbed elements from all its neighbours (and they have absorbed elements from the Slovenes). One only needs to compare the folk music of Bela Krajina, with its South Slavonic overtones, to the Alpine rhythms of Carinthia to realise this. Slovene culture as it emerged in the modern era is therefore quite similar to that of its neighbours. It is also in many ways quite distinctive, almost confirming the Herderian view that the genius of a particular people is conveyed primarily through its language.

Before the modernisation of the economy and cultural life, Slovene culture remained rather localised and peasant-based (regional variation in cuisine and viticulture is evidence of this), though not exclusively so, and its relationships with the more dominant cultures of Vienna and the Adriatic were complex and not simply ones of master versus servant, or conversely dominant versus stubbornly independent. The influence of the Orient and the New World is discernible from representations of turbaned Turks, elephants and tigers in peasant art,[3] to the African of Prešeren's poem 'Lepa Vida', which attempted to turn a folk theme into literary reality. Perhaps 'Lepa Vida' symbolises the greatest single characteristic of Slovene culture: the continual flow between the literary and the popular. This fact explains how the writings of intellectuals in the 1980s (discussed below) galvanised the Slovene public, creating a genuinely participatory democratic and pluralist political culture.

It has often been assumed that Slovene was an almost exclusively peasant tongue before the modern period and that somehow the peasants lived in a kind of Slavonic microcosm while the real business of life went on in German, Latin or Italian. However, specialist scholarship has emphasised that the nobility and the educated also often used the vernacular. Sigmund Herberstein (1486-1566) was chosen by the Emperor to visit Moscow in part

---

[2] Michael Burleigh has referred to this as 'ethnic totalities.' Burleigh, *Germany turns Eastwards: A Study of Ostforschung in the Third Reich*, Cambridge University Press, 1988, p.3.

[3] Zmago Šmitek, *Klic Daljnih Svetov*, Ljubljana: Založba Borec, 1986.

because of his knowledge of Slavonic languages. Although he was teased during his childhood in Vipava for speaking like a '*Schlaf*' (a local pronunciation of 'Slav'), he found his linguistic aptitude extremely useful later.[4] The Triestine bishop Bonomo translated Calvin, Erasmus and Virgil into Slovene,[5] while inventories from the early seventeenth century list Slovene-language Protestant books among the possessions of the nobility.[6] The accidental discovery in 1974 of a bundle of papers subsequently identified as the Marenzi-Coraduzzi correspondence from the last decades of the seventeenth century 'confirms that the nobility in Trieste used Slovene rather fluently.'[7]

Religious convictions were controlled by the centre and provided the main instrument of Habsburg domination beyond feudalism and the administrative structures of Inner Austria. Christianisation had first taken place in the seventh century when missionaries were sent from Aquileia to convert the heathen Slavs – a subject which later fascinated the poet France Prešeren and was the basis for his epic poem 'Krst pri Savici'. In the sixteenth century a Lutheran from Raščica, Primož Trubar, produced religious literature in Slovene and, like Luther, can justly be called the founding father of his language. Thanks to the efforts of a dedicated team of Evangelicals in Germany, a Bible was produced in 1584 by Trubar's successor Jurij Dalmatin (1547–89), making Slovene the twelfth language to receive a translation. The literary quality of Dalmatin's work was high and raised the quality of the written language[8] rather as the King James Bible elevated the English of the early seventeenth century. Only small scattered pieces of Slovene have remained from before the Reformation era, chiefly the Freising Fragments dating from 972, which are the

---

[4] Sigmund Herberstein, *Fontes Rerum Austriacum*, vol.I, pt.I, Vienna, 1855, p.70.

[5] On Slovene literacy see Primož Simoniti, *Humanizem na Slovenskem*, Ljubljana: Slovenska Matica, 1979.

[6] Maja Zvanut, *Od Viteza do Gospoda*, Ljubljana: Viharnik, Znanstveni Inštitut Filozofske Fakultete, 1994, p.35.

[7] Boris Pahor, 'Il Trattato di Osimo e la Cultura Slovena', *Corriere della Sera*, 20 June 1978. The texts of the letters have been edited by Pavle Merkù, *Slovenska Plemiška Pisma*, Trieste: Založništvo Tržaškega Tiska, 1980.

[8] E.g. see Micháel Glavan, *Dalmatinova Biblija in Slovenci*, Ljubljana: Jože Moškrič, 1994, p.29.

oldest extant Slavonic texts,[9] and the Celovški and Stiški manuscripts respectively from the fourteenth and fifteenth centuries. The appearance of important texts in Slovene from the Bible to Adam Bohorič's grammar in 1584, through to Prešeren's *Poezije* in 1847 created a historical and linguistic consciousness for the nation, and as such these works have been called 'a paradigm of Slavonic national evolution'.[10]

The evangelising of Trubar's associates, including itinerant preaching, had an immediate effect on transforming the Slovene peasantry. The popular imagination was set alight by the gospel word in the vernacular, the fire in the bellies of local preachers and Protestantism flourished briefly in some areas. In 1593 Franc Barbaro recorded: 'From Ribnica I arrived at Žužemberk, where the castle is in the possession of the heretics, and nearly all the inhabitants are Lutherans. A second church has been seized by the heretics, and there they now preach their heresies. I had intended to seize it back, but it was guarded by many soldiers and the Archduke's commissioner considered it unwise to expose himself to the danger of attack.'[11] In response to this outburst the Habsburg authorities attempted to stamp out all trace of the Reformation, burnt Slovene books and imposed the rule of the Jesuits on the peasants.[12] The approximate period 1630–1780 was a particularly low point in the history of Slovenian literary culture,[13] although local protests sometimes emerged. In 1646 a parishioner from Sveti, Peter pri Ložu, requested that the priest Michael Boltram, whom he considered good in other respects, should learn Slovene to communicate with his flock.[14]

---

[9] There is a facsimile of the 'Freising Fragments' (*Brižinski Spomeniki*) in Kos et al. (eds), *Zbornik*, pp.476-86.

[10] Rado Lenček, 'A Paradigm of Slavic National Evolution: Bible, Grammar, Poet', *Slovene Studies*, vol.6, nos 1-2, 1984, pp.57-71.

[11] Irma Ožbalt, 'Evangelini: the Protestant Intermezzo in Žužemberk', *Slovene Studies*, vol.6, nos 1-2, 1984, p.195.

[12] Predrag Belić, *Prva Tridesetletja Jesuitov in Slovenci*, Ljubljana: SAZU, 1989.

[13] Janez Svetokriški (1647-1714) published his sermons in Slovene as *Sacrum Promptuarium*, Mirko Rupel (ed.), Ljubljana: Akademska Založba, 1937, but little has survived that is not religious literature.

[14] Archiv Republike Slovenije, 'Vicedomski Urad za Kranjsko, 32, XVI beneficij sv. Petra v Ložu, 7-3'.

During this period many local animistic or even dualist peasant beliefs survived and coexisted with the official religion. In other words, Slovene literary culture continued not so much through the catechisms produced by the church but through very ancient folk beliefs which could be described as pagan. Festivals to celebrate the seasons were important occasions and echoed many pre-Christian practices known elsewhere.[15] In 1816 an ethnographer observed that 'the most important festivals of the Carniolans are consecration, marriage, pilgrimage and the fire of St John's Eve'[16] (a fire lit on the vernal equinox, which is a ceremony of pre-Christian origin). There is evidence to link the peasant cultures of the Friuli and Istria and the Quanero with the Slovene lands. The periodic lake of Cerknica was a focal point of a regional fertility cult that aroused the suspicions of the Inquisition in the sixteenth century.[17]

After the 'rediscovery' of popular culture from the late eighteenth century, some of the Slovenes' pagan gods such as Perun, Živa and Morana, and the bad spirits with their good counterparts, were revived within literary culture, creating a bridge with the popular.[18] Undoubtedly knowledge of the legends of Zlatorog (a goat with a golden horn) and other beasts has also enhanced tourism in the Triglav national park as well as exciting a new generation of children at bedtime. Some other uniquely Slovene folk customs such as the carnival festivals of '*Pustni torek*' and the '*Kurent*' of Ptuj have survived apparently almost unaltered into the modern age.[19]

Perhaps the greatest literary text to celebrate *Slovenstvo* before the modern era is an unusual baroque topography, *Die Ehre dess Herzogthums Crain*, written in 1689 by a local nobleman Johann

---

[15] Niko Kuret, *Praznično Leto Slovencev*, Celje: Mohorjeva Družba, 1967, 2 vols.

[16] Breton de la Martinière, *Illyrien und Dalmatien oder Sitten, Gebrauche und Trachten der Illyrier und ihrer Nachbarn*, Pesth: K.A. Hartleben, 1816, p.39.

[17] Cathie Carmichael, 'The Fertility of Lake Cerknica', *Social History*, vol.19, no.3, October 1994, pp.305-17.

[18] The former are dubbed '*črti*' in Slovene and the latter '*rusalke*' and '*sojenice*'. See, for example, Jakob Kelemina, *Bajke in Pripovedke Slovenskega Ljudstva*, Celje: Mohorjeva Družba, 1930.

[19] This end-of-winter festival in Ptuj in Styria is a carnivalesque occasion with zoomorphic costumes, which has survived since the Middle Ages.

Weikhard von Valvasor. As a young man Valvasor had travelled around Europe and North Africa on an extended version of the gentleman's 'grand tour' during the years 1659-72.[20] It became clear to him that his homeland was unknown outside the Habsburg Monarchy and as a result he dedicated most of the rest of his life to his studies of Carniola, developing a form of proto-nationalism. In the years that followed he corresponded with the Royal Society in London and was elected a Fellow in 1687.[21] His travels also convinced him of the uniqueness of his native landscape. In *Die Ehre* he wrote: 'I have seen many singularly wonderful caves in various lands and kingdoms, not only in Europe but also in Africa, but there is probably nowhere in the world that has the sort of caves that exist in this my fatherland.'[22] Although Valvasor's work was criticised by later generations, in many ways it was arguably the first text to create Slovenia as a distinct geographical and cultural region.[23] In addition, his ability to converse with local peasants in their own language gave his writing an ethnographic superiority to other contemporary accounts.[24]

If the Slovenes had links to wider geographical areas, then it is also clear that they had many cultural practices unique to their own areas. The hay rack (*kozolec*) is not found elsewhere in Central Europe and the painting of beehives, known as '*panjska končnica*' is also unique.[25] Beehive painting in Slovenia is an exuberant art form which uses bright colours and a mixture of traditional and biblical themes. Beekeeping has also been important across Slovenia

[20] On Valvasor's travels see Branko Reisp, *Janez Vajkard Valvasor*, Ljubljana: Mladinska Knjiga, 1983, pp.81-90.

[21] Branko Reisp (ed.), *Korespondenca Janeza Vajkarda Valvasorja z Royal Society*, Ljubljana: SAZU, 1987.

[22] J.W. von Valvasor, *Die Ehre dess Herzogthums Crain*, Laybach: Wolfgang Mainz Endter, 1689, Teil I, Buch I, p.240. A Slovene version of Valvasor's work was published in the 1960s: Mirko Rupel and Branko Reisp (eds), *Slava Vojvodine Kranjske*, Ljubljana: Mladinska Knjiga, 1968.

[23] Cathie Carmichael, 'Za Filozofa Preveč Romantičnega Pridiha: Nekaj Zapazanj o Valvasorjevi Etnografiji', *Traditiones*, vol.24, 1995, pp.95-107.

[24] Janez Šumrada, 'Valvasorjev Angleški Sodobnik Edward Browne v Slovenskih Deželah Leta 1669' in Andrej Vovko (ed.), *Valvasorjev Zbornik*, Ljubljana: SAZU, 1990, pp.54-102.

[25] On the hay-racks see Jaka Čop and Tone Cevc, *Slovenski Kozolec*, Žirovnica: Agens, 1993.

in historic times and a fermented drink, '*medica*', is prepared from honey. It is not perhaps so curious that one of the founders of modern apiculture, Anton Janša (1734-73), who advocated the medicinal use of propolis came from the hills north of Ljubljana. Valvasor, Janša, Trubar and the writers of the later modernist movement, or even the 'cultural revolution' of the 1980s, were to demonstrate that although the Slovenes belonged within European traditions, they were also continually producing work with a distinctive aroma. In the middle and late eighteenth century there was a re-emergence of Slovene linguistic culture after the long night of the Counter-Reformation. Baron Žiga Zois (1747-1819) sponsored the work of Anton Linhart (1756-95), who completed a history of Carniola in 1791 which united the Slovenes together as a historical people, although his chronological scope and empirical concepts would not correspond to what is considered historically accurate today.[26] In 1768 Marko Pohlin circulated his grammar, which was the first attempt to create a paradigmatic basis for the Slovene language, and in 1797-1800 a Slovene newspaper, *Lublanske Novice*, was published by Valentin Vodnik (1758-1819). Thanks to the work of these intellectuals, the Slovene language found a place again at the centre of life and culture in the Slovene lands.

Literature and the arts

The centrality of language to Slovenian culture meant that for the most part, literature developed far beyond the accomplishments in other spheres. The 'higher' arts did not enter the Slovenian canon until a relatively late stage. Although Slovenian literature and to a lesser extent the plastic and cinematic arts saw notable achievements, in other areas the record is fairly barren. This historic position began to change to a limited degree in the contemporary period, as will be seen in the following section. In the present section, Slovenian strengths and weaknesses in literature and the arts are reviewed.

Of all the arts, music is where Slovenia has least to offer. Specifically Slovenian music of distinction did not emerge in the

---

[26] Fran Zwitter, 'Prva Koncepcija Slovenske Zgodovine', *Glasnik Muzejskega Društva za Slovenijo*, vol.XX 1939, pp.355-72.

classical sphere, and although the work of Jakob Petelin-Gallus (1550-91), alias Jakob Handl, outside the Slovene lands has been compared to that of Palestrina,[27] it is little known and acknowledged not to have had much influence on the development of music in the Slovene lands. Traditional Slovenian music blends Alpine accordion, brass and vocal traditions with Balkan tones, and is mostly limited in character and variety. The most distinctive feature is vocal music based on traditional folk song and set for *a cappella* octets. The music generally progresses in steady *alla breve* phrases in rhythmic unison. In some cases it is intermittently broken by faster, punctuated *staccato* leaps of Alpine idiom, related to the patterns of yodelling. For the most part the music is built with solid, unadventurous harmony moving in blocks, generally lacking counterpoint, although there may be occasional solo lines or fugal descants.

The constraints on development in the fine and plastic arts were less pronounced or prolonged. In the twilight years of the Habsburg Monarchy Slovene art made the transition from the folk to the gallery, with the first Fine Art Exhibition being organised in Ljubljana in 1890 under the auspices of the Slovenian Art Society (Slovensko Umetniško Društvo). Perhaps the most important figure was Rihard Jakopič (1869-1943): apart from his leading role in translating Impressionism into the Slovenian context, he was also responsible for starting the first art school in Ljubljana, opening the first art gallery there and for initiating serious art criticism.

Impressionism played a significant part in the growth of painting in Slovenian culture. Its exponents came together as the 'Sava group' for five years after 1906. This contrasted strongly with the folk orientation found in the work of Maksim Gaspari (1883-1980), whose art society, Vesna, founded in 1904, was steeped in Slovene rural tradition. Sava encouraged the work of a series of Impressionist painters including Matija Jama (1872-1947), Matej Sternen (1870-1949) and Ivan Grohar (1866-1911). Sternen focused

[27] Georges Castellan and Antonia Bernard, *La Slovénie*, Paris: Presses Universitaires de France, 1996, p.121. The authors offer a rather paltry yet exaggerated overview of Slovenian musical development in the classical domain.

on portraits,[28] and the other two celebrated the Slovene landscape in gentle, muted colours. Grohar's '*Sejalec*' (The Sower) is perhaps the best established and most distinctive creation in Slovenian fine art, with the muted character of the title wearing traditional Slovenian peasant garb and seeming to emerge, ghostlike, as a shadow from the land.

The Slovenian record in the plastic arts is considerably more distinguished than in the fine arts. The creative force of true importance is the architect Jože Plečnik (1872-1957), who is to Ljubljana what Antoní Gaudi is to Barcelona, Frank Lloyd Wright to Oak Park, Chicago, and (perhaps to a smaller extent) Charles Rennie Mackintosh to Glasgow. As a young man Plečnik had travelled and worked in Vienna, Prague and Florence, and the influence of all these cultures is evident in his *œuvre*, as well as some of the simplicity of Japanese watercolours. After his return to the suburb of Trnovo in 1921, Plečnik's synthesis was to build a unique link between the predominant Baroque style of the city, with plaster pink and Maria Theresa ochre, and the geometric shapes of architectural modernism.

Ljubljana is unimaginable without the works of Plečnik. The pink and grey stonework of the National and University Library (NUK), finished in 1941, is a major feature of student and cultural life. So too is the Tromostovje (Three Bridges), constructed in 1931 – an elaborate trio of white bridges that transmute into the riverside stone façade of the fish market at the other end of which is a bridge guarded by green dragons, the symbol of Ljubljana. The Tromostovje is also in many ways the heart of Ljubljana, situated by the statue of the poet France Prešeren. In the 1980s this sculpture, which scandalised the inhabitants of Ljubljana when it was first unveiled because of its presentation of a naked muse above the poet's head, became a regular social meeting place and a venue for public gatherings, as well as for the sale of *Mladina*.

Among Plečnik's greatest work is the city cemetery at Žale (1940), a fitting epitaph to an ascetic Christian socialist whose love for quality in design and material made his work timeless. His creations fit far better with the spirit of the city than those of his near-contemporary Vladimir Subić, whose Nebotičnik

---

[28] See Moderna Galerija, *Matej Sternen: Retrospektiva Raztava*, Ljubljana: Moderna Galerija, 1976.

(Skyscraper) of 1931 was the tallest building in Ljubljana, although it is a miniature skyscraper by global standards. Nebotičnik, reflecting different trends of the 1930s including Constructivism, does not clash with nearby buildings of the post-war Stalinist period. The clash between the Stalinist and pre-Stalinist periods is epitomised in the egoistical impertinence of Drago Trsar's statue of Edvard Kardelj, on the one hand, and the sublime quality of the granite and bronze monument to Prešeren by Maks Fabiani and Ivan Zajc, erected in 1905, on the other. By contrast, the statue of the Slovene Partisan leader Boris Kidrič outside the Cankarjev Don (the main cultural centre in Ljubljana), is accepted and respected, as that of his junior Kardelj is not.

While the plastic arts have been important in shaping the light and attractive aspect of the Slovenian capital, giving it an air of cultural distinction, Slovenian culture has developed most strongly in the literary sphere.[29] The starting point for this is the work of the poet and writer France Prešeren. With Prešeren, Slovene began to find a new literary confidence, and his work is the most important single influence in the history of the modern language. He also gave voice to many of the characteristic attitudes that still define the Slovene personality. Although Prešeren sometimes wrote in German, his Slovene poetry was far superior in literary quality. The majority of his work was published in the collection *Poezije* ('Poetry'),[30] often still carried in pocket editions by Slovenian students a century and a half later. This marks Prešeren as the quintessential Slovenian writer whose work is thematically national, yet international in its sentiments.

---

[29] The assessment of Slovenian literature, as of the other arts, is necessarily limited by two factors in the present volume. The first is inevitably space. The second compounds the first: the decision to offer some sense of particular authors and examples of their work, rather than offering a list of names and titles. Thus the coverage in the present chapter is not only far from comprehensive, it also omits authors that might otherwise have been included in a different kind of survey giving less flavour of the literature itself. In its chapter on culture Castellan and Bernard, *La Slovénie*, offers a more extensive set of names, but only includes passing reference, however, to Vitomil Zupan, without treating the actual work in any detail. Antun Barac, *A History of Yugoslav Literature*, Ann Arbor: Michigan Slavic Texts, 1976, in its passages on Slovenia, offers a generally useful survey including many authors up to the Second World War not mentioned here.

[30] France Prešeren, *Poezije*, Ljubljana: Državna Založba Slovenije, 1949.

This is epitomised in 'Zdravljica' (A Toast), the lyric chosen by Slovenia for its national anthem.[31] In it Prešeren expresses the view that the world should live together in peace and harmony, indeed in a kind of brotherhood of all nations.[32] Its choice as national anthem would have satisfied the author who felt 'responsibility towards his people' and often sought to combine the themes of love, fate and patriotism in his work.[33] While 'Soneti Nesreče' (Sonnets of Misfortune) and 'Sonetni Venec' (A Crown of Sonnets) reflect the first two themes, it is the epic 'Krst pri Savici' (Baptism by the Savica) that ambitiously takes up the challenge of synthesis. The poem takes Christianisation as its setting and deals with the destiny of Črtomir, the leader of the Slav warriors who is unluckly not only in battle but also in love. On returning from battle, he is forced to renounce Bogomila, who has undergone conversion to Christianity, but who was formerly a priestess of the Goddess Živa. Ironically Bogomila's conversion was secured through a pact with God, in which she commits herself to Christian service in order to have Črtomir return safely from war. The tone and theme of this poem capture a melancholy mood that befits a people confronted by the challenges of destiny and global developments, and furthermore whose suicide rate is among the highest in the world.

After Prešeren, Slovene gained a firm footing as a modern literary medium. As elsewhere in the Habsburg Monarchy, the three decades before the outbreak of the First World War were remarkably creative and Vienna itself became a cultural Mecca for Slovenes. A number of Slovenes were acolytes of Hermann Bahr, the leader of the Modernist movement in Vienna which sought to transcend naturalism. The most significant of the Viennese Slovenes was the remarkable writer Ivan Cankar, whose face was immortalised by Slavko Tihec in a sculpture which stands outside the eponymous Cankarjev Dom. Despite Slovene views on Prešeren,

---

[31] In Slovene, *'pesem'* means both poem and song, and poems were often written to be sung – as was the case with some of Prešeren's work which was still sung in the 1990s. In keeping with the tradition of sung poetry, his work is characterised by relatively simple rhythms. Indeed, his poetry also borrowed from and adapted traditional popular songs, as with 'Lepa Vida' (Beautiful Vida).

[32] Prešeren, *Poezije*, pp.23-5.

[33] Castellan and Bernard, *La Slovénie*, p.35.

it is Ivan Cankar who holds the attention as the one Slovene writer who certainly commands a place in the pantheon of world literature. However, in spite of this, he is almost as little known outside Slovenia, as are other Slovene writers – although some of his work has appeared in translation. It seems likely that if Cankar's work had been written in German – as it might have been since he found his literary spirit in Vienna – rather than his native Slovene, it would have gained far more recognition.

Cankar wrote poetry, prose and drama. The first of these took up his early years and included *Erotika*, published in 1899, with its title offering nothing to mislead regarding the decadent *fin de siècle* world that influenced it. Copies of *Erotika* were ordered by the church to be burned. However, it is with his plays and especially his prose that Cankar made his mark. Although these differ in tone, there are inevitably common elements. While the prose contains elements of despair and occasional sentimentality, the plays comprise satirical thrusts at the hypocrisy and inward-looking nature of bourgeois life among the Slovenes – for example, *Za Narodov Blagor* (For the Good of the Nation), perhaps his best-loved play, and *Hlapci* (The Servants). In his prose Cankar represents the ambivalence of the Slovene in the twilight years of the Habsburg Monarchy. His own self-doubt runs through all his work and is manifested particularly clearly in the figure of the Bailiff Jernej, who struggles against legal injustice only to turn into a desperate and bitter parody of himself.

Hlapec Jernej (The Bailiff Jernej) is a metaphor for the position of the Slovenes in the Austro-Hungarian Empire.[34] In it Jernej, the bailiff of the title, has faithfully served his master, Old Sitar, for forty years. He has built the master's house and worked on every corner of the land. However, his position changes when Old Sitar dies. Young Sitar, who inherits the estate, immediately stops Jernej from sitting by the corner of the fire in the house, as he was accustomed to doing. Jernej initially finds it hard to take this and other actions of the new master seriously and laughs at them. For this he is dismissed. He then sets off for Ljubljana in search of his rights, assuming that he cannot be thrown out in this way, having built the house and lived in it for so long.

---

[34] Ivan Cankar, *Izbrana Dela* V, Ljubljana: Cankarjeva Založba, 1952, pp.417-98.

In Ljubljana he asks for justice in the courts, where however he is treated as a joke and is inevitably disappointed. Convinced of his rights, after working all his life on the estate, he heads for the imperial capital, Vienna, certain that he will meet the Emperor who will rectify the situation by dispensing justice and affirming his rights. Instead he is arrested as a vagrant, interrogated by men who do not speak to him in his own language, identified by his papers and returned home. Finally Jernej returns defeated to Sitar's house to collect the pipe he has left in it. The book ends with the house burning down, and the former bailiff, who has been standing with his fists on his hips, watching and laughing. He is then savaged by the villagers and thrown into the fire.

Jernej is a symbol for the Slovenes in the Empire, willing servants but not respected in the wider cosmopolitan environment.[35] Equally, Jernej can be taken as a symbol of the Slovenes in each of the 'houses' in which they found themselves throughout their history before independence. The text also implicitly offers a reflection on the responsibilities to be faced once rights have been attained through independence, both regarding others in the self-standing house and on questions of a future condominium that might be considered. However, its theme is also the universal struggle of the ordinary person for justice and a claim to rights, juxtaposing simple nobility and the world.

Cankar's writing encompassed rich use of language with elements of poetic vision and naturalism, all tinged with a mixture of irony, gloom and melancholy. He was concerned to capture the moral and material poverty that characterised the age in which he lived and the solitude of individuals either succumbing to their environment or struggling against it. The central characters of novels such as *Tujci* (The Outsiders) or *Martin Kačur* (Martin Kačur) are idealists sucked into the swamps of middle-class social decay. Some of Cankar's most moving prose concerns his relationship with his mother, whom he outpaced in experience and education and treated coldly, only to experience deep regret later in life. The short story *Skodelica Kave* (Coffee Cup) begins 'I have harmed a

---

35 The book's evident 'class' content, involving feudal-bourgeois repression and the assertion of rights by the 'creator' of the house who is eventually martyred for his revolutionary action made it a popular text under communism, despite the strong 'national' message.

person I loved on many occasions in my life.'[36] This tone is reflected throughout his work, which is often autobiographical and reflective about his early years. While *Podobe iz Sanj* (Reflections from Dreams) and *Moja Njiva* (My Field) fit this rubric, it is probably *Moje Življenje* (My Life) which is the most intimately written. Here his mother features as the person whose look searches so deeply that anything can be admitted without his realising it and who gently and silently makes her son profoundly aware of his sin. This epitomises the autobiographical portion of Cankar's *œuvre* in the way that *Jernej* is the touchstone of his fiction.

Cankar's life was cut short by the influenza epidemic that also killed his Viennese contemporaries Gustav Klimt and Egon Schiele. It is unclear how such a restless cosmopolitan would have adjusted to life in the new Yugoslavia. Given that the 'traditional' world had so definitively been swept away in 1918, it is conceivable that the writer would have been lost. Equally, given his prognosis for the South Slav state, he might well have found a new context in which to explore the Slovenian relationship with a broader set of communities.

The other main writer of the Modernist movement was Oton Župančič (1878-1949), an altogether more pragmatic figure than Cankar. In contrast to the pessimism and guilt of Cankar's work, that of Župančič is light and hopeful. He is probably best known for his creation of the children's book character Ciciban, known to all Slovenes. Like Cankar, he began his career at an early age by publishing poetry, such as *Čaša Opojnosti* (A Glass of Intoxication), and later translated this into theatrical work, such as *Veronika Deseniška* (Veronika of Desenice), which developed the genre of dramatic poetry established by Prešeren. Župančič was to become a bard of two world wars, as well as a translator of Shakespeare into beautiful Slovene. His work for the stage was given a boost by the foundation of the theatre company Ljubljansko Gledališče in 1892. The Modernist tradition was continued by the brief career of Srečko Kosovel (1904-26), particularly his *Integrali* (Integrals, 1924). He found the Karadjordjević kingdom a strange and hostile place and inspired the writers who were to form the *Sodobnost* group in the 1930s.

---

[36] Cankar, *Izbrana Dela* VIII, pp.151-4.

Slovene poetry and prose continued to play an important role in national culture into the second half of the twentieth century. The Christian Socialist writer Edvard Kocbek (1904-81) was a communist fellow traveller, closely associated with the liberation movement in the Second World War but always maintaining distance and dissidence. This made him acceptable both to the communist regime and to its young liberal critics. He is best known for his volume *Strah in Pogum* (Fear and Courage), published in 1952, which broke with the prevailing socialist realist traditions of the early Tito period. Kocbek's poetry captures the ambivalence of his position. Many poems were written during the Second World War, some reflecting his time with the Partisan movement in Slovenia. His writing also uses imagery common to communist literature, originating from Russian and Soviet writing. An example of this is the wind, which is frequently used to symbolise revolution in pre-Soviet and Soviet literature[37] and is a common image in Kocbek's work and is even the title of one poem, 'Veter' (The Wind). In this poem and others the image can be read on the revolutionary level, but it also operates as a more conventional spiritual, pastoral or romantic symbol. The way in which this wind imagery can operate on both levels is seen in 'Na Polju' (In the Field) which uses the short lines and curt rhythms common to much of Kocbek's most attractive writing. In this poem tree, word and man are loners in a ravine,[38] each suspicious of the others yet linked to them by a secret memory from ancient times. Each is a discrete part of the whole: tree is silence, word is bird, man is ear. Each of them waits, asking 'Where is the wind?'[39] The next stanza holds the key to the poem:

> *The question is love,*
> *love is the wind*
> *and the wind is the beginning*[40]

[37] We are grateful to Milena Michalski who drew this is our attention.

[38] In common with most other Slavonic languages (Bulgarian and Macedonian are the exceptions) Slovene does not use articles. 'Bird', 'tree' and 'man' could all be translated using the indefinite or the definite article. However, in this case the three are rendered in a de-anglicised form to reflect the starkness, brevity and gentle abruptness of Kocbek's line.

[39] '*Kje je veter?*'

[40] *Vprašanje je ljubezn / ljubezen je veter / in veter je začetek.*

With this the tree's leaves rustle, birdsong is heard, man starts to sing and the three join together as friends. The role of the wind as revolutionary inspiration can be taken to be the force that allows the three isolated elements to unite in order to free themselves so that a new, positive era can begin. Equally, it can be read on a more direct level as a simple, graceful elegy to the spirit and force of love.

Whatever his desire for social justice and his links with the communist movement, Kocbek like most other Slovenes was concerned with Slovenian culture and identity and saw the alliance with other South Slavs in rather pragmatic terms, dwelling on the the nation's complex over its small size which is so commonplace in Slovene self-portrayal. In the poem 'V seminarju' (In Seminarju) he speculates on what the impact on the world would be if seven million Chinese all jumped from a height of two metres. He continues rather wistfully, 'We Slovenes, for instance would need to jump from such a height that we would all be killed. That is why we have to sign up with our neighbours.'[41]

Kocbek was both a loyalist and a dissident. He criticised the slaughter of the Domobranci in the Trieste-based newspaper *Zaliv* in 1975. Nevertheless he had a troubled conscience about his own post-Partisan spell of favour with the communists, as his meditations on the redemptive qualities of imprisonment, 'Kopernenje po ječi' (Longing for Confinement), clearly indicate.[42] Kocbek's human and humanistic qualities were an important inspiration for the various contributors to the journal *Nova Revija* in the 1980s.

The importance of poetry in Slovene continued with the work of others, in addition to Kocbek, in the Tito period. Among the most important figures were those who together published the collection *Pesmi Štirih* (Poems of the Four) in 1953: Janez Menart, Tone Pavček, Ciril Zlobec and Kajetan Kovič. Each of the four acknowledged as their mentor Ivan Minatti, whose poetry reflecting the consoling power of nature – for example, *Pa bo Pomlad Prišla*

---

[41] Edvard Kocbek, 'Na vratih zvečer'/'At the door at evening' (trans. Tom Ložar), Dorian and Ljubljana: La Compagnie des Muses and Aleph, 1990, pp.110-11.

[42] Kocbek, 'Na vratih', pp.78-9.

(But Spring Will Come) – is nonetheless not obviously reflected in the collection or in the later work of these poets. Pavček's work has a musical aspect, while that of Kovič treats the anguish of the ideal meeting the real. Both Menart and Zlobec continued writing into the 1980s. The former produced a collection entitled *Menjave* (Changes) in 1984 which retained a mix of irony and neo-Romanticism, while the recognised style of the latter, poetry of resignation in love, continued in *Ljubezen Dvoedina* (Love Two in One) in 1993. However, this poetic mode was ostensibly at odds with the prominent role Zlobec took in social and political commentary as Slovenia's relationship with the Yugoslav federation deteriorated and Slovenia's independent statehood surfaced – reflected in his book-length essay-cum-autobiography, *Lepo je Biti Slovenec, Ni Pa Lahko* (It's nice to be Slovene, but not easy) of 1992.[43]

After the Second World War the tenets of socialist realism were introduced. However, while the principle behind this (that literature should contribute to the creation of socialist character and society) remained the official programme, it was not rigidly applied in Slovenia for long. Indeed, in so far as the literature could be dubbed realist, its character was social rather than socialist. It also took in Slovenian national questions as part of its remit. For example, one of the most prominent prose writers, Ciril Kosmač, treated the position of Slovenes in the mixed areas that had been part of Italy (the region from which he came), as in *Sreča in Kruh* (Bread and Happiness), published in 1946. While this novel reflected the ethos of socialist realism at the onset of the country's brief Stalinist phase, it was a later novel by Kosmač that broke the mould of socialist realism, following Kocbek's ground-breaking *Strah in Pogum*.

The novel in question was *Pomladni Dan* (A Day in Spring), published in 1953. The most interesting aspect of this work is its use of what is, effectively, dual narration. This is made to build the 'truth' from different viewpoints covering the period from the First World War to the period after the Second. One narrative voice is that of the 'author', the other that of his aunt. While the 'author' ostensibly tells the story, much of the book has passages in quotation marks where it is the aunt who is effectively telling that part of the tale. This stereophonic narrative thus bridges time and situation through the narrative of the aunt, reflexively inserted as a dominating layer within the author's narrative. This device is used to explore the differences between truth and an accurate record of events over three periods, the First and the Second World Wars and the present in which the novel is set.

The focal point for this is Kadetka, a young woman whose father was a Czech cadet in the Austrian army in the Idrica region in the First World War. The cadet was killed there after fathering the girl who was born illegitimate to her Slovene mother. The author decides to 'invent' a story about her shortly after he arrives home having been away for fifteen years, getting his aunt to supply the details that he needs to know. In the end, although Kadetka does not know it, her husband Gino, an Italian from the region who joined the Slovenian Partisans, is buried in the same grave as her father. Nor does she know, having been told that he died fighting, that Gino killed himself accidentally. The aunt's rendition to Kadetka therefore has elements of artistic necessity: the true facts about Gino's death would have made his personality incomplete, whereas the invented death on Domino Ridge seems appropriate.

As the aunt and the author agree, in a commentary on the nature of truth and art at the end of the book, the invented death is not true or, more properly, correct but it is 'more in keeping with the truth'. The 'author' considers whether the coincidences involved, although correct in terms of the record, would actually be believed by readers of a novel who might dismiss it as unconvincing artifice. Finally, he decides that he will write the novel, but warns his aunt that she will be annoyed because things will not be as they really were – he will deviate from the truth, just as she has, in order for the novel to be beautiful. She finishes by saying that it will be beautiful if it is in keeping with the truth. The narrative device and the commentary on the nature of truth and beauty are of intrinsic interest, yet they also serve to reinforce the events of the novel, which concern ethnic Slovene relations with others and the impact of the two world wars on the people and the region. Kosmač continued his move into experimentation in later work, such as the 1958 *Balada o Trobenti in Oblaka* (Ballad of the Trumpet and the Cloud).

Narrative strength is also very much in evidence in the work of Ivan Potrč. A committed communist supporter from before the Second World War, Potrč in his writing far transcends the ideologically obvious. His novels treat social problems, but in immediate, personal ways and in settings of rural Slovenian life. He had already published *Prekleta Zemlja* (Cursed Land) in 1936, marking him as a writer of note. However, his major novel is *Na Kmetih*,[44] published in 1953. In a more conventional way than Kosmač in *Pomladni Dan*, Potrč uses the device of a narrative within the narrative. This creates a frame for the events with which the novel is concerned to be told by the individual at the centre of them, Južek Hedl. The narrator relates to the reader what Hedl related to him while they were in prison about the circumstances that had brought him there.

The book is regarded as a treatment of the issue of collectivisation of Slovenian peasant lands after the Second World War, reflecting its location in the communist period. However, it is really a novel of passions in a small community and of both their impact on the fabric of that community and the contrast between the puritanical and conservative values professed by the people and their actual behaviour. The character of Slovenian rural life is captured as Hedl leaves his family with whom, apart from his mother, he cannot get along, especially his former Partisan brother-in-law who treats young Hedl, his mother and the others in an objectionable way. He goes to a neighbouring farm, where he has been helping out while the owner, Toplek, is dying and during which time he has been seduced by the man's wife, Toplečka. They begin to sleep together regularly after Hedl moves in, even before Toplek's death, which occurs when he discovers the lovers together and is about to strike Toplečka.

Scandal and opprobrium surround the Toplek farm, where Toplečka has become pregnant by Hedl and he is also now the lover of one of her two daughters, Hana; she has been away, and on her return provokes him into enjoying her favours too. In time, after Toplečka's new daughter is born, Hana also becomes pregnant. Against the background of his relations with the two Toplek women and reflections on his fate and concern for his

---

[44] The title literally means 'On the farm.' However, an excellent translation by Harry Leeming appeared as *The Land and the Flesh*, Ljubljana: Vilenica, 1988.

future, given that Toplečka refuses to sign the farm over to him
and Hana, and that the prospects of his inheriting his own family's
farm have become almost negligible, he returns to visit his family
on his sister's wedding day. After a clash with his hated brother-
in-law, he leaves in a state of despair and returns to the Toplek
farm. There, while Hedl is sleeping off his emotional distress,
Toplečka comes to him and, in the anguish and emotional intensity
of these events, he ends up strangling her with her own hair.
This leaves Hana alone on the farm, since her sister Tunika has
decided to marry, and Hedl is in prison, telling his story to the
narrator.

The character of Tunika provides a counterpoint in the novel's
course. She represents a lost, pure love. Once, picking cherries,
in a moment that he often recalls, and at other times, Hedl is
affected by her in a spiritual way that is quite different from his
sensual passions for the other women in her family. Finally, the
narrator, who believes that he will never find out what became
of Tunika after Hedl concludes his tale with the strangling, is
able to round everything off after Hedl has been taken away
from his prison cell. The narrator discovers a note given to Hedl
by Hana on a visit to the prison. It is from Tunika. She and her
husband Palek have escaped the arguments and petty emotions
of peasant life, which are so prominent in the novel, for a better
life on the collective. She also urges him to go back to the
waiting Hana. Crucially, she reveals that from that moment when
they were picking cherries she had been in love with him, but
had never wanted to be in his way while he was always otherwise
involved. It is the pathetic irony of this message that has silenced
Hedl's tale to the narrator after Hana's visit. It also provides a
light, if somewhat obvious, coda to the tale, giving the reader
space to reflect, with the same empty wonderment as the narrator,
following what has previously been an intense and pressing narrative
excursion through the emotional furrows of life on the farm. While
this setting is typically Slovenian, the passions and social pressures
the novel depicts are eternal themes of literature everywhere.

Narrative structure is also an important aspect of the work of
Vitomil Zupan, the remaining major prose writer of the post-1945
period. Zupan's most notable work is *Menuet za Kitaro (Na Petindvaj-
set Strelov)* (Minuet for [25-Shot] Guitar) from 1975, 'an artistic
synthesis of his earlier output', which was a great public success

as well as a hit with literary critics.[45] The novel is built on action in two time-frames. One is the Second World War, in which Jakob Bergant ('Berk'), a member of the Slovenian Partisans, retains a commitment to liberal rather than communist values. The other is 1970s Spain, where Berk meets a former Wehrmacht officer, Joseph Bitter, who had served in the Slovene lands during the war. Berk and Bitter, who must have fought on opposite sides in the same battle, begin a series of conversations on war and their perspectives on the experience of it. The book was problematic in official eyes, as was some of Zupan's other work, and the regime sought to discredit it along with the output of other writers.[46] This is because its characters' liberal politics combine with a realistic portrayal of the imperfections of the Partisan experience.

The novel captures the attraction of war for some, the folly of it for others and the relative detachment experienced by the ordinary soldier. This is epitomised in the death of Berk's friend Anton in the conclusion to the novel. Anton's death (echoing that of Gino in *Pomladni Dan*) is accidental and takes place at the end of the war when the Partisans' victory is assured. Ironicallly Berk managed earlier in the war to save the wounded Anton and help him to escape from the battle-line.

Anton and Berk are discussing the imminent victory. Berk's narrative considers the eternal need for enemies, while Anton, who served in the Spanish Civil War (as did many Partisans) and whose tales of Spain complete the link to the Berk-Bitter aspect of the book, once more recalls an incident from his time in Spain, at the end of that war. Then someone had said 'See you in the next war!' As Anton says this, he is killed by accidental gunfire as one of a group of Partisans celebrating in the room below bangs his automatic rifle on the ground and it goes off, sending a shot up through the roof into Anton's body. In contrast to the way in which accidental death is falsified to be closer to the beauty and truth of artistic creation in Kosmač, in Zupan's

---

[45] Alenka Koron, 'Nemirno Iskanje Moderne Proze: Zupanovo Pripovedništvo do *Menueta za Kitaro*' in Janko Kos *et al.*, *Vitomil Zupan: Interpretacije*, Ljubljana: Nova Revija, 1993, p.36.

[46] Castellan and Bernard, *La Slovénie*, p.113.

novel it is precisely the accuracy of this simultaneously pathetic
and bathetic death during a victory celebration, that underscores
the message that the world is not orderly with paths leading to
pre-ordained ends but characterised by people's needs, defined
by experience, and by chance. This questioning of the orthodox
view of Partisan heroism and destiny made the book outstanding
and provided a problematic addition to the canon of the Partisan
novel.

The last words spoken by Anton were taken as the title for
the 1980 film based on Zupan's novel, *Na Svidenje v Naslednje
Vojni* (See You in the Next War). The film, like the novel, is
one of the most important contributions to post-Second World
War Slovenian culture and, like the novel too, it reflects a dominant
strand in cultural output that was encouraged officially, but also
emerged as an obvious topic: the Second World War and the
Partisan struggle. It falls into the strong tradition in Slovenia, as
elsewhere in the world, of basing cinema on literature,[47] but
Slovenian films are almost entirely a product of the post-Second
World War era, with only two full-length feature films made in
the 1930s and original Partisan footage shot during the war.[48] *Na
Svidenje v Naslednje Vojni*, which is undoubtedly among the most
important of the country's films, was directed by a Serb, Živojin
Pavlović. Because the film posed questions about the Partisan
tradition more starkly than Zupan's book, it was subject to considerable criticism regarding its content leaving aside its quality.[49]
The protest only added to the film's influence in opening up
debate in Slovenia in the 1980s about the Partisan tradition.

While the discussions between Berk and Bitter in the film lose
the atmosphere created on the page, as the inevitable problems
of adaptation intrude (instead of being resolved), the film far
more strikingly captures the emotional link between the two men
with visual interplay. At a bullfight in Spain Berk sees Bitter,
who is sitting some rows ahead, turn around, giving a three-quarters
profile. This is momentarily echoed by the head of a Wehrmacht

---

[47] Film adaptation of classical Slovenian literary sources is treated in Stanko
Šimenc, *Slovensko Klasično Slovstvo v Filmu*, Ljubljana: Knjižnica Mestnega
Gledališča Ljubljanskega, 1979.

[48] See Stanko Šimenc, *Panorama Slovenskega Filma*, Ljubljana: DZS, 1996, pp.41-6.

[49] Šimenc, *Panorama*, p.94.

tank captain turning round to look behind, giving the same three-quarters profile. The spark of recognition in this flash elegantly and without effort conveys the connection to the viewer. It is a connection which will not be fully explained until much later in the film, when the whole of the scene from the Second World War reveals that, just as the two glance at each other without recognition in the Spanish arena, they had done so in the instant when Berk raised his head above a ridge in the 1940s.

The treatment of Anton's abrupt and accidental death at the end is equally affecting, and it gains added impact from a change in the nature of the accident. The scene is transposed to an outdoor location, where Berk and Anton sit at a table amid ruins, while in the background fellow Partisans celebrate by firing their guns. This catches Anton as he smiles after uttering the title phrase to the film. The film also captures Berk's liberal dilemmas through verbal reference, reinforced by visual context and atmosphere, thus avoiding the risk of laboured treatment of philosophy and doubt. The straightforward, businesslike brutality in the rendition of firing squads is offset by a scene in which a traitor, while being prepared for the firing squad by taking off his boots, escapes, chased by confused Partisans as his big white socks disappear into the woods. Most of all, in the Partisan scenes which are often dimly lit and in shadow, the grainy texture of the film accurately recreates the feel of wartime Partisan footage, despite being in colour.

By coincidence another non-Slovene director was responsible for a successful and notable series of films: this was František Čap, a Czech, who made a trilogy involving a young woman of her era, Vesna, beginning with the eponymous *Vesna* in 1953, *Ne Čakaj na Maj* (Don't Wait for May) in 1957, and *Naš Auto* (Our Car) in 1962. The series was popular because the films were comedies made with a light touch and marked the changes taking place both in the post-Second World War cinema and in society generally. *Vesna* was the first film to leave the war behind, which gave it great appeal to audiences beginning to tire of the war. The trilogy captured the changes in the lives of young people, reflecting 'the good life' of the 1950s and the changing social structure.

In perhaps the most enduring of the trilogy, *Ne Čakaj na Maj*, Vesna and her friends studying at Ljubljana University go on a winter vacation to the mountains by different routes (including some who parachute into the vacation resort, having flown around Mount Triglav). Vesna's boyfriend, Sam, has become one of the parachutists (although this was not the way he was supposed to arrive). He lands on the mountain and ends up meeting another girl, with whom he walks. Vesna, out skiing alone, sees the two and believes that Sam has arrived before her, then gone off with the other woman. She is at the resort with her aunt as chaperone, and is reunited with Sam following a dance. She boycotts the dance at first and goes to bed early, until the song of the film's title is sung. This engaging and popular melody draws her downstairs. At first she dances with another man, while Sam retaliates by agreeing to dance with the girl from the mountain. When Vesna runs off, he follows and her aunt arranges for them to be alone in Vesna's room.

The couple make up, and the rest of the film concerns Vesna's faking of pregnancy symptoms in order to make her conservative, professorial father accept her relationship with Sam. The father ends up preparing for the non-existent child, before all is revealed to him by the aunt who had also been making preparations but learned of the truth sooner. In the end, as Sam and Vesna circle above the castle in Ljubljana, the message is clear that the older generation, and the father in particular, will have to accept the ways of their children and that a young girl's heart cannot be constrained by her father's academic demands. The film, similar in tone to popular Western films of the era, was attractive because of its focus on younger people and their problems at a time when opportunities were being expanded and horizons broadened, as well as for the handsome leading actors (Metka Gabrijelčič looked stunning as Vesna) and for its handling of relations between the generations.

It is ironic that Čap, a non-Slovene, with his five films is among the most prolific directors of Slovenian cinema. Only nine others have made as many films, and one of them, Jože Gale, like Čap, made a popular series of films, starting in 1951, based on the children's character Kekec. One in the series, *Srečno Kekec* (Good Luck, Kekec), from 1963, was the first Slovenian colour film.

However, by far the most prolific and distinguished Slovenian director is France Štiglic, who has been responsible for twenty films.[50] Štiglic made the first Slovenian film after the Second World War, in effect the real starting point for Slovenian cinema.[51] This was *Na Svoji Zemlji* (On One's Own Land), based on a novel by Ciril Kosmač, *Očka Orel* (Orel, Father). Kosmač, who wrote for the screen as well, was also the author of the novel *Tistega Lepega Dne* (That Beautiful Day) on which Štiglic's eponymous film, often cited as a favourite by Slovenes, was based.[52] Made in 1962, this comedy is set in 1930 when 'part of the Slovene lands was in Italy'. The opening and close of the film make striking use of mirrors placed diegetically – i.e. within the action of the film, purely for cinematic effect – in plant collections, with the prancing Italian officer admiring himself in them at the start of the film, echoed by a prancing Slovene at the end. Between these cinematically remarkable moments, there is a tale involving a widower, Štefulc, who believes he has a right to be able to marry his deceased wife's younger sister, Zana, in order to look after their four children. He tries to put forward his case after he hears the banns for the sister's wedding being read in church, but in the end he accepts her marriage after it has taken place. At the fearsome mother's suggestion, he is married off to the other sister, Hedvika, played by the delightful Duša Počkajeva.

This action is set against the backdrop of quiet Slovenian assertion in opposition to Italian fascism, for which the focal point is forcing three pro-fascist Slovenes (who have been posting 'Only Italian to be spoken' notices) to sing a nationalist song in which the key line has the Slovene lands stretching to the Adriatic Sea – meaning that they should incorporate those very lands in which the story is set that were under Italian rule before the Second

---

[50] This is twice as many as the next in the list, Matjaz Klopčič, whose ten films have not had such great resonance.

[51] There had been work on three other films made in Yugoslavia after 1945 before this, but these were not Slovene. There was Slovenian involvement in the first of these, *V Gorah Jugoslaviji* (In the Mountains of Yugoslavia), in 1946. This was a Soviet-Yugoslav co-production on which one of the great early Soviet directors, Abram Room, and the renowned cameraman Edvard Tisse worked as well as Vjekoslav Afrić, on the Yugoslav side. As a Soviet-Yugoslav co-production, this is not counted as a Slovenian film by Šimenc (*Panorama*, p.69).

[52] This is covered by Šimenc, *Slovensko*, pp.58-63.

World War when the story is set. It is somewhat ironic, therefore, that the dominant aesthetic timbre of the film is redolent of Italian neo-realist cinema in its crisp lighting and contrast, as well as the relative lack of cutting that permits scenes to unfold before the viewer's eye.

Similar cinematography marks another of Štiglic's most successful films, *Dolina Miru* (Valley of Peace). Also co-written by Štiglic, it follows two children orphaned by the Allied bombing of Ljubljana towards the end of the Second World War. Lotti is an ethnic German who speaks both German and Slovene, while Marko is purely Slovene. After Marko has first pulled her under cover with a number of other children (mostly pro-Partisan ones who had been beating up two Hitler Youth Slovene children as the bombing raid began) to shelter from an air raid, he realises that the bombs are falling near his home. He races over to search the apartment for his family, only to open the bedroom door and find nothing but rubble on the other side of it. During another raid both Marko and Lotti escape from the orphanage in which they have been placed and set out for the farm of Marko's uncle, a place which Marko defines as the 'the Valley of Peace' that Lotti has said must exist. On their journey they meet a black American airman who has been shot down while his captain has been killed. Neither has seen a black man before and it is only because they trip up while trying to run away that the airman, Jim, is able to begin to communicate with them by speaking German to Lotti.

The empathy between these two is cemented in the film through Lotti's dolls. In the scene where Jim buries his captain by covering him in leaves and branches, Lotti does the same for her doll, previously decapitated by a dog as the two children were hiding from a German tank. Later, as the three of them are hiding in a large deserted house, Jim makes Lotti a new doll, giving it wiry black hair and making its face black with charcoal. Lotti takes the doll and clings to it as she did the old one. The racial dimension of the story is treated with touches of humour, such as when Lotti, being carried by Jim through the woods, licks her finger and tries to wash the colouring off his ear.

Eventually the three make it to the small farm of Marko's uncle. However, the uncle has already left 'for the mountains' and taken his cow with him. It is there that first the Germans and then the Partisans, both of whom have been searching for Jim, catch up with them (although Jim had escaped earlier when the Germans came across Marko and Lotti and chase after him). For the Germans the important thing is to prevent Jim and the children from being able to inform the Partisans of the imminent German offensive which the three are suspected of having seen. Inadvertently the Partisans looking for Jim and the children discover the German presence. Jim is fatally wounded helping them see off the Germans in woods near the farmhouse. Before he dies he returns to the farmhouse and sends the children away. At the top of a mountain between one valley and another, Lotti closes the film by telling Marko that the valley had not been the valley of peace and suggests that maybe the next will be the right one.

This optimistic ending maintains the positive tone found throughout the film, despite death and loss, with the touching qualities and humour in the relationship between the two children themselves and between both of them and the pilot reinforced by bright and sharp visual tones which capture the rippling detail of grass, leaves and water in the Slovenian valleys, mountains and rivers under strong sunshine that encompass the action. Moreover, the radical sub-text that ethnic and racial barriers can be transcended gives the film a special quality for its time and context. Štiglic's film is in the Partisan tradition, but it is a very rare kind of war film.

A strong stylistic contrast to *Dolina Miru* is provided by one of Štiglic's more important later films, *Povest o Dobrih Ljudeh* (A Tale of Good People), made in 1975.[53] Shot in colour, with heavy shadows and dark green natural backdrops predominating, the film is pervaded by a gentle, intimate atmosphere. Set in rural isolation, it juxtaposes an elderly couple and their sublimely tender relationship with the confused passions and relationships of younger members of their family who come to live with them at the beginning of the action.

An old couple, Josef and Ana, worry about the difficult relationship between Ivan and his wife Marta who has a daughter, the blind Katica, whom Ivan has taken as his own. That marriage finally collapses after Marta has been found with Peter, a fugitive from the law, who has appeared as the old couple's grandson.

---

[53] This film was based on a novel by the same name written by Miška Kranjca.

Peter's presence has also raised the first stirrings of love in Katica and it is she who tells Ivan that Marta and Peter are together as lovers in the barn (where an unexpected and incidental mirror echoes the use of mirrors in *Tistega Lepega Dne*). Ivan, after contemplating violence, simply warns Peter that the police are coming. Peter escapes, but there is no repairing Ivan's and Marta's marriage. Peter reappears with the beard he has worn earlier to visit the house as a stranger, but he is unable to stop Marta leaving to find her way in the world. Ivan too leaves, before Peter again has to flee the police. He is followed by Katica who gets him to come to her in a field dotted with white flowers while she sings the simple plaintive tune that is her theme. He leaves her there. She tries to follow, but has no idea where he has gone and, as her hand is seen barely missing the branch of a tree that might have changed her course, she walks through rushes into the river. The film ends with a pan shot across a sky that is pale and bright, contrasting with the prevailing sombre tones. The implication is that Katica has been swallowed up by the river.

However, it is the focus on the old couple that gives the film its real quality. The ageing couple are covered in great visual detail, as the camera softly and slowly follows the lines on their faces. In the darkness, with the slightest glimmer of light making their watery eyes glint, they discuss death and their responsibility to each other – Ana tells Josef that the Angel Gabriel came for her, and when he asks why she did not go with him, says that that Josef knows nothing and would not be able to care for himself. In a later scene they celebrate fifty years together with the younger cohort. Toasts by both Peter and Ivan to the meaning of the old couple's 'golden marriage' provoke the wordless reaction that the viewer witnesses in Marta: she realises that she cannot emulate, or fit with, this old-fashioned idyllic relationship. The stability of Ana and Josef's relationship is aerated with poetic visual detail and tender discourse. This treatment is universal, yet at the same time it catches the milieu of small-scale, conservative rural life in Slovenia, and the values of the 'good people' who live that life and endure.

There should be no doubt that Štiglic's films are worthy of international note and stand comparison with many films that have registered international critical appreciation. Yet Štiglic, typically, is unknown outside the Slovenian cultural environment. In part this reflects the relatively small scale of Slovenian cinematic output – by 1997 the total number of Slovenian full-length feature films was a little over 130, making an average of two a year since the first film was made. It is virtually unavoidable that for a form such as film, which is expensive even if subsidised, a small potential audience limits the resources likely to be allocated or money recuperated. For an independent Slovenia no longer adhering to the principles and practices of communist Yugoslavia, the challenge of Americanisation is great. Whereas communist Yugoslavia supported and protected national cinemas and gave every film school graduate the chance to work on a live project in line with its nationalities policies, since 1991 the dominance of Hollywood has created the genuine fear that Slovenian cinemas 'will soon be completely Americanised'.[54]

These pressures are peculiar to the cinema, but the impact of change has increased difficulties across the whole spectrum of cultural life. Both the continuing effect of international influences and the withdrawal of theatre and other subsidies have created problems for those in the cultural sphere. This is the essential problem faced by virtually every aspect of Slovenian activity in the creative arts: the country is not large and the Slovenes are a small people. The products of Slovenian cultural and creative life, even at their best, have traditionally found the greatest difficulty in registering outside the Slovenian context, even in a minor way, because the language is barely known by non-Slovenes. If it cannot be understood how can it be recognised?

Of course, Slovenian literary and cinematic work may have failed to find an international audience, as the Archbishop of Ljubljana was reported to have said, because Cankar, to take the most striking example, simply never reached a world-class standard in his writing.[55] The other perspective on Cankar's standing would be that he is not recognised as a world-class writer simply because he wrote in Slovene and his work is therefore largely unknown. Although some of it appeared in translation after 1945, this was often, as with other works, translated into English and other

---

[54] Šimenc, *Panorama*, p.88.

[55] This was reported by Tom Ložar at the American Association for the Advancement of Slavic Studies 29th Annual Convention, Seattle, 22 November 1997. The following paragraph is based on his comments

languages by Slovenes.[56] So even where Slovenian literature is registered – as in the *New York Review of Books* which was reported to have published one poem by Kocbek, badly translated – the net effect is negative: this one poor choice comes to represent all Slovenian culture and cuts off other opportunities for aesthetic consideration. The reality of the Slovenian position is that Slovenes are generally so 'grateful if anyone recognises them' that all publishing outside Slovene becomes 'quasi-vanity publishing'.[57]

While Slovenian achievement in some areas of the collective arts has limited appeal, in others there is work of note that has none the less been largely overlooked, as with other small peoples, because the language at the heart of most of Slovenian cultural consciousness is a barrier to outside appreciation. While the work of Plečnik speaks for itself to those who visit Ljubljana and are susceptible to the plastic arts, in film and literature, where there is work that deserves to be tested internationally, there is little chance of the material being accessed. Although in some cases, such as Harry Leeming's rendering of Potrč's *Na Kmetih* as *The Land and the Flesh*,[58] translations exist that might draw an audience, the work of Slovenian creative spirits has mostly remained in the shadows, with literature and cinema a small, virtually uncharted backwater, centred on language and land, diminishing rather than enhancing the profile of Slovenia and the Slovenes.

Avant-garde, alternative and contemporary culture

There is one way in which Slovenian cultural expression has escaped the confines of Slovenia itself and where the Slovene language is spoken. This is in the broad area of cultural activity that developed in the country during the 1980s in particular, and produced an avant-garde and alternative dimension to the national culture. This work, which operated in the popular idiom, also made some impact outside the Slovenian context – although this was not always well received given the radical approach adopted, invoking traditional and totalitiarian symbols to challenge the pre-

[56] This is a phenomenon that prompted Ložar to ask, 'Why is it that Slovenes think that they know English well enough to write it for publicaton?'

[57] Ložar, as above.

[58] Even this, however, is marred by poor production in the Slovenian edition.

vailing order. This defines much of it as quintessentially Slovenian, precisely because its driving force is an attack on all that is parochial. While not all contemporary Slovenian cultural activity fits this category, it is such work which has defined its essentially Slovenian character by consciously seeking to be non-Slovene, thus gaining for themselves some notice outside the country.

After 1991, Slovenian literary organisations strove to make contemporary literature more accessible through publication of translations and a guide to work in translation by Slovenian authors. This was undertaken by the literary magazine *L.S. (Litterae Slovenicae)*.[59] Contemporary Slovenian writing has also benefited from a readership in other publications such as *Le Livre Slovène*, promoting Slovenian literary culture.

Among writers of the present time the central figure and probably the most translated is Drago Jančar. His intense style is marked by strong storytelling, whether it is the treatment of fate and irony in the short story that gives its name to the collection *Smrt pri Mariji Snežni* (Death at Mary-of-the-Snows), or the individual's quest for an unattainable liberty in the historical novel *Galjot*. The latter takes a seventeenth-century character, Johan Ot, and his conflict with the prevailing conventions and institutions of life in Habsburg Central Europe. The former takes a character from the brilliant Russian writer Mikhail Bulgakov's *Belaia Gvardiia* (The White Guard) – a Tsarist doctor and officer who escapes the Bolsheviks in 1918 after being wounded through angelic intervention – and transposes that officer under his changed name, Vladimir Semyonov, to the Slovenian-Austrian border on the River Mura. There, having been prevented by the angel from committing suicide in the face of inevitable capture by the Bolsheviks, he finally does so in fear of the arrival of the Soviet Army in 1945 – even though it does not, in fact, come as far as the Mura. Thus the overwhelming sense of eventual fate is imposed.

While Jančar's work seems superficially to be distinguished by the author's ardent prose style, what marks his work as 'modernist' and 'avant-garde', as with many other contemporary Slovenian writers in the 'New Slovenian Prose' movement that includes

---

[59] 'Contemporary Slovenian Literature in Translation', *L.S. (Litterae Slovenicae)*, no.2, 1993.

Jančar,[60] is an underlying obsession with Post-Modernist ideas such as 'ludism' and 'inter-textuality'. It is the cross-referencing of time and space drawn from other sources, accompanied by play with language and structure that infuses these texts with subversive tones. It was because this approach ran against the social and realist expectations under communism that it attracted writers and was problematic officially, despite the fact that the ideas often stemmed from left-wing and Marxist thinking.

Avant-garde experimentation was even more pronounced in the theatre, where numerous alternative and youth groups developed from the 1950s onwards. It was in that decade that playwrights such as Dominik Smole laid the foundations for new theatre. Smole's *Antigone* (1959), for example, leaves the heroine of the title out of the Sophoclean original. Instead the defiance, sacrifice and humanity of Oedipus's daughter is seen only in the reflections of her in the words of others as the dramatic action unfolds. The power of Antigone's presence through her absence was broadly understood as a metaphor: Smole and a number of others had gone 'underground' following the banning of a publication *Revija 57* and the imprisonment of its editor Jože Pučnik – later to emerge as a political figure in the democratic opposition at the end of the 1980s. Smole and his colleagues formed a small theatre group called Oder 57 that performed *Antigone*, and met with sympathetic understanding from political officials, who took its meaning well.

From this the sense that theatre was a popular and accessible medium encouraged a proliferation of interest and activity. It also engendered a spirit of experimentation, inevitably with differing degrees of success. Some pieces might be direct political criticism of the authorities, while others could be obscure but still expressing the spirit of openness as well as a reproach against those in the regime who would limit expression. This continued even into the more radically open 1980s. However, drama had just as much of an individualist, existentialist character as a political one. One of the most striking plays of the 1980s was written by one of Smole's underground colleagues, Dane Zajc. His *Medeja* is focused

[60] For an overview of contemporary Slovenian prose, see the essays accompanying the collection 'Contemporary Slovene Short Stories', *L.S.*, no.1, 1991, pp.187-216.

on the idea of what is lacking in life and the imperative for action, as random, mindless forms strive for identity, and both Medea and Jason are given refractions of themselves that emphasise their lack of individuality, as well as their confusion in striving for it. Medea finds this is death, which permits an ultra-modern Jason to interpret it as fulfilment rather than tragedy.

However, while the avant-garde of the 1950s continued its work into the 1980s, it was a new, even more radical alternative movement that managed, in part through its reputation for shock, to transcend the Slovenian milieu. In the 1980s the growth of this alternative culture, built on the foundation laid by the avant-garde with its fascination for Post-Modern inter-textuality, was important not only artistically, but also politically. By force of circumstance it chimed with concern for the core of traditional Slovenian culture and its values, the Slovene language itself.

Post-Modernism, in its various forms, captured Slovenian intellectual life in the 1980s. Of all the cities in Europe, Ljubljana was probably the one most affected by the cultural theory that came from the 1968 generation of Post-Structuralist Parisians including Julia Kristeva, Roland Barthes, Jacques Derrida and Jacques Lacan. Intellectuals in Ljubljana at that time also embraced a number of other intellectual trends, including the Civil Society ideas popularised in Central and Eastern Europe (they were propagated in Slovenia by Tomaž Mastnak) and added to this a late 'Punk' trend and the convoluted Lacanian vocabulary of former Maoist Slavoj Žižek, one of Slovenia's foremost thinkers – celebrated inside the country for the fact that he appears to be known outside it.

This cultural outpouring also had a truly popular dimension. At a time when it was rare in other communist countries, Ljubljana's walls were covered by radical or ironic graffiti, calling for democratisation, the release of Janez Janša or even, occasionally, for a return to the Habsburg Monarchy. The graffiti artists also definitively rejected Western culture in the form of McDonald's and Coca-Cola, and to this day Slovenia has remained almost free of the more disposable elements of Western life, preferring to continue living with its own styles and tastes in food and drink.

Unavoidably language, which had received particular attention in the 1980s, was the subject that seemed to galvanise the Slovene public more than any other during the decisive political events of 1988. The cause of Slovene was championed initially by academics, but this consciousness was soon translated into broader, more political terms. This process accelerated after Professor Jože Toporišič pointed out in 1978 that the language was in an endangered position. He claimed that Slovenes would either continue to assimilate linguistically and become a minority within Slovenia, or change the nature of their relationship with their southern neighbours.[61] In 1987 Dimitrij Rupel advanced this argument further in the so-called '*Prispevki za slovenski nacionalni program*' (Contributions towards a Slovene national programme), published by *Nova Revija* as its issue 57 – deliberately echoing, as well as considerably amplifying the content of *Revija 57*, which had appeared thirty years before in 1957. Rupel called Slovene a 'second-class language' within Yugoslavia, and described the fear that Slovenes experienced when 'stammering' Serbo-Croat.[62]

But language was only one aspect of the remarkable efflorescence of Slovene culture in the 1980s. The launch of *Nova Revija* in 1981 became the platform for a group of anti-Leninist cadres who were inspired by the Polish Solidarity movement, as well as developments in post-Kavčič politics in Slovenia itself. Other journals, such as *Časopis za Kritiko Znanosti*, the student journal *Tribuna*, the Maribor-based *Katedra* and, most fundamentally, the putative organ of the League of Communist Youth, *Mladina*, created a heady atmosphere of cultural and intellectual expression and exchange, as well as political subversion and humour.

In the late 1980s each edition of *Mladina* would be eagerly anticipated, with each week's magazine seeming to have at least one article, or a devastating cover, that would both increase circulation and be the talking point of young and old for that week. *Mladina* blended serious investigative journalism with political and cultural commentary. It featured a semi-ironic comic book section, the political 'barometer' measuring the fortunes of public figures,

---

[61] Jože Toporišič, 'A language of a small nationality (Slovene) in a multinational state' in William R. Schmalstieg and Thomas F. Magner (eds), 'Sociolinguistic Problems in Czechoslovakia, Hungary, Romania and Yugoslavia', *Folia Slavica*, vol.1, no.3, 1978 (special edn), pp.480–6.

[62] Dimitrij Rupel, 'Odgovor na Slovensko Narodno Vprašanje', *Nova Revija*, VI, 57, 1987, pp.57–73.

and above all the world of Diareja, the creator not only of the strip cartoon filled with blob-shaped sterotype figures, but also of the searing cartoons and picture collages that formed the cover of each edition. Whether the image was conscripts building a villa for the defence minister, or the Serbian leader Slobodan Milošević wielding his sword in medieval armour atop a white charger and re-fighting the 1389 battle of Kosovo Polje, the *Mladina* cover set the agenda.

It was the articles inside that really provided the explosive detail, exposing the army's role in arms sales to Ethiopia at the time of the conflict and famine there, that ended in the international mobilisation of support through the Band Aid concerts of 1987, or the Agrokomerc corruption scandal in Bosnia and Hercegovina. At the same time, there were articles provocatively proposing a western Yugoslav Federation that would take Slovenia, Croatia and Bosnia-Hercegovina out of Yugoslavia, and asking 'How would you like to live in this country?' The apparent contradiction between criticism of Bosnian corruption and the proposal of a new common state is easily explained: the magazine's role was exploration and provocation. Its ideology was liberal iconoclasm: if there was a taboo or a totem anywhere, it would be smashed. Therefore just as thinking about dividing the Yugoslav lands was subversive, so was a series of interviews with the competing claimants to the Yugoslav monarchy and articles about them, predicated on a continuation of Yugoslavia. *Mladina's* incisive and humorous way of addressing key issues that deeply concerned people was typified by the invention of the Lipa, a fictional Slovenian currency that would be stable as a benchmark against Dinar hyper-inflation in Yugoslavia.

During 1988 *Mladina* was selling out a 50,000 print-run each week, often by the end of the day of publication when the street vendors' cry '*Nova Mladina!*' would ring out in the centre of Ljubljana.[63] At the same time research revealed that each edition was read by seven people, which meant that every edition of the magazine was reaching at least 350,000 people out of a total population of around 2 million. Thus perhaps half the adult population was reading *Mladina* each week, giving its amalgam of *The Economist*, *Newsweek*, *Private Eye*, the *National Enquirer* and *Time*

[63] '*Nova*' means new.

Out cultural salience of which others could not dream. *Mladina* defined a generation, as it shook Slovenia and Yugoslavia, and often, by no more than printing a joke for the sake of being provocative, shaped changing values.

One of the most memorable of the *Mladina* covers was the '*Dan Mladosti*' (Day of Youth) poster in 1987 which caused that particular edition of the magazine to be banned. This was based on the poster designed by the Novi Kollektivizem studio for an event on the annual day of youth celebrations marking the official birthday of Tito. Initially well-received for a brief period, it was abruptly banned when it was found to be based on a Nazi poster and had substituted the figure of Tito for that of Hitler. The authorities were outraged because it equated communist and Nazi versions of totalitarianism. Designed as an ironic artistic joke, the allusion to Nazism was a step too far. But *Mladina* laid bare the connection by revealing the Nazi past beneath the communist one.

This type of work and reference was typical of a linked set of artistic essays that were gathered under one umbrella, NSK, with which Novi Kollektivizem was associated, and which was supported by *Mladina* because NSK's mission was similar to that of the magazine itself to challenge the taboos of society by a variety of means. Parts of this movement, above all the musical group Laibach, became the first significant Slovenian cultural export. The acronym NSK was itself provocative, standing for '*Neue Slowenische Kunst*' (New Slovenian Art). The use of German was a deliberate comment on the nature of being Slovene, at once appearing to threaten Slovenian culture and putting it into focus.

NSK was formed as a loose-linked collective of artists in different creative fields, with a common commitment to an alternative vision.[64] That vision mixed traditional folk elements and totalitarian expression to create a unique set of abstractions. In addition to Laibach's music, NSK included drama, architecture, design, paint-

---

[64] In the late 1990s, interesting research on NSK was being carried out by Alexei Monroe at the University of Kent at Canterbury, and we are grateful for his assistance in amplifying our own experience and knowledge of NSK. Some of his unpublished written work informed the following paragraphs, particularly on Plečnik's design and its use by NSK's architectural department. We anticipate that this material will eventually be published, expanding understanding of a curious and important cultural phenomenon.

ing and sculpture. All were bound by a philosophy that challenged national identity by affirming it and transcending it. The group used common and inter-related subjects and themes. One drama group, Scipion Nasiče Teater, took for its name the same subject as one of the artistic group Irwin's deliberately shocking creations, 'The Resurrection of the Sisters of Scipion Nasiče'. Similarly and more potently, the idea of a Slovenian Acropolis was a motif common to a range of NSK activity. The inspiration for this was a design by Plečnik for a national parliament building that would have far exceeded in scale any other building in the country. It would have been 120m. tall, and had a conical roof supported by twelve columns over a hidden cupola. Plečnik called this design *Slovenska Akropola – Parlament Naše Svobode* (Slovenian Acropolis – Parliament of Our Freedom). The design was of special importance to the architectural group Graditelji which used it as a trademark emblem in its heyday in 1986-7. Strongly influenced by architectural idioms with totalitarian echoes like neo-classicism and Soviet modernism but also by the Bauhaus, Graditelji produced plans for an industrial city called 'Laibach' (the German name for Ljubljana). From one angle the plans show Plečnik's parliament building on a hill dominating the city with a cross-section below. It was a utopian vision divorced from industrial reality.

Pleúcnik's design was also integral to the art group Irwin's 'Slovenske Atene' (Slovenian Athens), which developed the Slovenska Akropola motif, transforming it into a collection of mythic visions of Slovenia. The ensemble of five paintings takes a Slovenian archetype (and a regular NSK reference), Grohar's Impressionist sower, and superimposes it on each of five characteristic Slovenian settings: the Alps, the forest, the Karst, the field and the sea. Each of the five paintings is crowned by an image of the Virgin and Child. Taken together, the paintings form a unity that evokes a mythical, unreal Slovenia. Its grand scale, with each painting measuring around 3.5m. by 1.5m., captures the monumental character of Plečnik's design. Yet the rich, typically Slovenian imagery of the painting is the antithesis of the architect's cosmopolitan vision.

Scipion Nasiče Teater also made use of the Plečnik design. The group proposed an 'artistic event' to mark the Day of Youth in 1987 (the occasion for which the notorious poster was designed) to be held beside Lake Bohinj in the Alps. Draft designs show that it was to centre around Plečnik's design, representing what was essentially Slovene, and Vladimir Tatlin's celebrated 'Monument for the Third International' of 1919-20, juxtaposed as an internationalist and communist marker.

The most renowned use of the Plečnik image, however, was by the Laibach music group. Its 1987 album, *Slovenska Akropola*, had the design dominating the cover, while the record itself, a collection of the band's work up to that point, is a link to other NSK activity and a summation of the Slovenian 'question' with which NSK generally, and the group in particular, were grappling at that time. The album was the first work of the group officially available since it was banned in 1983. In the mean time, Laibach had been recording and performing elsewhere in Europe and had built itself an international profile. Hence, by 1987 it was on the cusp of considerable international success and was the most successful of all Slovenian, or Yugoslav, cultural exports. With its version of 'Life is Life' set for chart success and a period of disco popularity, there was little sense in continuing a ban in its home country.

Although Laibach recordings and performances were banned in Yugoslavia until 1987, with the release of *Slovenska Akropola* and *Opus Dei*, its music could be heard on Radio Študent. This popular station was another source of radical irony testing the staid communist way of doing things (including a decision to defy the authorities by playing jazz when the Slovenian communist leader Edvard Kardelj died in 1979). By giving air space to the notorious group, Radio Študent was playing its role in challenging the *status quo*. Laibach's notoriety and banning resulted from its provocative flirtation with totalitarian chic, explicit rejection of the Partisan myth, and deliberate use of German as a Slovenian antithesis. Its mission was to shock. The group's name was itself part of this: by taking the German name for Ljubljana, it was challenging Slovenian insularity and parochial national attachment to language, at the same time as implying that beneath the surface of all that was Slovenian lay a structure of Germanic influence. This approach only made sense because of Slovenian sensitivity to Germanic influence and communist sensitivity about fascism. The point was to be offensive in order to provoke.

Laibach was often associated with fascist symbolism and suspected by some in the West of being open to abuse by fascist elements, but in reality Nazi kitsch, as part of a totalitarian contextualisation of Laibach's 'industrial' music, made sense when the main questions of the day concerned Slovenian identity. Laibach's purpose was always to ask questions and set out paradoxes. By 1987, when it could issue records and play 'homecoming' concerts again, the shibboleths they were challenging had begun to change and their own concerns had been internationalised by their success. Although the band's reputation from its Slovenia-and-communist-challenging days lingered on in many minds, most likely because of its adoption of Nazi kitsch and wearing of uniforms, the targets shifted as the 1990s progressed.

By 1994 the totem to be felled was NATO, which was the title of Laibach's album that year. The mission was to take NATO where it had refused to go – to Bosnia and Hercegovina, where its intervention was much debated internationally and eventually came about in 1995. NATO had become the new orthodoxy and posing an alternative was Laibach's new mission. Once NATO had found a path to Bosnia and Hercegovina, Laibach's mission to provoke took other directions. In 1998 it played in Belgrade, and the lead singer Peter Mlakar made a speech asking the Serbs how Serbia had come to be so small and suggesting that it was because they had forsaken God. A similar diatribe against the English (possibly meaning British) was delivered at a concert in the Royal Festival Hall in London in the summer of that year. However, the most striking feature of the band's latest incarnation was a pronounced emphasis on what was Balkan and Yugoslav. Ironically, ten years after it had prodded the dominant Slav identity with Germanic neurosis, it now emphasised Balkan characteristics to challenge European comfort and especially the dominant opinion in some of the former Yugoslav lands, including Slovenia, that their countries are not Balkan or Yugoslav but European.[65] What Laibach once opposed had become its weapon.

The essence of the NSK message, always with a suspicion of tongue-in-cheek, was to live in a 'state of mind', not a state with physical borders. This universal state could issue passports to its citizens if they signed the pledge on the application form to

---

[65] It is notable that from 1992 onwards Irwin dropped the use of explicitly Slovenian images and symbols.

support the integrity of the NSK state on a 'best-effort basis' and not misuse the passport for 'criminal, ideological, religious or political purposes conflicting with the contents of NSK and/or jeopardising the reputation and good name of NSK'.[66] The theme of NSK citizenship was encapsulated in the slogan 'Art is fanaticism that demands diplomacy'. While NSK clearly had a playful approach to artistic creation and associated activity, its essential mission remained a serious attempt to challenge and exceed the commonplace. This was an approach that brought some critical interest and success internationally.

The international success of Laibach especially, and of other parts of NSK, such as Irwin and Red Pilot, was in strong contrast to other areas of Slovenian culture. It was those in the alternative movement challenging limited and parochial versions of that culture who did most to make a Slovenian imprint on the international scene. A short film using the image of Russian roulette minus the qualities of courage and honour to characterise the Yugoslav war of the 1990s, *Balkanska Ruleta*, directed by Zdravko Barašič, was selected for the Cannes International Film Festival in 1998. A little less significantly, the touching and nostalgic *Adrian*, directed by Maja Weiss, was shown at the London Film Festival later that year. However, these exportable portions of Slovenian culture, by being cosmopolitan in outlook, were in many ways the antithesis of the national tradition.

Much of Slovenian culture, for better or worse, was largely hidden from the outside world. While development in some areas, such as music, was negligible, literature – focusing on the most valued facet of Slovenian existence, the language – was extensive in a highly literate population. Yet to a large extent it was precisely that prized language that made Slovenian writing inaccessible to non-Slovenes. In addition to this, the native Slovenian cultural world is small and there is much in its creative arts that is closed and self-referential, even where the themes are universal. While this is predominantly true of literature, it applies also to other art forms, even where language is not relevant.

Because Slovenian culture was inevitably immured from the

---

[66] 'NSK Passport Application Form', available from NSK Information Center Ljubljana. Further information available at http://Iois.kud-fp.si/~lukap/embassy/, at August 1998.

wider world, it was also insular and its proponents were concerned not with reaching out but with the centrality of culture to Slovenian identity. There was certainly work such as Cankar's writing, Štiglic's cinema and surely Plečnik's architecture that would not be out of place in the international canon. In most cases, however, this was obscured by Slovenia's all but unknown minor profile, whatever the importance of their culture to the Slovenes themselves.

It was ironic that the contemporary movements of the 1980s, which established themselves in opposition to traditional Slovenian cultural symbolism by absorbing it, managed to break the bounds of isolation. Slovenian cultural idioms could reach beyond a domestic audience when specifically Slovenian references were used to attack parochialism and insularity with outside and more cosmopolitan influences. This was the crux of the challenge to be faced. The traditional role of culture as the bastion of Slovenian identity, inward-looking and a protection against the outside world, ran contrary to the desire to be embraced by the world. Culture was the underpinning for Slovenian identity, yet while it preserved that identity, it also inhibited its international development.

This was the essential challenge faced by Slovenia in all aspects of life. Following independence, what was true of culture applied in other areas. A small country, a small population and a deep attachment to their peculiar features had to be reconciled with internationalisation, if the Slovenes were to prosper not only spiritually but also politically and economically in the world that had been joined. However, just as Slovenian culture until the early modern period had been not only a barrier to assimilation but also a crossroads where cultural evolution was concerned, it was possible that the internationalised cultural movements of the 1980s could show the way forward to a new maturation. Their experience and relation to traditional Slovenian culture also suggested the difficulties that might be faced.

4

ECONOMY AND SOCIETY

Although it could be said that cultural distinctiveness was the most important feature of Slovene development, this did no more than provide the underpinning for social evolution which was itself closely linked to economic advancement. This economic improvement and concomitant social change were shaped by experience of both royal Yugoslavia and communist Yugoslavia. As a result, when economic necessity, *inter alia*, precipitated Slovenia's independence in the 1990s, it had the strongest of the former communist economies.

With independence the economy was transformed not only from communism to the market, but also from industrial manufacturing to being a service-based-economy – although in both cases necessarily oriented to external trade. This prompted a rapid phase of social transformation, as the result of which economy and society both emerged strongly at the end of the twentieth century –although there were latent problems. It is the purpose of the present chapter to see how the transition of the 1990s to a post-industrial economy and society built on the transformation already experienced throughout the century from the agricultural and rural bases with which it began.

Economic development through Yugoslavia

Both the monarchical and communist versions of Yugoslavia brought development to the Slovene economy to such a degree that by the time of Slovenia's independence with the dissolution of federal Yugoslavia its economic position was the best of any former communist country. This was the product of modernisation throughout the Yugoslav period, especially during the second version of the South Slav state.

Having entered the South Slav union as one of the least developed areas of Austria-Hungary, Slovenia was undoubtedly the most developed and prosperous part of Yugoslavia by its end. While the first Yugoslavia saw some development of industry and manufacturing, it was in the early communist period in particular, with the catalyst of later developments, that Slovenia was transformed from a country economically as agrarian as it looked, even at the end of Yugoslavia, to one based on modern economic activities – industry, manufacture and, increasingly, services.

The Slovene lands entered Yugoslavia on a largely agricultural economic base, but one in which industrialisation and modernisation had begun. Although a majority of Slovenes worked on the land, the proportion doing so dropped considerably during the second half of the nineteenth century. Whereas in 1857, 83 per cent of Slovenes had lived off the land, by 1910 this figure had dropped to 67 per cent. This process continued into the first Yugoslav period, with 58.8 per cent of the population engaged in agriculture in 1931 and only 48.9 per cent in 1948.[1] Apart from the areas close to Trieste, where there were major landowners, most of the agricultural life in Slovene lands was taken up with smallholdings. Many of these faced great difficulties in the later nineteenth century, giving rise to sales to landowners and often emigration by the erstwhile smallholders. To prevent this trend, farming 'societies' or 'associations' were formed. This made life easier for those living from the land because they were better able to get their produce, such as milk, to towns through cooperation and pooled resources. However, this only eased a trend, which was complemented by growing industrial and commercial activity in the towns.

The principal heavy industries during the nineteenth century were coal and steel. Although these were less developed in Slovenia than in other parts of Austria-Hungary, a small but significant amount of heavy industry was developed. This grew from 116 businesses with 6,600 employees in 1852, to 441 with 36,200 employees by 1912 – with faster growth after 1880.[2] However, this

[1] *Zgodovina Slovencev*, Ljubljana: Cankarjeva Založba, 1979, p.541; *Slovenija. Geografska, Zgodovinska, Pravna, Politična, Ekonomska in Kulturna Podoba Slovenije*, Ljubljana: Založba Mladinska Knjiga, 1998, p.73.

[2] *Zgodovina Slovencev*, p.527.

still only involved two out of every seven workers.[3] In addition there was also significant activity in other spheres of industry which benefited from modern technology, such as chemicals and pharmaceuticals, shipbuilding (primarily around Trieste), timber and textiles (introduced by a Briton, William Moline).[4] With the exception of wood, which was also linked to the production of part- and wholly finished manufactured goods, these industries were not particularly significant at the time. However, each provided a basis for later development.

The growth of Slovene industry was facilitated by two factors. The first was the extension of the railway system. Up to 1894, railway communications through Slovene lands were limited; there was a main line running south from Vienna, through Maribor to Celje, Zidani Most, Ljubljana and then to Trieste. This was supplemented by two branch lines, one connecting Klagenfurt (known in Slovene as Celovec) to Maribor, while the other linked Zidani Most and Zagreb. In 1894 a significant new extension to the rail network linked Ljubljana with Novo Mesto, followed by a further extension in 1898 connecting the former with Kočevje. In the twentieth century there were further additions to this network, facilitating the shipment of both raw materials and manufactured goods.

The second factor which affected the development of Slovenian industry was capital accumulation. External capital invested in the Slovene areas was ten times greater than internal capital, and most of it was of German or Czech origin.[5] For example, the modernisation of the Jesenice steelworks was capitalised from Berlin and Vienna, and coal production by French capital (in 1880). However, relatively large sums of 'Slovenian' capital were also made available through the development of the banking system. This involved, first, the development of mutual societies – beginning with that at Ljutomer in 1872, and growing to involve a number of similar societies and land banks, which were linked in the League of Slovene Mutuals, formed in 1883. This created a significant degree of autonomy from Viennese and other banks,

---

[3] *Ibid.*

[4] Joško Šavli, *Slovenija: Podoba Evropejska Naroda*, Nova Gorica: Humar, 1995, p.165.

[5] *Zgodovina Slovencev*, p.530.

while also providing funds for local investment.[6] This was only made possible by the formation in 1900 of the Ljubljana Credit Bank with initial capitalisation amounting to 500,000 crowns, which made business loans possible.[7] However, the most significant banking success emerged from Trieste – perhaps not surprisingly since it was the major port of the Empire and a major commercial centre. This involved Jadranska Banka, formed in 1905. This bank became so successful that it grew to have operations in Vienna, Ljubljana and several other places in the Habsburg South Slav lands, as well as ownership of the Frank Sasker Bank in New York and Banco Yugoslavo de Chile.[8] Thus, while agriculture remained the dominant feature of Slovenian economic life before the First World War, there were elements not only of heavy industry but also, crucially, of manufacturing and commercial enterprise.

Economic development in the Kingdom of Serbs, Croats and Slovenes continued, with industrial, manufacturing and commercial activities slowly eroding the position of agriculture within the Slovene lands. However, this development was not as intensive as it might have been. This was due largely to the economic policies of the various inter-war governments, as well as to a (perhaps consequent) relative lack of interest by foreign capital. Neither the politicians in question nor the potential investors appeared committed to the rapid economic development of Slovene lands or indeed of Yugoslavia as a whole. The outcome of this was a country still primarily agrarian on the eve of the Second World War. Badly weakened socially and politically by economic debility, it had fallen into complete dependence on Hitler's Germany.

The governments of the newly-formed but troubled South Slav state were faced with serious dilemmas. The union had brought together the relatively well-developed and prosperous former Habsburg lands of Slovenia, Slavonia and Vojvodina, with the economically and even agriculturally backward territories of Dalmatia, Bosnia and Hercegovina, Serbia, Montenegro and Macedonia. It

---

[6] Šavli, *Slovenija*, p.167.

[7] *Zgodovina Slovencev*, p.532. This capitalisation was made possible by the Czech bank, Živnostenska Banka, as well as a group of Slovene businessmen.

[8] Šavli, *Slovenija*, p.167.

was necessary to decide whether to emphasise the modernisation and rapid advancement of agriculture to help the poorer areas, or to accelerate improvement in the relatively mature regions. Given the links between national and political tensions, it was inevitable that the decision would favour agrarian betterment.

Despite this, there was still notable industrial and commercial modernisation in Yugoslavia between the two world wars. During the 1920s more than 1,000 new businesses were established, and their overall value grew by over 30 per cent. In the Slovene lands alone this meant 150 new industrial enterprises, leading to a position where, at the beginning of the Second World War, there were 785 industrial businesses in Slovenia. These were mostly small companies, with many within the major existing sectors. These were wood-cutting (118 businesses), textiles (109) and construction materials (101).[9] Other areas which saw notable development were metal and textile manufacture, while coal and steel remained important – although the coal industry suffered several crises in face of competition from cheaper operations in Bosnia and Serbia.[10]

This growth in the number of industrial units was facilitated by rapid electrification. This had an equivalent impact to the extension of the railway network and establishment of credit banking in the Habsburg period. Indeed, the process of electrification had begun under Austria-Hungary, but it was wholly and systematically extended in the South Slav state. As a result there came to be 595 hydro-electric power plants and 154 fossil fuel power stations in 'the Slovene space'.[11] This encouraged a situation in which the number of Slovene industrial units approached a quarter of the total of 4,000 in the whole of Yugoslavia.

This growth was not enough, however, to absorb those made unemployed in agriculture. This was a result of the combined effects of worldwide depression and technological improvements that created conditions in which the land could no longer sustain

---

[9] Jože Prinčič, *Slovenska Industrija v Jugoslovanskem Primežu, 1945-1956*, Novo Mesto: Tiskarna Novo Mesto-Dolenjska Založba, Seidlova Zbirka, vol.2, 1992, pp.8-9.

[10] Janko Prunk, *Kratka Zgodovina Slovenije*, Ljubljana: Založba Grad, 1998, p.116.

[11] Prinčič, *Industrija*, p.9.

such large numbers as in the past.[12] Smallholders were generally on the margins of survival, and this, along with the number of agricultural workers made jobless, generated social problems.[13] Nonetheless, even though the economic depression of the early 1930s seriously stalled further growth for a period, the Slovene economy was modernised in major ways between the world wars as part of the industrial development in Yugoslavia as a whole.

By the eve of the Second World War the industrial contribution to national income had increased by 5 percentage points to 29.7 per cent. Industrial growth in the Slovene lands was two and a half times faster than in Serbia, six times faster than in Bosnia and twenty times faster than in Montenegro. As a result, the Slovenian share of total Yugoslav economic output reached twenty per cent.[14] This was a position that would be maintained and consolidated after the Second World War, when the Slovenian economy would be forcibly industrialised and rapidly modernised under the communists.

While some might suggest that there is 'no point' in trying to illustrate the post-war economic development of Slovenia within Yugoslavia[15] because of the distortions of communist rule, compounded by the abnormality of the 'self-management' system adopted by the Yugoslav communists, it is impossible not to do so if one is to consider the economic dimensions of Slovenia's independence. It is certainly true that self-management gave rise to a constant strain between efforts to maintain state control of economic activity and the imperative of decentralisation.[16] However, the overall economic transformation of Slovenia in the context of communist Yugoslavia was so great that a clear picture can be drawn despite the problems of self-management. That change

---

[12] On the impact of these trends on royal Yugoslavia in general, see Joseph Rothschild, *East Europe between the World Wars*, Seattle: University of Washington Press, 1974.

[13] Prunk, *Kratka*, p.117.

[14] Prinčič, *Industrija*, p.8.

[15] Žarko Lazarević, 'Economic History of Twentieth-Century Slovenia' in Jill Benderley and Evan Kraft (eds), *Independent Slovenia: Origins, Movements and Prospects*, Basingstoke: Macmillan, 1994, p.62.

[16] There were numerous studies of this economic system and its political ramifications. See, for example, Rusinow, *Experiment*.

is summarised in the decline of agricultural employment from around 50 per cent at the end of the Second World War to 20 per cent by 1971, and only 8 per cent on the eve of independence in 1991.[17] This marked the comprehensive modernisation of the Slovene economic space.

Full industrialisation was a major part of the process of modernisation, although the manner in which it was introduced generated problems. Immediately the Second World War ended, the communists began to renew the entire Yugoslav economy, including Slovenia. The renewal of existing industry in all sectors was seen as the first phase of complete industrialisation,[18] imitating what had occurred earlier in the Soviet Union. Because of Slovenia's relatively advanced economic position, Edvard Kardelj and Boris Kidrič decided in 1949 that its industrialisation and modernisation should be completed within two years, while the same processes in the other Yugoslav republics would have to continue.[19]

Concomitant with rapid industrialisation was the decline of agriculture. Here private farming was squeezed not only by normal processes of economic modernisation but also by ideology. The Yugoslav communists sought to nationalise the land and collectivise agriculture. However, conscious of their need for support, they allowed the maintenance of very small private farms: while private ownership was anathema to communist ideology, in terms of both food and politics, the authorities could not afford to alienate the agricultural sector completely, when so much of it in Slovenia was traditionally based on smallholdings anyway. All additional land was appropriated into state farms. It was into these farms that investment flowed in the 1950s, as there was an attempt to make Slovenia and Yugoslavia as a whole self-sufficient in food.

Over time, efforts to emphasise state-run agriculture receded for both practical and ideological reasons – as did similar efforts, in other sectors of the economy. In the 1960s greater attention and support were given to private farming, and, crucially, it became

---

[17] Lazarević, 'Economic', p.62.

[18] Prinčič, *Industrija*, pp. 21-2 and 30.

[19] Prinčič, *Industrija*, p.175. Both Kardelj and Kidrič were leading Slovene figures in the communist movement. With great authority in Slovenia itself, based on their wartime roles, the former was the Yugoslav party's chief ideologue, while the latter was minister for economics, in Belgrade. Cf Ch.2, n.49.

possible for private farmers to purchase new technology. Following changes in the early 1970s and the adoption of the 1974 constitution, there was considerable support for private sector agriculture. In particular, the right to lease extra land in order to extend the area farmed was introduced. This buoyed up the agricultural sector in Slovenia which was already productive and making a contribution to food self-sufficiency.

From the mid-1950s similar trends began in all sectors of the economy. The ten years to 1955 had included a substantial amount of forced industrialisation as the Yugoslavs ambitiously attempted to ape the Soviet Union. Having been forced by the Soviet-Yugoslav rift to re-evaluate this approach pragmatically and ideologically, there was found to be reason to end the march of coal, steel and state control. Instead there was an attempt, in the context of the doctrine of 'self-managing socialism', to create a more balanced economy. In principle more decisions were decentralised, but this turned out to be more principle than practice. There was also a move to encourage more variation in industrial production. In particular there was stress on the development of manufacturing and service industries in Slovenia.

By the 1960s the emphasis on modern manufacturing processes, new technologies and liberalisation of the market had become the central refrain of Slovene political and economic thought, which was amplified by the opening of borders to trade and travel. The Slovene leaders of the 1960s, notably at the time of the government of Stane Kavčič, tried to take Slovenia to the forefront of economic development. In particular, government policies favoured the most modern sectors of the economy with investment – electronics, banking and finance, and service industries. While the Kavčič government ended in 1972 under federal pressure, the programmes it had put in place, despite a more conservative and less competent administration in Ljubljana during the rest of the 1970s, began to bear fruit, with Slovene manufacturing proving both to be dominant in the intra-Yugoslav market and to be an export motor.[20]

By the 1980s, however, a number of problems were beginning to dominate the policy agenda and to impoverish the economy.

[20] See John Allcock, 'The Economy' in Gareth Wyn Jones (ed.), *Eastern Europe and the CIS, 1997*, London: Europa, 1996, p.731.

First, much of the growth brought by 'warm breezes from booming economies' in Europe,[21] coupled with loans for development from international financial institutions, was going into reverse as the warm breezes turned chill in face of world recession. The flow of loans ebbed. Secondly, while the boom of the 1970s which had avoided any real unemployment in Slovenia, as well as producing a comprehensive system of liberal social benefits, there were now increasing problems of over-employment and poor productivity. These did not prevent goods from having a strong place in the Yugoslav market, or greatly impede strong export performance in Europe. However, these conditions created a situation in which, in the 1980s, it would become necessary for the Slovene authorities to begin to prune the social welfare system. Thirdly, the costs involved in production of crops on a large number of smallholdings was too great. Most of all, however, it was federal policy and the relationship with the federal economy and federal budget which impacted on the Slovene economy and on Slovene economic thought.

Difficulties between the Slovenes and the federal leadership were present from the outset. This was because of the differences between the economies of the different parts of Yugoslavia and their different needs. Such differences could be found even at the close of the Second World War. One example concerned an aluminium factory at Strnišče, where the Nazis had already built 70 per cent of it and installed half of the plant during the occupation and left the fittings in a warehouse. While the federal proposal was to dismantle the factory and move it to Dalmatia to be close to bauxite sources, Slovenia also had bauxite – the reason for the Nazis having wanted to build the plant there – in addition to which it had the necessary power, communications network and workforce. It was only when Tito could be persuaded to override the federal ministry that, at the end of 1945, work on the plant was continued.[22]

Slovene investment was largely financed by the republic itself, and from 1953 all basic investment was generated internally. Up till that point there had been some basic investment from federal funds, to which the Slovenes had contributed anyway, and from

[21] Lazarević, 'Economic', p.61.

[22] Prinčič, *Industrija*, p.23.

international, primarily Western sources, including UNRRA (the United Nations Reconstruction and Rehabilitation Association) in the early post-war years, and the United States, Britain and France after the Soviet-Yugoslav split.[23] However, the question for the Slovene economy was not the degree of investment in the republic itself but the extent to which Slovenia contributed to federal funds for redistribution in less developed regions and the way in which those funds were used. In 1953 and 1954, for example, it was calculated that Slovenia lost 23,927 and 30,427 dinars, respectively, through the federal fund. This represented around one-sixth of the republic's 'national income' and half of the actual investment in Slovenia.[24] These arrangements continued until the eve of dissolution, with Slovenes increasingly frustrated at the way this use of resources restricted their own economic development.

The restrictions on economic development were twofold. The first was that the republic was deprived of funds, which it could have used itself for investment, in what appeared to amount to exploitation of Slovenia. The second was that the actual use of the funds in other parts of the federation served to reinforce old, poorly performing industries or systems of personal patronage. This created a bigger economic divide between Slovenia and those other areas and in the 1980s placed severe impediments in the way of the modernisation, restructuring and market reforms that were needed as communism came to an end. Of these two reasons the latter is overwhelmingly the more significant, and became the major element in the economic motor for Slovene independence.

Slovenia was in a position to establish fairly quickly and easily a Western-type market economy and to be capable of integration with Europe. This was because with a variety of advantages from early market reforms to a diversified economy and a highly-skilled workforce, it would need much less restructuring than the other parts of the Yugoslav federation, as well as other countries in Central and Eastern Europe. Because of this it was not frustration at exploitation through (misused) federal funds that generated economic pressures for Slovenia to leave the federation; rather,

[23] *Ibid.*, pp.23 and 123.

[24] *Ibid.,* p.159.

independence 'became the "emergency exit" condition for macro-economic stabilization, supply side restructuring, and systemic transition'.[25] This made the potential benefits of independence considerably outweigh the possible deficits.

Both royal and communist Yugoslavia provided a fertile context for the Slovene economy to mature. Slovenia thus came to be the most successful and modern economy in Central and Eastern Europe. That economic standing was the result of both intervention and evolution throughout the lifetime of the South Slav state. However, by the time the second, federal version of that state dissolved in the early 1990s, the Yugoslav context which had fostered growth and development in the Slovenian economy for seventy years had become the greatest impediment to its further improvement.

Economic restructuring and independence

The Slovene economy needed independence for successful reform. However, independence itself did not remove the need for reform. In many ways economic restructuring would be easier without the need for (unattainable) agreement with the other Yugoslav states. However, the problems of transition were temporarily compounded by the conditions in which independence was achieved and, especially, by the adjustment to independence. As will be seen below, the Slovene economy generally emerged from the first years of independence well, although there were some problems. What the period of transition made clear was that, like other small economies, Slovenia would need to find its place in the international economic setting through openness, if it were to realise its potential. First, though, it was necessary to negotiate the basic challenges of transition and restructuring.

Slovenia was one of the former communist countries which needed to make a double transition.[26] It was necessary not only

[25] Jože Mencinger, 'Costs and Benefits of Secession' in Danica Fink-Hafner and John R. Robbins (eds), *Making a New Nation: the Formation of Slovenia*, Aldershot: Dartmouth, 1997, p.205. Mencinger was an architect of federal market reform in federal Yugoslavia and later a member of the board of the Bank of Slovenia.

[26] These were the states that, like Slovenia, emerged from the conglomerate

to restructure all aspects of the economy towards full market mechanisms, but also to do this while negotiating the path to full independent international status, including the development of state institutions. This also affected the allocation of resources. Most notably, public expenditure – which as in all the former communist countries, was already high – had to be stepped up in areas such as money, diplomacy and defence, hallmarks of independent statehood, where Slovenia was forging key institutions – establishing its currency the tolar, opening embassies, procuring vehicles and so forth. [27]

Restructuring meant the elaboration of the legal, institutional, attitudinal and operational framework for a market economy. As in the other former communist countries, this was far from an overnight process. However, because market reform had begun before the end of the communist period, Slovenia had a comparatively advanced starting point. On the other hand, the peculiar qualities of the Yugoslav self-management system, with collective ownership, meant that establishing ownership was problematic. This was significant because ownership was one of the key elements of restructuring, along with investment, banking and finance, business practice and monetary and fiscal policy.

Aside from being beneficial to the overall health of the economy, monetary and fiscal policy were important for restructuring of the economy as a whole. First, there was a need for macroeconomic stabilisation to ensure an environment which would most reduce the pain involved in the process. Secondly, it was necessary to provide centrally the kind of financial discipline that would be vital to the successful operation of a full market economy. Thirdly, and most crucially in the short term at least, there were costs associated with restructuring, especially in the major state-backed sectors of industry.

Monetary discipline was important for securing external financial

---

communist federations in the Soviet Union, Czechoslovakia and Yugoslavia and had to build institutions for their new states. For Slovenia, see *Slovenija. Geografska, Zgodovinska, Pravna, Politična, Ekonomska in Kulturna Podoba Slovenije*, Ljubljana: Založba Mladinska Knjiga, 1998, p.162.

[27] See Marko Lah and Andrej Sušjan, 'The Public Sector in Transition' in Fink-Hafner and Robbins, *Making a New Nation*, p.195.

support to withstand the period of shock. Fiscal policy was vital in two ways: first, to introduce measures to increase revenue and reduce the scope of arrangements whereby employees might get part of their salaries in benefits, such as air travel, so as to avoid taxation; and secondly, by increasing revenue to be able to provide state support for restructuring – whether retraining of personnel, cushioning the impact on weak major industries through continuing subsidy, providing social protection for casualties of the restructuring process, or, indeed, strategic investment.

These were all effects of new business requirements. Enterprises were required to leave the old protectionist system behind and adopt new practices geared towards competitiveness and profitability. Whereas in the past the self-managing socialist system had provided the right to work, meaning that virtually every competent individual was employed somehow with restructuring, jobs were shed where there was overmanning and businesses could not sustain them. The 1986 unemployment figure of 13,964 had risen almost tenfold by 1993 to 137,142.[28] However, despite the introduction of accountability and profit mechanisms, there were still indications of companies performing 'less well' that would have to become 'more competitive'.[29] To some extent this judgement applied to a number of the largest industries which had remained protected, simply because tackling their imbalances would have caused major social problems.

Potentially more damaging, however, was the position of small firms. The evidence showed that this sector was 'very volatile,' with the number of businesses, their workforce numbers and their results undergoing considerable change.[30] This reinforced the impression that there was a relative lack of successful innovation and entrepreneurship in Slovenia – businesses that became estab-

---

[28] *Slovenija*, p.165.

[29] Boris Šustar, State Secretary for Industry, Ministry of Economic Affairs, 'The Integration of Slovene Industrial Enterprises into the Common European Market' in Vincent Edwards (ed.), *Proceedings of the Fourth Annual Conference on Convergence and Divergence: Aspirations and Reality in Central and Eastern Europe and Russia*, Chalfont St Giles: CREEB, Buckinghamshire Business School, Buckinghamshire Chilterns University College, 1998, p.4.

[30] Šustar, 'Integration', p.9.

ished appeared to be strong in maintaining efficiency and activity but not generally in breaking into new territory.[31]

To some extent the success of business as a whole depended on restructuring the banking and financial sector. This involved an audit of existing banks by the Bank Rehabilitation Agency set up in 1991, as well as diversification and the formation of new banks. The major Slovene bank before independence, Ljubljanska Banka, was rehabilitated and renamed Nova Ljubljanska Banka in 1992, with the Agency releasing government-backed thirty-year bonds offering 8 per cent interest to cover the bank's bad debts.[32] A similar approach was taken for other banks. International financial confidence in Slovenia seemed high, with bond issues being greatly oversubscribed.

Part of the rehabilitation process was to break up banking activity. As a result of this and the emergence of new banks in 1994, thirty were operating in Slovenia at the end of 1996, when one of them, Banka Noricum (of Ljubljana), was merged with Banka Celje. Another, Komercijalna Banka Triglav, had earlier become the first Slovene bank to go into liquidation. Of the twenty-nine banks operating in 1997, three – Nova Ljubljanska Banka, Nova Kreditna Banka Maribor and Komercijalna Banka Nova Gorica – owned 52 per cent of all assets.[33] The first two of these had state stakes in them, as did a third, Poštna Banka. All others were private, and seventeen had foreign equity. Of these, three – Bank Austria, Banka Creditanstalt and Volksbank-Ljudska Banka – had majority foreign ownership, and a fourth, Société Générale, was wholly foreign-owned. This represented a fairly strong banking sector, with significant international involvement, although most capital continued to be provided by individual savers. However, it was also a situation in which

[31] For example, in one small business the 'entrepreneurial' director whose initiative had been essential to establishing it before the end of the communist era sold his share of the business out of frustration when the others involved preferred to maintain the steady business the firm had obtained rather than striving for new ventures. This corresponds with some of the social characteristics considered in the final section of this chapter.

[32] Evan Kraft, Milan Vodopivec and Milan Cvikl, 'On Its Own: the Economy of Independent Slovenia' in Jill Benderly and Evan Kraft (eds), *Independent Slovenia: Origins, Movements, Prospects*, Basingstoke: Macmillan, 1994, p.213.

[33] *Slovenija*, p.313.

rationalisation and consolidation, particularly, in view of a prospective move towards the European Union by 2005, meant that there were pressures – political and business – for mergers and takeovers that would reduce the number of banks operating.[34] However, alongside this it would also be necessary for the banks to create affordable business loan packages in order to prevent enterprises seeking loans from going to banks outside the country to get better interest rates.

In addition to banking, the restructuring of the financial services sector also included the creation of the Ljubljana stock exchange. However, this institution performed in relatively limited ways in its first five years. It served to trade bonds of various kinds, including government issues – although it was notable that when the government issued Eurobonds in 1997, it chose the Luxembourg stock exchange rather than that in its own capital to do so. Otherwise the Ljubljana exchange was used to exchange ownership of equity, with a total of seventy-three companies in different categories being traded. This amounted to an indirect form of swap-shop rather than a means for capital realisation – as would normally be expected of a stock market. The total estimated capitalisation of the stock market was a very low 7.5 per cent of Gross Domestic Product in 1997.[35] The absence of capital on the stock exchange was a symptom and indeed cause of a prevalent lack of investment throughout the economy.

Investment in the Slovene economy was low for a number of structural reasons. First, undoubtedly, was the absence of an investment culture: individuals simply did not understand how investment and share systems worked – leading to poor judgements when vouchers were issued for shares in enterprises in connection with the privatisation programme.[36] This point can be extended to the

---

[34] The pressures to alter course from the break-up of banks in the first half of the 1990s to the consolidation of banking was the subject of discussion between one of the authors and an executive from one of the more prominent smaller banks in August 1998.

[35] Economist Intelligence Unit, *Country Profile, 1997-98*, London: Economist Intelligence Unit, 1997, p.20.

[36] Under the privatisation scheme all citizens were given ownership certificates. These were offered in six categories, defined by age, ranging from a value of 100,000 tolars for the under-18s to 400,000 for those over 48. Individuals could use their certificates to obtain and sell shares either in a mutual fund or in a

operation of portfolio investment through private or institutional schemes. Secondly, a source of investment which was available, the injection of external capital through the stock market, was severely hampered by restrictions imposed by the government because it judged too much capital to be flowing into Slovenia, pushing up the value of the tolar. A high value for the tolar was counter-productive to the necessary export strategy. The government was thus in an awkward predicament. Its response was to require foreign investors to maintain special custody accounts for their securities – which prompted criticism from major international investors, such as the European Bank of Reconstruction and Development (EBRD), as well as causing heavy falls on the stock exchange and a drought of foreign investment.

Finally, Slovenia faced difficulties over foreign direct investment (FDI). While there was certainly external interest of this kind, it was too small to meet the country's needs. This remained the case, even though there were substantial increases after 1995 – for example, there was a jump from $198.5 million in 1996 to $320.8 million the following year. Of this foreign stake in the economy, 34.3 per cent originated in Austria, 18.5 per cent from Croatia, 14.1 per cent from Germany, 7.5 per cent from France, 7.4 per cent from Italy, and 4.7 per cent from Britain. In some cases this type of investment was targeted at particular businesses. The French stake was substantially the result of the car-maker Renault's commitment to the Revoz car plant in Novo Mesto, while Croatia's share of FDI was principally due to its co-ownership of the Krško nuclear power plant.[37] In part, what this picture confirmed was that the Slovenian market was small and therefore, unable to attract plentiful foreign investment for its strong manufactured goods sector unless a clear and successful export profile, as well as a position in the domestic market, could be demonstrated – as in the case of Renault and Revoz. However, this was more likely to apply to 'niche' industries – such as the electrical starter motors for automobiles manufactured by Iskra and exported to major car manufacturers throughout Europe. Psychologically this was judged to be a problem – Slovenes needed FDI, but often seemed to regard filling niches in the market as beneath the

particular firm. See *Slovenija*, p.172.

[37] Economist Intelligence Unit, *Country Report*, pp.21-2.

standing they expected.[38] The shortage of investment was not a straightforward matter.

The issue of ownership was not straightforward either. While Slovenia had passed a law on the transformation of ownership – privatisation – in November 1991,[39] there were long delays before the process of putting ownership into private hands really got under way. In the autumn of 1995 representatives of both the EU and the World Bank tempered eulogies to the Slovene transition with strong comments about the dilatory pace of privatisation. This was largely due to the complexity of the question. Whereas privatisation was a major problem in all the communist countries, in the former Yugoslav states, notably Slovenia which was eager to privatise, the old system of social ownership meant that there were philosophical as well as legal and practical dimensions to defining ownership in the first place. Once this could be established, then the transfer could proceed apace, and this is what happened. Between the real beginning of the privatisation programme at the end of 1994 and the first quarter of 1996, the number of businesses transferred grew to about one-third.[40] By the middle of 1998, 95 per cent of all enterprises had been privatised – with those that remained including such operations as public utilities.[41] Almost all economic ownership had passed into private control, confirming the shift to market mechanisms.

The question of ownership of land and property was by no means so easily settled. Much of the land in Slovenia was nationalised under communism. The authorities remained reluctant to restore land to the Roman Catholic church, for example; the communists had confiscated 35,000 hectares of high-quality forest it had previously owned, and after fighting a legal battle throughout the 1990s, the church was favoured by a Constitutional Court ruling in December 1996 which found that, according to the denationalisation law, as much of the forest land as possible should be restored to its previous owner. Political opponents of the church in and around the government argued that the land in question was

[38] This point was made in discussion by Janez Damjan of the Economics Faculty, University of Ljubljana.

[39] Allcock, 'Economy', p.733.

[40] *Ibid.*

[41] Šustar, 'Integration', p.4.

now a part of the national heritage and wealth, and sought legislation that would prevent restitution, although Prime Minister Janez Drnovšek, in an attempt to accommodate the church, undertook to ensure that there would not be a majority in parliament for such legislation. On a lesser scale, the claims of individuals from Austria and Italy were also troubling. Despite Slovenia's creation of a fund to compensate Italians who left the country after 1952, the Italian side would not relent. Thus ownership would remain an important issue economically – and politically (see Chapters 5 and 6).

The difficulties in each of these areas of restructuring were compounded by severe contraction and depression, linked to the break with the Yugoslav federation and its impact on the economy. Indeed, Slovenia's experience of economic decentralisation and market features in the 1980s meant that, as one well-placed analyst concluded, 'the necessity of rapid restructuring was produced more by the secession and ensuing collapse of Yugoslavia than by the transition itself.'[42] The events of 1991 forced production down by 9.3 per cent, and in 1992 there was a further fall of 6 per cent.[43] Along with this, as noted above, there was a large growth in unemployment, adding to public spending.

The most obvious impact of the Yugoslav dissolution was in trade. Slovenia had not been dependent on 'cheap' raw materials from other Yugoslav republics – contrary to most assumptions.[44] However, a significant part of its manufacturing output had been sold into the Yugoslav market, particularly to Croatia. However, from 1993 overall recovery began and foreign trade grew, including that with Croatia – which, however, was in third place among Slovenia's trading partners with Germany and Italy accounting for the largest individual shares in 1997.[45] By that year trade had been re-oriented, with a significant increase with member states of the EU. This had already accounted for two-fifths of exports

[42] Mencinger, 'Costs and Benefits', p.211.

[43] *Ibid.*, p.210.

[44] See Milica Žarković Bookman, 'The Economic Basis of Regional Autarky in Yugoslavia', *Soviet Studies*, vol.42, no.1 (January 1990), p.100.

[45] Exports to Germany were valued at $2.554 billion, those to Italy at $1.103 billion and those to Croatia at $859 million (Economist Intelligence Unit, *Country Profile*, p.42).

at the end of the Yugoslav period, but had risen to nearly two-thirds.[46] There was also strong trading with the states of CEFTA, the Central European Free Trade Association. Slovenia had restored itself as a successful exporter.

Despite the strong recovery, there was a long-term significant impact on certain businesses which were closely tied to coordinated production and sale in the Yugoslav federation. For example, the TAM factory in Slovenia was integrated into the production of tanks in federal Yugoslavia – activity which was halted because of independence and the outbreak of armed conflict. The company went into liquidation and was reconstituted with only 2,000 of its previous 8,800-strong workforce and a focus on the non-military area of its business.[47] In 1996 TAM collapsed when that activity, the production of buses, could not be sustained in face of global competition.[48] While the impact of the double transition had been successfully negotiated in general, there were thus casualties in specific areas.

The break with Yugoslavia had an important impact in two further ways. The first of these affected Slovenia's relations with international financial institutions. Aside from the need to establish links between the newly-independent country and these bodies, Slovenia's position was affected by the question of unresolved debt from the federation. However, the country's good will on this matter helped win a favourable reception, as it volunteered to take on an 18 per cent share of the unallocated debt of the erstwhile federation. Although the newly-formed Federal Republic of Yugoslavia, comprising Serbia and Montenegro, in 1996 sought to block this through legal action in Britain, the case collapsed.[49] This left Slovenia unhampered in its external economic relations.

The second way in which the Yugoslav divorce seriously affected Slovenia was to do with perception. Although there had only been armed conflict involving the country for a period of ten days in 1991 and that conflict had been very limited, the association with Yugoslavia left many under the impression that Slovenia

---

[46] Šustar, 'Integration', p.3. This translated into actual figures as $5.4 billion.

[47] Allcock, 'Economy', p.731.

[48] *Slovenija*, p.242.

[49] Allcock, 'Economy', p.731.

was as dangerous as parts of Croatia or Bosnia and Hercegovina, where major armed conflicts continued up to 1995. Although there was nothing to corroborate the suggestion that the Slovene authorities could do little in this period to 'enhance...the security and confidence of its own population',[50] who in fact were more secure than the population of London, there could be no doubt that proximity to its conflict-ridden former partners gave a contrary impression. Among the problems of securing investment already noted, there was also a sense that potential business partners, who had not actually experienced the tranquillity of the country, did not want to take risks in what they presumed to be a war zone.

This impact was also strongly felt in the tourist industry, which had been a major source of external income before the war and independence. However, the events of 1991 almost wiped out foreign tourism for a period. While in 1990 Slovenia had welcomed 1,095,000 foreign tourists, there was a drop in 1991 to 299,000, and almost no activity in 1992, by which time hostilities in Croatia and Bosnia and Hercegovina had reached their peak.[51] This reflected in part the perception that Slovenia was involved in the conflict, and in part, the fact that much of Slovenia's foreign tourism derived from Germans and Austrians in transit to the Dalmatian coast in Croatia. With war in Croatia and Bosnia and Hercegovina over, in 1996, after slow improvement during the years after 1992, Slovenia received 831,895 foreign tourists – representing $1.22 billion in earnings.[52] While this meant that there was some way to go, it also demonstrated a real recovery in that sector. The prospects for reaching pre-war levels seemed generally good.

Slovenia had sought independence to ensure reform, and the balance-sheet certainly suggested a positive outcome. However, there were significant costs and the mere fact of independence did not bring automatic reform. Transition was made more difficult by the need to create new institutions and to negotiate the difficulties caused by the break-up of Yugoslavia. Despite this, the transition in Slovenia had recast the economy in a post-modern mould, as will be seen in the following section.

[50] *Ibid.*

[51] *Slovenija*, p.281.

[52] *Ibid.*, p.280.

Economic structure and economic performance

The importance of tourism reflected the increasing overall emphasis on service industries in the country's economic structure. That structure changed as the economy developed positively, though not without complications. Measures of economic management had to balance requirements in an economy which at times suffered from its apparent strengths. Exports were essential, but various pressures conspired to make them over-priced. As will be seen below, this weakened economic performance, but that performance was still high. However, economic success for this small country was dependent on export and openness.

In 1996 the service sector accounted for 57.1 per cent of GDP, while manufacturing industry represented 28.8 per cent, with agriculture and construction at around 5 per cent each, leaving other sectors such as mining to account for the rest.[53] The structure of exports was generally diverse, meaning that success was not dependent on any one sector. In manufacturing, for example, transport equipment, machinery, electrical and optical equipment, basic metals and fabricated metal products, and chemicals and chemical products each accounted for 12-13 per cent, while a range of other manufactures accounted for the rest, with textiles and textile products the highest at 9 per cent.[54]

However, it was service industries which provided the major share of wealth and their invisible earnings made the most significant contribution to the country's current account trade balance. While services constituted only around one-fifth of total exports, the sector consistently registered a surplus, whereas there was an increasing deficit in goods. This meant that, following a strong current account surplus of $600 million in 1994, there was a drop in subsequent years, with a small deficit in 1995 and small surpluses in 1996 and 1997.[55] The signing of an association agreement with the EU in 1996, removing tariffs in most areas, made the prospects for further development positive. In addition, business was generally optimistic about the scope for advances in Central and Eastern Europe – especially, in the former Yugoslav lands

[53] *Slovenija*, p.176; Economist Intelligence Unit, *Country Profile*, p.9.

[54] Šustar, 'Integration', p.9.

[55] Economist Intelligence Unit, *Country Report,* 2nd quarter, 1998 p.5.

once Serbia was in a position to normalise. The prospects for economic performance appeared fairly bright, although there were a few dark clouds.

There were several areas in which economic health was, or was perceived to be, vulnerable. One of these was the Slovene sense that the high level of exports to Germany left the country exposed, even if that trade was broadly structured. This was thought to make the country susceptible in the event of German economic weakness, or open to pressure. However, this was no more than hypothetical, given that the German economy had been at its weakest (because of the costs of unification) during the period in which this trading relationship had emerged and it was unlikely that any German government would have reason to try to interfere in this way, even if it could force the large number of businesses involved to toe the line.

A more significant potential shadow on the economy was the fact that day-trips, almost entirely by Italian and Austrian shoppers, accounted for a substantial part of the tourism total. Most day-trippers were taking advantage of lower petrol prices in Slovenia and, in the case of Italians, the gambling facilities. As petrol prices were set to rise as taxes were harmonised with those in EU countries, there was sure to be some impact on this kind of tourism – the question was how extensive it would be.[56]

A third area of vulnerability was the growing deficit in goods trade – especially if service sector performance failed and so removed protection in the current account. Most of the growing trade gap in goods was not caused by consumer spending but by investment, as companies seeking to restructure purchased new infrastructure. As restructuring was set to continue, it seemed likely that for some time the import of investment goods would do so too. This would mean a widening gap for some time to come and was responsible for the appearance of a current account deficit in the first months of 1998. The likely effect of this would be to slow the pace of economic growth.

There was also vulnerability from indirect foreign investment. Ironically for an economy in need of investment, significant capital appreciation in the country created unwelcome pressures. In part, capital appreciation was due to high interest rates in Slovenian

---

[56] *Ibid.*, p.12.

banks. On the one hand this meant Slovenian businesses looking for cheaper private loans outside the country to finance investment, with the net effect of bringing foreign capital into the country. On the other hand it meant that there were benefits for those with money to place it in Slovenia, given the high return. While capital appreciation had been necessary, it became a burden as Slovenia's economic masters were put in a double bind that would require adept management to overcome.

Policy was caught between the need to reduce inflation – with the interest rate mechanism a key instrument – and at the same time to reduce pressure on exports caused by currency overvaluation, which in turn was generated by the capital appreciation induced by high interest rates. Both currency appreciation and inflation damaged exports, with one overvaluing goods and the other undermining them. In either case there had to be an impact on export performance and consequently on the current account and overall economic performance. As it was, the authorities opted to stem the inward flow of capital by imposing restrictions on foreign investment and capital flows. These began to deter adequate external investment (as discussed above). However, ratification of the EU association agreement by all involved in 1998 meant that these restrictions could not be maintained. Export goods would continue to be more expensive, pushing exports down.

Inflation was one of an interrelated set of factors which also hampered the economy's progress. It was indeed a key weakness. Although it had been reduced from an annual rate of over 100 per cent through the 1990s, the need to balance anti-inflationary policies with maintenance of other areas of the economy meant that the 1997 level of 8.3 per cent would not fall significantly, although projections of gradual reductions to 6.4 per cent at the end of the decade were sound.[57] However, inflation was continuously under pressure from rising pay which grew by 12.1 per cent in the year to December 1997.[58] This was seemingly paradoxical, given an official unemployment rate of 14.1 per cent in the same month. Given that high unemployment usually correlates with low wages, this was surprising. The explanation was found

[57] *Ibid.*, p.8.
[58] *Ibid.*, p.17.

in the economy's need for highly skilled labour and the fact that the vast majority of those unemployed had previously been in the unskilled manual sector. This fact also meant that although the actual number, rather than the percentage, of the unemployed was relatively low at 127,000,[59] it could not be absorbed by a small amount of growth or a limited public investment programme, as would normally be expected. Instead there would have to be significant government training for skills acquisition to meet the needs of an advancing economy.

Unemployment and rising wages were linked to increasing profitability. Corporate business results showed a net overall profit in 1997 for the first time since independence.[60] This was reflected also in the consistent growth of GDP since the end of the in-dependence depression in 1993. However, the net effect of the pressures outlined above meant that the annual rate of growth was slowing, having reached 3.8 per cent in 1997.[61] As with other aspects of the economy, there could be no doubt that the picture was positive, but there were obstacles to be negotiated.

Perhaps the biggest impediment of all was the mixture of the country's size and its psychological disposition. It did not have a domestic market to satisfy its own abundant economic activity. Nor did it have the resources to ensure adequate levels of in-vestment. In both cases the international dimension of the economy was vital. If Slovenia did not trade, it would not prosper. Moreover, as with countries like Britain, it was clear that Slovenia's comparative advantage would be in the service sector, whether in tourism or in financial services. Success in that sector required an open eco-nomy and flexibility. However, as will be seen below in the present chapter and later ones, this implied changes in society as well as in cultural and political values.

In general Slovenia's economy emerged well from its first years of independence in spite of notable problems. Although it was still export-oriented, the balance of its external trade had shifted from manufacture, which nonetheless remained strong, to services. Overall, the structure of the economy and of exports was both wide-based and complex. Nonetheless there were difficulties in-

[59] *Ibid.*, p.16.

[60] *Ibid.*, p.20.

[61] *Ibid.*, p.7.

volved in steering a way towards macro-economic stability and prosperity. These were numerous and, as we have seen, interwoven in such a way that measures in one area, such as control of inflation, had an adverse impact by capital accumulation and currency appreciation, and hence downward pressures on exports. Yet exports were critical to the Slovene economy. Indeed, what the period of transition made clear was that, as with other small economies, Slovenia would need to face the challenge of finding its place in the international economic setting through openness if it were to realise its potential. This would augment the changes precipitated in society by the shift in the economy during the 1990s.

Society: demography and dislocation

The economic transformation forced the pace of social change. In the course of the twentieth century there had been great changes in the Slovene population, mostly after the Second World War. These changes, especially in education, occupation and outlook, were part of a process that entered a new and even more rapid phase with the transition from communism. Significantly, many of them were equivalent to changes that had occurred, or were occurring, in the advanced industrial and post-industrial societies of Western Europe. While in many ways the changes represented the strength of Slovene society, they also generated demographic pressures and social dislocation. We should now look more closely at the Slovene social fabric.

There is an obvious and almost intuitive division in Slovene society and character. This might be seen as the clerical-liberal pattern which influenced political development, and in turn reflected a rural-urban and agricultural-business cleavage. It extends to parochial-cosmopolitan divisions. The former is focused on Slovenia and all that is Slovene, and is represented by someone who never travels far from the valley where he was born. The latter is oriented to global trends and European values, and represented by a citizen far more likely, as a stereotype, to have travelled the world than to have ventured down the road. However, this division within society is neither as complete nor as pronounced as it superficially appears to be. While it does have some validity and translates into other areas of life, Slovenia's economic success and relative social stability would not have been possible if its society were truly reflected in these stereotypes.

The reality was that Slovenes shared the characteristics of diversity found in modern Western societies, despite this broad-brush picture of social schism. These were the characteristics of countries with advanced economies, of the kind with which Slovenia emerged from Yugoslavia. However, there was also limited evidence to confirm certain distinctive social features. Some of these were outlined in perhaps the most important study of Slovene society, Janek Musek's 'psychological portrait' of the Slovenes.[62] This book used the methodology of social-psychology to draw an 'average' national character. It found that Slovenes were relatively introverted, depressive, rigid, tending to psychotic aggressiveness in thought (although not deed), oriented towards work and productivity, and conscientious. Musek pointed out that these dominant features corresponded with high levels of independence and productivity, as well as suicide, personality disorders (including alcohol and drug abuse), and road accidents.[63] Thus, while Slovenes could be said to reflect the characteristics of Western societies, it was also possible to categorise them as suicidal, envious, modest and diligent.

Beyond this analysis, other research has given greater definition to the characteristics of Slovenes. These include high respect for authority, individualism and self-control, resistance to change, inflexibility, low levels of ambition and a sense that one's life is inevitably controlled from outside.[64] All of these, in particular the last three, indicate the obstacles to the highest levels of success in the country's transition stage because, while not absolute, they

[62] Janek Musek, *Psihološki Portret Slovencev*, Ljubljana: Znanstveno in Publicistično Središče, 1994.

[63] Musek, *Portret*, p.184. There was testimony for the high suicide rate when a man jumped from the *Nebotičnik* building – a 1930s 'skyscraper', though in reality not so tall – in Ljubljana on 6 August 1998, to record the 400th suicide of the year (*Radio Ljubljana*, 6 August 1998). As for alcoholism, over 25 per cent of the population drank more than the equivalent of half a litre of wine per day. Nevenka Černigoj Sadar and Alenka Brešar Iskra, 'Determinants of Self-Reported Health' in Nevenka Černigoj Sadar (ed.), 'Quality of Life in Slovenia', *Družboslovne Razprave*, vol.XII, no.22-3, 1996, p.199.

[64] This analysis is based on work in progress at the time of writing and discussion with Janez Damjan.

were restraints on the type of entrepreneurship and innovation emerging which was required to make the most of economic changes. The degree to which those barriers could be overcome was important for the future of Slovene society.

Changes earlier in the twentieth century indicated that Slovenes, while reluctant and slow to embrace change, were capable of making real adjustments. Because of changes in the socio-economic structure of the land, only 5 per cent of the population was employed in agriculture by 1998, with the overwhelming majority of the active working population employed in other sectors. Concomitant with this was the expansion of education. Illiteracy rates were traditionally low – the rate was only 8 per cent in the first Yugoslav period – but the creation of universities in Ljubljana and, later, Maribor meant a highly educated population. The creation and, then, expansion of Slovene-language television had the same effect.[65] This represented a major social change, especially after the expansion under the communists in the 1960s, and was a major underpinning for economic development.

This type of change was also significantly affected by other policies in the late 1960s, notably the opening of borders. This had a completely different impact in Slovenia than in other parts of the Yugoslav federation. One of the mainsprings for the freedom to travel and the improvement of relations with Western Europe was a programme to unburden the Yugoslav economy of excess labour, allowing workers from economically developing regions to seek employment (and to return hard currency revenue) as 'guest workers' in countries which needed them such as Germany, Switzerland and Sweden.

However, Slovenia had more of the characteristics of those advanced European economies than its federal partners – it too had labour shortages and was in effect importing labour from the other Yugoslav states. The benefit for Slovenia was therefore not a reduction in excess labour, since this was not a problem. However, Slovene companies could establish important business contacts and, crucially, ordinary people could travel freely and easily in a way that those in the rest of Yugoslavia could not. For Slovenes freedom to travel did not mean freedom to go on a major trip, whether for work or for a vacation, by air or by train. Rather,

---

[65] See Prunk, *Kratka*, pp.153–5.

it meant the possibility of regular drives of two hours or less, in so far as these were affordable (and mostly they were) to shop and have coffee in Italy or Austria.[66] Slovenes, far more than other Yugoslavs, were exposed to what would later be somewhat narcissistically termed 'European standards' and, more important, absorbed them.[67]

In the post-Yugoslav period, with an eye on membership of the EU, the notion of European standards became ever more appropriate. With its per capita GDP slightly lower than that of the lowest-ranking existing members of the EU, but growing, Slovenia was a relatively affluent society. This was certainly true of those in gainful employment, even though there was a problem of structural unemployment caused by the shift to intellectually more demanding work in the key sectors of the economy – high-quality manufacturing of electronic and chemical products and the various service industries. This went with the emergence of great flexibility in the labour market. Before 1989 this had been quite rigid, whereas by 1994 11.1 per cent of workers were on temporary contracts or in part-time employment and freelance arrangements.[68] Jobs had become less secure and had moved away from manual labour.

However, despite a growing and demanding economy, unemployment was embedded in the socio-economic fabric. Only 15 per cent of those unemployed found work within six months,[69] largely because those made jobless in the course of transition were unskilled or low-skilled, whereas any opportunities being created were for those with high skill levels in technological or service industries. As a consequence, wages rose quickly despite the existence of a labour surplus. The effect of this was to widen

[66] Slovenes could get special travel documents, effectively a 'local passport', to enable regular travel across the borders with Italy and Austria.

[67] For reference to the nebulous character of this Slovenian concept of 'European standards', see Ljubica Jelušič, 'Slovenska Javnost o Varnostnih Dilemah Svoje Države' in Anton Grizold (ed.), *Razpotja Nacionale Varnosti. Obramboslovne Raziskave v Sloveniji*, Ljubljana: Zbirka Teorija in Praksa, 1992.

[68] See Ivan Svetlik, 'Quality of Working Life' in Černigoj Sadar (ed.), *Družboslovne Razprave*, p.24.

[69] Sonja Drobnič, 'Labour Market Dynamics in Slovenia: Transitions from Unemployment' in Černigoj Sadar (ed.), *Družboslovne Razprave*, p.151.

disparities in income and lifestyle, and so increase social stratification.

The key to this changing picture of the labour market was education and training, which were vital to job acquisition and to progress within employment. Hence social policy had to be geared towards these requirements in order to alleviate unemployment and meet the needs of employers.[70] This meant that the 10 per cent rise in the numbers attending university in the 1996-7 academic year to 50,667 would not be a transient cause of pressure on the educational system.[71] It would be necessary to forge an integrated, global education, employment and social policy.[72]

Education and employment were inevitably linked to quality of life. Slovenes with the kinds of jobs predicated on education and offering some degree of autonomy tended to be happy in their work and in their lives generally, although in the 1990s this seemed more true of men than women, who were now more than half of the population.[73] Increasingly, as in other post-industrial societies, it was women who were dissatisfied, as they succeeded in their work while striving to maintain family lives, either in the mould of traditional housewife (despite full-time employment) or attempting to get men to adapt to an arrangement in which the woman's work was given space and priority. Both situations created stress and neither on the whole had a successful outcome. As a consequence it was possible to see a similar pattern emerging as in many post-industrial states as women, unhappy with the quality of the men available to match their own working lifestyles and aspirations, would settle down only at a later age and be far more demanding in their choice of partner – and possibly even choose to live without a man at all.

Nonetheless, the overall image was of a fairly contented country. The greatest problem areas concerned accommodation and leisure time. This applied especially to those between twenty-five and fifty-

---

[70] See Milan Vodopivec, 'Elementi Strategije Gospodarskega Razvoja Trga Dela' in *Slovenija po Letu 1995. Razmišljenja o Prihodnosti*, Ljubljana: Fakulteta za Družbene Vede, 1995, pp.281-96.

[71] Economist Intelligence Unit, *Country Profile*, p.17.

[72] Zdenko Medveš, 'Strategija Razvoja Vzgoje in Izobraževanje v Slovenski Prihodnosti' in *Slovenija po Letu 1995*, p.279.

[73] *Slovenija*, p.70.

five years old and was linked to the conflicting needs of maintaining a two-job family and raising children.[74] While over half of the Slovenes took vacations outside the country (the majority in Croatia) and over half engaged in some other activity (e.g. an additional job, sport, adult education, moonlighting), elements of a more traditional society remained: in particular, most leisure and social contacts took place within families. It was possible that this was connected in part with the demands of the two-jobs-plus-children lifestyle, which mostly was only made feasible by family support – usually from the children's grandmothers.

Along with the continuation of aspects of the extended family in Slovene life went a shortage of housing.[75] This led in the 1990s to a growing trend towards private house-building. While this had been the way in which Slovenes had gained their own homes in previous times, especially during a boom in the 1970s, it now became a pronounced phenomenon – with the modestly large 'house in Gorenjska' (typifying suburban comfort) being the ambition of a typical thirty-something Slovene. This enabled them to escape cramped conditions with a high number of inhabitants per dwelling, which continued to apply to older people and those with low educational achievement.[76] By 1997 Slovenia had a remarkable owner-occupier level of 87 per cent, in excess of the 81 per cent figure for the Republic of Ireland – the highest level among existing EU countries and 20 per cent higher than at the beginning of the decade.[77] Although there had been a tradition of small-scale agricultural ownership even under communism, this was a remarkable trend. Slovenia had rapidly formed an owner-occupier society.

This process of private house-building had a striking impact on the environment. While a population of a little under 2 million managed to be spread through 5,700 settlements, between seven-

---

[74] Nevenka Černigoj Sadar, 'Social and Material Determinants of Leisure' in Černigoj Sadar (ed.), *Družboslovne Razprave*, p.133.

[75] See, for example, Barbara Verlič Dekleva, 'Urban Mobility and Housing Shortages: the Case of Slovenia' in Frane Adam and Gregor Tomc (eds), 'Small Societies in Transition: the Case of Slovenia', *Družboslovne Razprave*, nos 15-16, 1994, pp.117-33.

[76] Srna Mandič, 'The Changing Quality of Life During Transition – the Housing Component' in Černigoj Sadar (ed.), *Družboslovne Razprave*, pp.32-3.

[77] Mandič, 'Changing Quality', p.36.

ty-eight and 250 could be described as urban, depending on the criteria used.[78] Of these only the capital, Ljubljana, with 268,000 inhabitants and Maribor with 133,000 were large towns. Municipalities generally had less than 20,000, with only three having more than 50,000.[79] This polycentric distribution of the population was reinforced by the pattern of new house construction, where the larger towns were overlooked and the greatest growth area was that of privately built houses in what, somewhat misleadingly, were described as 'suburban' areas. These were moderately large houses in small settlements where those working in towns chose to live and from which to commute. The 'suburban' label was applied because of the link to urban workplaces, although the properties themselves were well away from the existing fringes of the towns. These sites were chosen because such larger, better-quality homes in a greener and more peaceful environment cost less, particularly for those raising families, as well as being a lifestyle symbol for successful urbanites in their thirties. It also seemed likely that despite the enormous move away from an agricultural society, people were at most four generations away from life on the land, and there was still a strongly implanted attachment to living in the countryside.

This pattern of housing has implications for other areas of life. For example, it has caused a decline in use of public transport and a consequent wasting of the public transport infrastructure. In 1984, over 30 per cent of people in Ljubljana and Maribor were using public transport, but a decade later only around 18 per cent did so. Correspondingly, there was a great increase of private motor vehicles not only to help get around inside the urban area but also to commute from the small satellite communities in the countryside.[80] Car sales were one of the growth areas in the 1990s.

Overall, Slovenes were well-educated and prosperous, although it seemed they were often dissatisfied with their lot. In the 1990s there had been considerable social change, accelerating trends

[78] Barbara Verlič Christensen, 'Quality of Life in the Living Environment of Slovenia' in Černigoj Sadar (ed.), *Družboslovne Razprave*, p.41.

[79] *Slovenija*, pp.157-8.

[80] Verlič Christensen, 'Living Environment', pp.52-3.

from previous decades, but while well equipped for transition in many ways, the population was also ageing and stagnating. Around 40 per cent were dependent,[81] a share that was set to rise as low fertility rates, reduced mortality rates and longer life-expectancy combined to take Slovenia into the twenty-first century with a declining active workforce and a larger inactive part of the population. As an official study noted, there were two likely consequences of this: either the size of the relevant part of the population would need to grow or the demands of the economy would lead to inward migration.[82]

This would possibly create social pressures of other types, particularly in the area of ethnic relations. While much was made of Slovenia's 'ethnic homogeneity' at the time of independence, around one-tenth of the population were non-Slovenes. While these groups were not subject to discrimination in a legal or political sense, there was no doubt they were prone to social exclusion and varieties of informal discrimination – such as expressions of opinion that migrant workers should be dismissed before ethnic Slovenes.[83] This problem needed careful management.

The economic transformation which had driven social change in the 1990s would therefore require further changes. The twenty-first century would continue the trends of the twentieth which had seen enormous changes, especially in the second half. Slovenes had become a modern, post-industrial, highly educated, industrious and older population. While this had proved a great resource, low fertility rates indicated latent decay in this transformed social fabric, as well as the possibility of greater ethnic complexity. These processes had been catalysed during the twin transition from communism and Yugoslavia to democracy and independence. Overall, the traits of Slovene society bore many similarities to those of the EU members the country was preparing to join. However, these changes which demonstrated the strength of Slovene society also induced incipient demographic dislocation and social stress.

Throughout the course of the twentieth century, Slovene

[81] Economist Intelligence Unit, *Country Profile*, p.16.

[82] *Projekcije Prebivalstva Republike Slovenije, 1995-2000*, Ljubljana: Zavod Republike Slovenije za Statistiko, 1994.

[83] Peter Klinar, 'Social and Ethnic Stratification: Global Social and Ethnic Relations' in Adam and Tomc (eds), *Družboslovne Razprave*, pp.103-13.

economy and society had been transformed. The monarchical and communist versions of Yugoslavia had provided fecund soil for the Slovenes to develop a strong and mature economy, which then emerged from Yugoslavia as the strongest of all the former communist Central and East European states. This position was the outcome of policies and experience in the Yugoslav framework which saw Slovenia become a prosperous net export economy. By the end of the South Slav state, despite the beneficial effects of the Yugoslav environment, continued development and necessary reform were blocked by that context.

Independence ensured reform and on balance the outcome was clearly positive. But there were problems as independence required the creation of new institutions and there were various issues arising from the Yugoslav break-up to be handled. In spite of this, the economy was reshaped. While it continued to be predicated on export, the nature of external trade had shifted from high-quality manufactured goods, which nonetheless remained important, to a vibrant service sector. However, although the trade tended to be successful, the maintenance of macro-economic stability was problematic as both inflation and the currency appreciation resulting from measures to deal with it – depressed export potential. Like other small economies, Slovenia's needed to be open and integrated in an international setting – something that would be helped by EU membership. This kind of openness and the economic structure which emerged inevitably triggered social change.

Through the economic transformation of the twentieth century, enormous changes had occurred, taking the people from the land into a post-industrial setting. A highly educated and diligent population, albeit with tendencies to depression and related disorders, was also becoming an older and stagnating population. Although the Slovene population had been a major resource as economic development occurred, it also contained elements of decay as the century ended – notably, through structural unemployment among the less educated and a falling birth rate. This meant that a society which had come far in the twentieth century, largely steered by cultural distinctiveness but with many similarities to the societies of EU countries, would enter the twenty-first century with a continuing trend of change and facing new social questions. The resolution of these would depend on political developments.

5

POLITICS

Slovene politics from the mid-1980s was characterised by a strong degree of consensus, in spite of a multiplicity of parties in the 1990s. At the core of this generally stable political arrangement was a strong centrist element associated with liberal reform communists in the final stages of communism, who paved the way for democracy and, following the advent of democracy and independence, provided most of the ballast to government coalitions after 1992 in the form of a re-invented Liberal party. The key to this political development was the nature of the political system established by the constitution and by electoral legislation. These were geared towards the formation of strong, stable coalition government, in many ways developing the style of politics which, despite personality problems, had emerged in the later years of communism. However, a system predicated on forming effective and stable coalition government also carries with it the spectre of stasis and ineffectiveness. While Slovenia experienced a generally consensual and positive political life in the 1990s, the effect of the political system developed from the communist period into democracy could also be negative at crucial moments.

Political System

There were two key elements which set the framework for political life after the end of communist rule – the constitution and the electoral law. Together these shaped an environment in which significant change was hard to precipitate easily, in which there was a necessity for compromise, coalition and a high level of consensus. If these were absent, government in any active, policy-making sense would be stifled. It was important, therefore, that the third factor in political life – the parties which inhabited this framework – should be capable of finding ways to cooperate and

135

form working partnerships if the country was not·to drift. In a time of transition this was especially important. While the way politics developed is the subject of the rest of this chapter, this first section focuses on the political system itself – constitutionally defined institutions, electoral mechanisms and political parties.

Formally the Slovene constitution appears to place the greatest weight on the role of parliament in the organisation of the state.[1] However, its prerogatives are not as great in practice as some attempted to make them at the time of change,[2] or as might be inferred purely from reading the constitution. In reality there is a more important and effective role for the prime minister and the government than might appear in theory. The centrality of parliament is indicated by its being treated first in the constitution; it is bicameral, with the parameters of the two chambers defined by Articles 80-101.[3] The more important lower chamber is the National Assembly, while the upper house is the National Council.[4] The former consists of ninety members directly elected by secret ballot as representatives of the people. It also includes one place each for representatives directly elected by the autochthonous Italian and Hungarian communities – an arrangement to which these minorities 'shall always be entitled'.[5] Furthermore, there is

---

[1] The pro-democratic push experienced in many other Central and East European countries was present in Slovenia, although its effects were more limited over time. However, the initial thrust of putting parliament in control of everything, rather than creating a division of responsibility led to absurdities such as con-stitutional provision, under Article 92, that the National Assembly 'shall determine the deployment of the defence forces'.

[2] Drago Zajc, 'The Changing Political System' in Danica Fink-Hafner and John R. Robbins (eds), *Making a New Nation: the Formation of Slovenia*, Aldershot: Dartmouth, 1997, p.167.

[3] *Constitution of the Republic of Slovenia*, Ljubljana: Časopisni Zavod Uradni List Republike Slovenije, 1993.

[4] The original terms '*Državni Zbor*' and '*Državni Svet*' should properly be translated as 'state' rather than 'national' assembly and council, but 'national' has been adopted as a convention and is therefore used here.

[5] *Constitution* Article 80. The distinction drawn between the autochthonous but very small Italian and Hungarian minorities reflects arrangements under communism, where there was an effort to accommodate minorities, but it has been challenged by critics, primarily outside Slovenia, who note that the distinction between autochthonous and immigrant minorities means that the considerably larger Croat, Serb and Slav Muslim minorities are not accommodated by similar

an effective right of veto for these representatives over any piece of legislation which affects the exercise of their minority rights, as no such measure can be passed without their consent. Once elected and confirmed, deputies to the National Assembly obtain a substantial degree of legal immunity. This is the case not only regarding their freedom to state opinions and cast votes in the parliament and parliamentary bodies, but also in the sphere of criminal offences for which the penalty is less that five years' imprisonment – unless the consent of a majority in the National Assembly in support of legal proceedings has been given (equally, the Assembly has the authority to designate immunity for a deputy, even where the individual in question has not claimed it as a right). Once in place, deputies retain their seats for the duration of the parliament – a four-year period, fixed by the constitution, with elections to be held at some stage during an approximately six-week period between fifteen days and two months before to the fourth anniversary of the first day on which the parliament convened.[6]

The first session of each parliament has to be held within twenty days of the election. The first priority for each term of the National Assembly is to choose its president. This is the individual selected by a majority of all elected members to have responsibility for managing parliamentary business, as well as to deputise temporarily for the President of the Republic in the event of his dying in office or being so incapacitated as not to

---

political arrangements. To a large extent this may be explained by a trait in the Slovene national character which leads Slovenes who emigrate to assimililate with the host community, and fosters the expectation that immigrants to Slovenia will do likewise. This creates conditions for low tolerance of 'foreigners'. (Janez Damjan, 'The Slovene National Character', Ljubljana: unpublished paper, 1998.) The indigenous Italian and Hungarian communities are distinct because they have always coexisted side-by-side with Slovenes rather than having come to 'join' them. To some extent this approach appeared to be changing when discussions on relations between Slovenia and Croatia introduced the notion of formally recognising and giving status to the Croat minority – something Slovenia was prepared to accept for the sake of good relations with its neighbours. This was a matter of great importance for Slovenia's ambitions regarding NATO and the European Union.

[6] *Constitution*, Article 81. There is provision, however, for exceptions in time of war and emergency.

be able to continue his task effectively; or while the President is outside the country.

The business of the National Assembly is to enact legislation which can be formally initiated in one of three ways. The first of these is the most obvious and the one which mostly operates in practice – proposals being brought before the Assembly by the government. However, there is also provision for individual members of the Assembly to introduce legislation, as well as for a process to be initiated by a petition by a minimum of 5,000 voters. In 1992-4 this meant 167 government-proposed statutes, fifty-one put forward by individual deputies and just one originating from outside parliament.[7] In whatever way a piece of legislation is initiated, to be completed it requires a majority of all members to be present at the time of voting, and the support of a majority of those voting.[8]

The legislative process in the Assembly is supplemented by the work of standing committees. These replaced a structure of committees which had been in place under old arrangements and continued to operate *de facto* until standing orders were passed in July 1993. This set of standing committees is designed to complement the work of the government, with one for each ministry plus a number of others to consider non-executive issues, such as elections and administration. In total, twenty-two committees operate and have an influential position through the reports they produce as well as their ability to propose amendments to legislation.[9] This structure in the National Assembly generally appeared to work as a vast amount of legislation arising from the transition was enacted.

In contrast to the legislative powers of the Assembly, the role of the National Council is essentially consultative. Despite this, it does have limited authority to initiate legislation, as well as a formal veto which returns legislation to the Assembly but can

---

[7] Zajc, 'Changing', p.168.

[8] Exceptions to this basic rule are possible: except where defined by statute or by constitutional provision for a greater majority, such as matters of defence, a two-thirds majority of those present and voting is required to enact legislation (under Article 124). The overturning of bills returned for reconsideration by the National Council requires a majority of all elected deputies to vote in favour. Constitutional change requires a two-thirds majority of all elected deputies according to Article 169.

[9] Zajc, 'Changing', p.168.

easily be overturned by a majority in the lower house. In addition to these powers, the National Council has the right to require that a referendum be held or call for the establishment of a parliamentary inquiry. As with the National Assembly, a majority of all members must be present for a vote to be taken, and a majority of those present must take part for a decision to be adopted – except in the case of calling for a referendum where, according to Article 99, a majority of all members is required.

The membership of the Council is quite different from that of the Assembly. Its genesis lies in the parliamentary structure under communism, where there were three Chambers: of Associated Labour, of Communes, and of Socio-political Organisations. These were made up of representatives of, respectively, employed labour, local communities and five officially recognised organisations, such as the Socialist Alliance and the Socialist Youth League. Mostly these chambers were required to work together to pass legislation. In theory it was a delegate system in which each member was mandated to represent a particular view by his or her organisation or community.

This system of representation of bodies within society was transposed into the creation of the National Council, where the forty-strong membership has the following composition, according to Article 96 of the constitution: four councillors to represent each of three groups – employers, employees and, collectively, farming, small business and independent professionals; six to represent non-profit non-governmental organisations; and twenty-two to represent 'local interests'. Thus the Council retains a link with the elements of 'civil society' on a putatively 'non-political' basis, and acts as a force for consolidation, if not for corporatism. Although nowhere near as strong as the Assembly, and with councillors who do not share the legal immunity of deputies in the Assembly, this body, through its composition and its exercise of limited powers, plays an important role as the second chamber in the legislative process.[10]

---

[10] As Mitja Žagar notes, some observers objected that the weakness of the National Council meant that the Slovene parliament could not be regarded as bicameral. This seems curious and inaccurate, given that the Council is clearly a second chamber and that its formal powers, aside from the calling of referendums, have superficial parallels with the United Kingdom parliament, which is not usually seen as monocameral – although there is much of difference in substance.

The formally limited role of the National Council is parallel
to that of the President of the Republic – although he is chosen
directly by general election. The President is elected for a five-year
term and can serve for a maximum of two consecutive terms.[11]
He is head of state and commander-in-chief of the defence forces.
These largely formal roles are supplemented by a number of powers
and functions. These are to call elections for the National Assembly,
to proclaim statutes already passed by parliament, to appoint state
officials in a manner subject to regulation by statute, to accredit
and revoke the accreditation of Slovenian ambassadors to other
countries as well as to receive the credentials of ambassadors to
Slovenia, to publish adherence to international agreements, to
grant pardons, to confer honours and decorations on behalf of
the state, and to perform other duties in accordance with the
constitution. In addition, the President may be asked by the National Assembly to offer an opinion on particular issues, and retains
powers of legislation by decree, on the recommendation of the
government, in the event of Assembly sessions being suspended
because of war or a state of emergency. Mostly these are limited
powers and functions.[12] However, there is theoretical scope for
the President to impede legislation by failing to proclaim it once
it has been passed by the National Assembly – although this is

---

[11] The calling of the presidential election is the responsibility of the president
of the National Assembly, and the election has to have been held no less that
fifteen days before the expiration of a term in office. The exception to this is
provision for time of war or a state of emergency: should the election be due
during such a period, it will be deferred until six months after the end of the
period.

[12] The President's exercise of these relatively limited powers and functions is
normally constrained only by the relationship with the voters. However, there
is a mechanism, akin to that in the United States, by which the National
Assembly can impeach the President if, according to Article 109, 'in the course
of carrying out his office, the President of the Republic acts in a manner
contrary to this constitution, or commits a serious breach of the law'. In such
a case the National Assembly would register a complaint with another body,
the Constitutional Court, which has the option to suspend the President's exercise
of powers and functions while the matter is under consideration, and determine
whether or not the complaint was well founded. The complaint would then
be either dismissed or upheld, and if it is upheld, a vote of two-thirds of the
judges in the Constitutional Court can dismiss the President from office.

almost as inconceivable in reality as the British monarch refusing to sign acts of parliament.

The power to appoint state officials is significant to the extent that this includes nomination of a prime minister to the National Assembly. Thus what could be a merely formal role in a system providing a parliamentary majority for one party or another may become a quite creative one as the President consults leading members of the National Assembly in order to identify the prospective leader of a coalition government. Should no candidate emerge to obtain the support of a majority in parliament, then the President can dissolve the Assembly and call new elections.[13] While the President has an important and potentially influential role to play in the selection of a prime minister, the nomination of candidates for that office is not exclusive to him. While his nomination has precedence, it is possible for political groupings in the Assembly, or simply a group of ten or more deputies, to nominate a candidate. Should this happen and the President's nominee does not receive the support of more than half of all deputies in a vote, then the nominees of others will be considered in the order in which they were nominated. If this fails to produce a prime minister with support from over half the Assembly's membership, the President is bound to call new elections unless a majority of members present and voting decides within forty-eight hours to hold a new round of votes.

In the event of moving to a second round of votes, only a majority of those present and voting is then required to choose a prime minister. The same nominees are considered again and this time ordered according to the number of votes obtained in the first round of voting. In the event of a tie, any new nominations made before the sequence of voting will be put to the vote – with any new candidate nominated by the president coming first. If, following all these attempts, no prime minister is chosen, the President is then obliged to call new elections. Thus the process overall gives the President a potentially influential position. It also emphasises the way in which arrangements are designed to consolidate power through a strong degree of consensus.

[13] The President can also do this in the event of the National Assembly passing a vote of no confidence in the prime minister and failing to elect a new prime minister.

It is then the task of the prime minister, once chosen, to nominate the candidates for the fifteen ministerial posts provided for under the 1993 Law on Government.[14] According to Article 112 of the Constitution, each of these has to appear before a commission of the National Assembly and answer any questions posed before being confirmed by a full vote of the Assembly. Subsequently a minister can only be dismissed by a further vote of a majority of all deputies in the Assembly, on the recommendation of the prime minister, or following an 'interpellation' (under Article 118 of the constitution), regarding the work of an individual minister, initiated by at least ten deputies – that is, a vote of no confidence.

Ministers, under Article 110 of the constitution, are formally accountable not to the prime minister but to parliament and are deemed to be 'independent within their own particular portfolios'. However, this apparently direct link between ministers and the Assembly is qualified by the responsibility of the prime minister, under Article 114 of the constitution, to ensure the 'political unity' of the government and to coordinate the work of ministers and the ministries, while the ministers are collectively (and possibly confusingly) charged with responsibility for the government as a whole while being individually responsible for their own ministries.

Over time, the prime minister and the government have acquired more power in practice than the formal provisions of the constitution might suggest – at least, once a prime minister has been able to establish some authority and form a coalition, as with Janez Drnovšek in the mid-1990s. In effect, this meant a relatively stable government being able to shape legislation to strengthen its authority. However, because of the necessity of coalition governments, the problems of reconciling individual responsibility for ministries with collective responsibility for government, and prime ministerial authority with the accountability of individual ministers to the Assembly, presented real problems. This was the case especially, as will be seen below, during Janez Janša's tenure as defence minister, when ministries seemed to become personal fiefdoms and ministers were effectively battling with each other from their ministerial bases.

---

[14] The number and composition of the ministries can be varied by legislation in the National Assembly.

The key to making the formal arrangements work is the formation of coalitions. This is made necessary by the distribution of support between a number of parties and, in particular, by an electoral system which favours the building of coalitions and consensus. The Law on Elections to the National Assembly identifies three principles which it is intended to embody:[15] a proportional distribution of seats; a clear link between the voters and their representatives; and encouragement of stability of legislative and executive power.[16] The rules incorporated in the law successfully hit each of these targets by establishing a complex mechanism for electing deputies.

The electoral system for the Assembly was a qualified version of proportional representation. Strict proportionality was limited in two ways. The first was a threshold to exclude parties gaining less than 3 per cent of the vote. The second was the provision to vote for individuals rather than simply for a party list, even though those votes were then translated into a proportional vote for a list; despite this, by means of a complicated system, the popular vote for an individual continued to have some relevance, as will be seen below.

The whole of Slovenia was divided into eight electoral units, approximately equal in the proportion of the electorate they contained, and each of these was subdivided into eleven districts. Within the electoral unit each party puts forward a list of eleven candidates. However, each of those eleven had to be assigned as an individual to one of the eleven districts within the unit. This meant that in each district the voter would cast a vote for a named individual, but the individual who secured the greatest number of votes in one electoral district was not elected to represent that district. Instead, the number of votes he or she obtained in the district was added to the number obtained by others across the electoral unit, and the resulting figure was then transformed into a proportion of the vote across the whole electoral unit. Of the eleven seats from that unit the party list gained a share in the National Assembly proportionate to its share of the vote.

The initial vote for individuals in the districts became relevant

---

[15] *Uradni List Republike Slovenije*, no.44, 12 September 1992.

[16] Franci Grad, 'The New Electoral System' in Fink-Hafner and Robbins (eds), *New Nation*, p. 175.

at this point, since it provided the mechanism for deciding which of the eleven candidates from a list in an electoral unit was elected to represent the party in the National Assembly. Rather than simply being ordered by the preference of the party (that is, a ranked list), the candidates from a particular party within an electoral district were ranked according to the individual vote they scored at the electoral district level. At the top of the party list in a particular electoral unit was the individual who had obtained the highest district vote for his party in that particular unit.

The electoral process is not complete at this point, however. The proportionate element of the vote at this stage is not rounded up but left at the point where it contributes to the election of one whole individual.[17] In practice this worked as follows. Because each unit was divided into eleven districts, to gain one seat in the Assembly a party required one-eleventh (or 9.09 per cent, recurring) of the total vote. This meant, in effect, that if a party's share of the vote was 9.1 per cent, it gained one seat; if it gained an 18.2 per cent share of the vote, two of its candidates were elected; and where the share of the vote was, say, 16 per cent, then a little over 9 percentage points of this would be used to elect the candidate, while a little under seven percentage points – the remainder – would be added to the national pool as an actual figure. In practice the total number of electors per electoral unit was around 110,000. This meant that for a party to gain a seat, it needed to receive 10,000 votes. If it gained 16,600 – a 16 per cent share – the remaining 6,600 votes would be transferred to the national pool.

Any votes which did not make up a share of the vote for one individual, or which did not contribute to the election of one individual from the electoral district, were classified as 'remainder' votes. These were then redistributed – that is, all the 'unused' votes from each electoral unit were put together at the national

[17] Thanks are due to Dennison Rusinow for knowing enough to point out the right direction for trying to understand this aspect of an enormously complex electoral arrangement – one which bemused even Slovenes who had read the Electoral Law. Grateful thanks are also due to Jurij Rifelj of the Slovenian Foreign Ministry who took time out of working at Ljubljana's Washington embassy and was impressively the first person encountered who was able to explain the precise workings of the electoral system – and who also revealed the fact that the system was to be replaced.

level and proportional levels were established. These shares of the remainder vote at the national level were then translated into a proportional share of the seats in the Assembly not allocated by the first part of the electoral procedure (this time the shares were rounded up, leaving no remainder for a further tier of re-distribution). The number of seats available at the national level would depend on the number across each of the units for which there was insufficient support within the unit for the seat to be taken. So within a particular unit it might be that one party gained 33,000 votes, giving it three members of the Assembly and 3,000 votes remaining for the national level, while three other parties would each gain one seat with precisely 10,000 votes. With no other party reaching the 10,000-vote level, the position regarding that unit would be that six seats were allocated as a result of the constituency vote, while five would remain available to be distributed on a proportionate basis with no remainder at the national level.

The candidates at the stage of national redistribution were drawn from two national lists. Half the seats allocated went to candidates on a list – one for each party – of those obtaining the highest individual district votes but who did not secure election on that basis at the first stage. The other half of the seats were allocated under the remainder procedure to lists provided by and ranked by the parties at the national level – thus, for example, each party could try to ensure that its leader found a seat in parliament by this route, if not by virtue of district-level popularity. While ensuring that party leaders would get a seat by this means if by no other, the electoral system as a whole ensured that no more than half the number of deputies chosen under the remainder option are selected because of their place on a party's national list. In practice this meant that around quarter of all deputies were elected by this method, given that in reality about half of the seats were allocated under the first stage of the procedure – an outcome which may indicate a relatively even distribution of support among parties.[18]

This complicated procedure (derived from, among others, the Finnish and Austrian systems) served to meet the three aims of the Electoral Law set out above. In particular, it placed apparent

---

[18] See Grad, 'Electoral System', p.179.

stress on links between the individual deputy and the electorate, although any real sense of identification was heavily diluted by the electoral process. Similarly, the mechanism ensured that even if party leaders were not elected in the first stage through the mixture of popularity and proportion the system provided, they could be guaranteed a place in the Assembly under the party-ranked section of the national redistribution. Because of the role of individuals at the district level, the system also opened the way for individuals (or groups of individuals across an electoral unit) to stand for the Assembly independently, permitting the possibility that independent candidates with very strong local support could be chosen.

Overall, the procedure served to elect eighty-eight of the ninety members in the National Assembly, some of whom might well have been Italians or Hungarians, whereas the two members elected outside this overall process were certainly chosen respectively by the Italian and Hungarian minorities.[19] However, despite the provision of reserved seats for minorities, the possibility of independent candidates having opportunities, and the emphasis on the individual candidate in a proportional system, the electoral system actually worked in favour of around half a dozen political parties, from among which coalitions would be formed with a view to generating a consensual and stable governmental environment.

The 1996 elections saw seven parties obtain seats in the Assembly – two more than in 1992 – as well as the representatives of the Italian and Hungarian minorities. As will be seen below, the boundaries between the stability the system was intended to foster and stasis are blurred.[20] While the system encouraged cooperation and coalition government, it also required sufficient harmony and consensus between a number of parties for there to be effective

[19] At the time of writing, discussions had begun between Slovenia and Croatia about the institution of 'minority' provisions for Croats in Slovenia. Two possibilities were latent in this: that a 'reserved' minority seat might appear at some stage for Croats and for other minorities in Slovenia – notably the Muslims and Serbs, both of whom formed a larger share of the country's inhabitants than the Hungarians or possibly the Italians.

[20] Because of this it was decided to replace the complex electoral mechanism with a more straightforward one, similar to that in France. It was intended that the new mechanism should be in place in time for the 2000 elections.

government; thus the character and platform of each of the main parties were important. Of the parties gaining seats in the Assembly following the 1996 election, four were left-of-centre and three right-of-centre. The most significant of the centre-left parties was the Liberal Democratic Party (Liberalna Demokratska Stranka – LDS). It had the largest number of seats of any party (twenty-five), and its leader Janez Drnovšek was charged with forming a government – as he had been at the 1992 elections in a broadly similar situation. The roots of the LDS lay in the most reform-oriented sections of the old League of Communists of Slovenia – the 'communist party' – before the introduction of competitive, pluralist elections in 1990 (Drnovšek, at that stage, was Slovenia's representative to the collective State Council of the old SFRY). In part the LDS was able to preserve its position because it represented continuity with a relatively positive period in the near past, and because of the undoubted advantage in organisation and experience it inherited from the communist period. Most of the other parties were relative amateurs by comparison. The image of Drnovšek and his party as a competent team was reinforced by this. In policy orientation the key elements of the LDS programme were its outward-looking programme of integration with international and, particularly, European organisations, such as the European Union and NATO – as well as a domestic programme focusing on measures such as privatisation and economic stability to facilitate European integration. In general, and in its policy orientation, the LDS could be said to lay claim to the traditional inheritance of the Liberals in Slovenian politics: serving the national cause through integration in a wider framework which *inter alia* allows the development of business.

The other centre-left parties were the United List of Social Democrats (Združena Lista Socialnih Demokratov – ZL), the Democratic Party of Slovenia's Pensioners (Demokratična Stranka Upokojencev Slovenije – DSUS) and the Slovene National Party (Slovenska Narodna Stranka – SNS). The first of these, like the LDS, had its roots in the old communist party. The ZL was linked with some of the less radical sections of the old League of Communists (though not the most conservative). Its platform remained linked to ideas of social justice and social provision, as well as social ownership and protection of jobs, rather than privatisation and full economic reform. However, after the 1996 election its leader Borut Pahor began a major overhaul of the party, seeking to modernise it and put it more in line with the times and in touch with its potential constituency.

The DSUS emerged from the LDS and maintained close links with it. It was perhaps more properly regarded as an interest group, given that sectional interest was the only real point of distinction between it and the LDS. Its focus was obviously on the needs and concerns of the ever-growing number of pensioners in an ageing population. Closely aligned with the LDS and reflecting a purely sectional interest, the DSUS was the smallest of Slovenia's parties.

The SNS was perhaps the most curious of Slovenia's political parties. As with the other centre-left parties, its roots lay in communist rule. However, the platform adopted by the SNS was starkly nationalist and anti-communist, although retaining an attachment to the more authoritarian aspects of communist rule. Its leader, Zmago Jelinčič, was accused of being a fascist at some points, and was shown to have been involved with the secret police under communism.[21] Despite the possibility that it might disappear completely following the revelations about its leader's past, the SNS still managed to retain one-third of its seats in the 1996 election, giving it four.

The centre-right parties which emerged tended to be somewhat more parochial, focusing on Slovenia and Slovene identity and seeking to protect it from alien interference or absorption. If the LDS can be said to have adopted the traditional mantle of the Liberals in Slovenian politics, then there were two parties which lay claim to the inheritance of the Slovene People's Party (Slovenska Ljudska Stranka – SLS; see pp. 28–41). One of these maintained the name of the SLS, while the other derived from the tradition and heritage of the SLS, but sought to give it a more contemporary and broadly European flavour. Thus the Slovene Christian Democrat Party (Slovenski Krščanski Demokrati – SKD) looked to the same parts of Slovene society as those which had traditionally supported the SLS, but also, as the name could be taken to indicate, sought a more modern aspect, laying claim to the humane post-1945 tradition of right-of-centre Christian Democratic parties

---

[21] In some ways, there is clearly a parallel in this regard between Jelinčič and the Russian Vladimir Zhirinovsky.

in countries such as Germany and Belgium. Under its leader, Lojže Peterle, the SKD led the government coalition which negotiated Slovenia's political road to independence, pushed to a considerable extent by its then coalition partner, the Democratic League (Demokratska Zveza – DZ).

The SLS, led by Marjan Podobnik, joined the Drnovšek coalition government despite clear points of difference with the LDS. This indicated that another aspect of Slovene tradition, the Liberals and the SLS forming coalitions in spite of policy differences, still had life. The SLS, while broadly committed to policies in line with those of the LDS on economic reform and stabilisation, was more hesitant over agreement on the European Union and noticeably reluctant over possible moves towards membership of NATO.

The question of NATO membership was also pertinent to the position of the last of the centre-right parties, the Social Democratic Party of Slovenia (Socialdemokratska Stranka Slovenije – SDSS). This party had very different roots from those of the other parties on the centre-right. Its leader, Janez Janša, had been a prominent figure (see pp. 152-3 and 187-9) first as a journalist with *Mladina* and then as a politician in the years surrounding Slovenia's emergence as an independent state. Janša had established himself in the role of arch-critic before entering politics and becoming defence minister in the period before and immediately after independence. The SDSS appeared to have taken on a role, very much in the Janša tradition, of being the focal point for disaffection and criticism, rather than of seriously seeking to play a constructive role in power. Even so, it was not impossible that Janša himself, who had previously harboured ambitions to become President, but who had probably realised that this was not feasible, still had hopes of becoming prime minister – a more obviously purposeful political role.

While the constitutional and political framework did not preclude the emergence of a significantly greater number of political parties, it seemed much more likely that the system would be consolidated around these parties, or replacements for them, in the course of political evolution and that the overall number would remain about the same. This meant that the prospects for radical political change were not great although, again, the possibility could not be excluded. In general, the division of political

power under the constitution had made the prime minister and
the government answerable to the National Assembly, but conditioned by the various roles played by the President, the National
Council and the Constitutional Court. This division of power,
which broadly created an environment for consensual and cooperative rather than conflictual and adversarial politics, was accentuated
by the complex electoral mechanism and its impact on those
parts of Slovenia's political make-up which emerged with the
most central role – the National Assembly and the government.
In all aspects, arrangements were geared towards consensus and
stability.

This stability, as will be seen below, held within it the possibility
of stasis. Crucially it also reflected the consensus and solidarity
which emerged around the ideas of democracy and independence
during the latter period of communist rule and carried Slovenia
into independence. This set the political complexion of post-independence Slovenia.

The homogenisation of Slovenian politics in the 1980s

One of the key factors in the emergence of Slovenia as an independent international actor and in the broadly consensual character of its political system was the way in which all parts of the
political spectrum coalesced while developing the character of
their plurality. The context for this process was the ´crisis in the
Yugoslav federation of which Slovenia was a part. At the heart
of the process of convergence was the issue of Slovene identity
and language, but this core issue was conflated with others such
as economic well-being, approaches to democracy, and aspirations
for the future. As will be seen, each of these elements was involved
in one defining event, the trial in 1988 of four Slovenes by a
Yugoslav military court in Ljubljana. That trial and its circumstances
forged Slovenian solidarity. It also acted as the catalyst for Slovenian
democracy and turned the country in the direction of eventual
independence.

. In the course of the 1980s there had begun to be limited
nationalist political pressure.[22] There was also movement on the

---

[22] Steve Reiquam, 'Is Slovenian Nationalism on the Rise?', *RFE*, 9 August
1983.

question of Slovenia's status and position regarding the Yugoslav federation, as intellectuals engaged in discussions with their Serbian counterparts. This had given rise, among other developments, to the outlining of perspectives on a Slovene national programme in Issue 57 of the cultural publication *Nova Revija*, which was banned by the authorities. However, as a later review of the *Nova Revija 57* affair by many of those involved in the banned issue noted, that edition represented the interest of the liberal wing of the communist party leadership at the time in face of rising centralist ambition in Serbia, and was no more than the focus of discourse which had been developing in the journal before Issue 57 and which continued immediately afterwards.[23]

However, there had also begun to be significant pressure for economic change and, crucially, for the democratisation of the communist system. The latter pressures came in particular from younger people and especially from the communists' own youth movement. Crucially, those pushing for the expansion of pluralism were quietly encouraged to do so by the communist party leadership under Milan Kučan, who had become party leader in 1985.[24]

There was a focal point for this discourse: the weekly magazine *Mladina*, published under the auspices of the communist youth movement (Zveza Socialistov Mladine Slovenije – ZSMS). Kučan had let the editors of *Mladina* know that there would be no serious problem with their challenging the taboos of communist monism – with one exception, the Yugoslav People's Army (Jugo-

---

[23] Niko Grafenauer calls it the Slovene party leadership's 'mode of survival' while Alenka Puhar points out that the following issue, no. 58, containing material connected to Issue 57, was being prepared throughout the period in which Issue 57 was a political affair and subsequently was published without problem: Grafenauer, 'Sedemletica' (p.2) and Puhar 'Prispevek k anatomiji politične gonje' (p.121) in Puhar (ed.), 'Zadeva 57', *Ampak*, vol. XIII, Jan.-Feb. 1994. The original material, edited by Jože Pučnik, is 'Prispevki za slovenski nacionalni program', *Nova Revija*, VI, 57, 1987; the Serbian precursor to this is the infamous 'Memorandum' of the Serbian Academy of Sciences and Arts (SANU), a version of which is reproduced in *Naše Teme*, vol.33, nos 1-2, 1989.

[24] As noted in Chapter 4, Kučan was an able young politician. In many ways his becoming leader of the League of Communists of Slovenia represented the return of the liberalising agenda of the Kavčič era. He was able both to pursue the combined agendas of political and economic reform and skilfully to manipulate situations for his own political benefit.

slovenska Narodna Armija – JNA).[25] This shibboleth inevitably became the prime target for *Mladina*, precipitating the 1988 trial which in turn defined the Slovenian political agenda in the subsequent years. Numerous articles as well as anti-military cartoons appeared in *Mladina*,[26] reflecting the enormous gulf in opinion between Slovene society and the Yugoslav military, and it was in this environment that relations between them came to their nadir with the trial.

The *Mladina* defence correspondent who had been one of the sharpest thorns in the army's side, Janez Janša, was arrested on 31 May 1988. He was a graduate of defence studies at Ljubljana and had been writing on military matters for many years, but his articles had become increasingly critical. Subsequently three others were arrested, two of whom, like Janša, were journalists at *Mladina*, David Tasić and Franci Zavrl, the editor.[27] The other person indicted was a non-commissioned officer, Ivan Borštner, who had been working in a communications and signals unit of the JNA. Support for the accused was tremendous, there were large public rallies and, at the suggestion of Slovenia's communist leaders, a Committee for the Protection of Human Rights was founded within the party-linked Socialist Alliance of Movements. This was not, an unequivocal expression of support from the party leadership, but it was a sign of concern. The somewhat ambivalent position was confirmed when Kučan spoke to a Communist party meeting in June and reaffirmed the need for legitimate discussion about the JNA. However, he distanced himself from *Mladina*.[28]

At the trial in July the four accused – always summarised together by their initials 'JBTZ' – were charged with offences relating to the disclosure of secret JNA documents. Borštner admitted this offence – he had become aware of a particular signal relating to

---

[25] Interview with Milan Kučan, *Death of Yugoslavia*, programme 1, Brian Lapping Associates, 1995.

[26] See James Gow, *Legitimacy and the Military: the Yugoslav Crisis*, London: Pinter, 1992, pp.78-9. The following section broadly draws on material treated at greater length in that volume.

[27] Zavrl had previously been sued for libel by the JNA for writing an article in *Teleks*, another weekly publication.

[28] BBC, *SWB*, 30 June 1988.

a possible declaration of a state of emergency in Slovenia, and it concerned him so deeply that he felt bound to make it known. However, none of the journalists admitted the allegations. All were eventually found guilty. Borštner was sentenced to four years' imprisonment, Janša to eighteen months and Tasić and Zavrl to six months although on appeal Zavrl's sentence was tripled to eighteen months. In practice, as Zavrl was to relate, the authorities in Slovenia were so relaxed in their enforcement of these sentences that, having been allowed day release to continue editing *Mladina*, he had to break into the prison on one particular night to fulfil the terms of his arrangement.[29]

It was not so much the sentences given by the military court which galvanised Slovenia as the fact of the trial itself and the way it was managed. Because the trial was conducted in Serbo-Croat and not Slovene and held behind closed doors, the Slovene public became convinced that it was nothing more than an army frame-up to take revenge on Janša in particular and *Mladina* in general, and the Slovene political leadership felt compelled to become involved.

There was good reason for this. The document leaked by Borštner – Ljubljana Military District Command Order 5044-3, dated 8 January 1988 – concerned a plan to destabilise Slovenia, declare a state of emergency and replace the liberal Slovene political leadership and press with more conservative figures, who would have been markedly preferable to the JNA command. *Mladina* continued to play its role, asserting that the government had known about the plan – which indeed it had, as was confirmed by two sets of stenograms taken at the relevant meetings, to which *Mladina* had gained access thanks to an anonymous leak which, it emerged, came from Kučan.[30] It was he who, on the first occasion in March, had tried to accommodate the military in order to buy time, but who had at the same time facilitated the spread of rumours about a potential clampdown. He had then ensured that JNA attempts to bully the Slovene leadership were made known and that opposition (notably that of Kučan and the head of the security service, Stane Dolanc) to such measures was

---

[29] Interview, *Death of Yugoslavia*, programme 1.

[30] In contrast to Gow, *Legitimacy* (p.81), there were two sets of notes, rather than one, taken at two separate meetings. See *Death of Yugoslavia*, programme 3.

expressed at the meetings. In all of this Kučan was seeking to protect himself and the Slovenes as a whole, and as a result greatly increased his popular support.

Support for Kučan's leadership was strengthened further by the reaction to the JBTZ trial. The two elements which drove this reaction were the apparent threat to Slovenia of martial law and, above all else, the slight felt at the JNA conducting the trial in Serbo-Croat and not in Slovene, even though the defendants were Slovene and the trial was held in the capital of Slovenia. The Slovene language, as noted in this volume, is the essence of the nation's cultural identity and something of which the people are fiercely proud. The use of Serbo-Croat insulted them deeply.

There were various protests and challenges against the conduct of the trial on the grounds that the failure to use Slovene in Slovenia had been unconstitutional.[31] In the end, a commission established to investigate the propriety of the trial found that it had been improperly conducted – a factor which caused the authorities to be lenient towards the JBTZ four. For the Slovene leadership and the Slovene people the trial had been an attack on them and their land.[32] Focusing on the language issue but embracing a range of other considerations, Slovenian politics became homogenised, yet in that homogenisation, galvanised by fear and ferociously conscious of issues of sovereignty and constitutionality, the shoots of pluralism were growing rapidly and beginning to bloom. The Communist party under Milan Kučan's leadership had first embraced the notion of 'socialism on a human scale' and then, with the creation of the Committee for the Protection of Human Rights and other bodies, the pheno-menon of pluralism under the party umbrella. By the second half of 1989 it had extended its understanding of pluralism to encompass the notion of multi-party elections. The Slovenes were leading a push towards pluralism.

The key to the Slovenes' push for change, underpinned by their quest for self-protection following the JBTZ trial, was amend-

[31] See Gow, *Legitimacy*, p.84.

[32] Dimitrij Rupel, later to be leader of the Social Democratic Alliance, president of the National Assembly, foreign minister and mayor of Ljubljana, in an interview; Milan Andrejevich, 'The Yugoslav Crisis and the National Question', *RFE*, 17 August 1989.

ment of the constitution. Slovene politicians began to draft amend-ments – a process in which they were not alone among the Yugoslav states as Serbia initiated a radical process of constitutional change. The thrust of the Slovene amendments which emerged in 1989 was to clarify Slovenia's relationship with the Yugoslav federation and its other members.

The most striking posited its membership of the federation on a voluntary basis with the right to self-determination and thus secession. Although these were elements which had been present in various formulations in each of the federal and republican constitutions under communism, the Slovene amendments spelled them out clearly as part of a 'psychological war' against the con-servative forces in Belgrade. Other amendments included the defini-tion of economic authority, the equal-rights status of the Yugoslav languages in accordance with the constitution, and the exclusive right of the Slovenian authorities to declare a state of emergency on Slovenian soil. An amendment to remove the Communist party's leading role was the most radical of all since it asserted a pluralist, liberal future for Slovenia with or without the other Yugoslav states. The shift to multi-party pluralism was the hallmark of Slovene consensus.

This shift was marked by the effective end of the League of Communists of Yugoslavia at the beginning of 1990. As the Slovene communists walked out of the Emergency 14th Congress of the League, they ensured that this congress would be the last. The Slovenes' walk-out was judged to be their only possible response to the total defeat of their reform proposals by the conservative majority, led by Serbia under Slobodan Milošević. The tensions that had been building up since 1987 erupted on this very public stage, and the Slovenes were taunted by delegates from Serbia and Montenegro. The Slovenian delegation requested a com-promise whereby at least some of their proposals would be accepted so as to avoid humiliation on every issue and therefore catastrophe. This only encouraged the majority, who rubbed salt in Slovenian wounds by clapping and cheering as the Ljubljana delegation made its exit.

Following this drama, there was an emergency meeting of the League of Communists of Slovenia on 4 February, at which the Slovene party abolished itself and with it, *de facto*, the League of Communists of Yugoslavia. From the ashes of the Communist party arose the (League of Communists of Slovenia) Party of Democratic Renewal, which stressed both continuity and a new start. This twin label demonstrated the desire to retain traditional support entwined with the need to renew its identity and attract those whose support was not guaranteed in anticipation of competitive, multi-party elections in the spring.

The outcome of the April elections in Slovenia was cohabitation. Kučan, the former communist, was elected president, but at the same time a fragile coalition of erstwhile opposition parties held a weak parliamentary majority and formed the government under Prime Minister Lojže Peterle. This phase of cohabitation forced Slovenia to retain something of the consensus which – despite strong difference on some issues, notably the church – had brought Slovene leaders and the people through the difficult path to democracy. The outcome of the elections confirmed both the transfer of rule from the party to the state and the seismic shift in legitimation of the political community from anything federal to the wholly Slovene level. This was to have consequences as the next broadly consensual course began to emerge – the redefinition of Slovenia's relationship with the federation, including the possibility of independence. While some parties, notably the Democratic Alliance and the Social Democrats, sought to develop the idea of independence, others saw this as potentially too costly, although in the end, by 1991, they would be persuaded that no real alternative existed. While there were already disputes which sometimes became bitter and recriminatory and were to be more prominent later, it was the overriding consensus on the need for stability and commitment to Slovenia which shaped not only the route to independence but also much of post-independence Slovene political life, which is considered in the following section.

Between stabilisation and stagnation

Consensus and stability marked Slovenian politics during the process of gaining independence and for the years following its attainment. This reflects the characteristics of 'semi-consociational democracy and neocorporatism' identified by some observers of Slovenian political life.[33] In essence this means that political life has developed

---

[33] Frane Adam, 'After Four Years of Democracy: Fragility and Stability – Lessons

with a large degree of overlap between parties on core values, such as the establishment and consolidation of democracy, the development of a market economy (crucially, with elements of protection built in) and on major issues such as potential membership of the EU or NATO. The 1992 electoral law reinforced this tendency towards consensus by creating a government-forming mechanism which depended on it. However, underlying core consensus does not mean complete agreement and harmony in politics; as will be seen, the broadly harmonious Slovene experience in the period after independence was accompanied by discord generated by the personal rivalries and issues of the past.

The six-party DEMOS (Demokratična Opozicija Slovenije) coalition which emerged from the first competitive multi-party elections in the spring of 1990 led Slovenia on its path to independence. However, this grouping of parties was a fragile alliance forged primarily around the common element of having opposed the communists (later supplemented by general agreement on the politics of independence.) Cohabitation with Kučan, the former communist leader, as President as well as coalition in government were characteristic of Slovenia's cohesion in this period, but with independence accomplished, both cohabitation and coalition became far harder to sustain, as a number of less strategic questions and personal clashes weakened the government of prime minister Lojže Peterle.

Already in early 1992 the coalition was beginning to fracture. The fault-lines between Peterle's Christian Democrats (SKD) and DEMOS partners such as the Democratic Alliance, the Social Democratic Party and the Green Party included the issues of abortion and privatisation. As a result, these three coalition partners soon left, arguing that the coalition had done what it had set out to do – ousting the communists and steering a course relatively safely out of the Yugoslav federation. However, this did not prompt immediate elections since Peterle was able narrowly to survive two votes of no-confidence.

Nonetheless, his had become a wounded government, in ever more disarray as ministers resigned and others were less than clear

From an Accelerated Evolution of the Political System' in Frane Adam and Gregor Tomc (eds), 'Small Societies in Transition: the Case of Slovenia', *Družboslovne Razprave*, nos 15-16, 1994, p.42.

in their support for Peterle, given the emphasis he appeared to place on a backward-looking social policy, aiming to restore the primacy of Roman Catholic values that for many were from a previous age. At the same time, the government was moving slowly in the area of economic restructuring, an issue regarded as urgent and vital by most in the Slovene political élite. In a sense the biggest problem for Peterle was not that consensus had broken down in Slovenian politics, so much as that he and the Christian Democrats had quickly sought to move outside the consensus by promoting social policies which were simply out of line with contemporary Slovenia.[34] The Peterle government therefore could not last.

Peterle was replaced as prime minister by Janez Drnovšek even before the new electoral system (which, as will be seen, would favour Drnovšek and his Liberal Democratic Party as the pivot of coalitions and the core of political consensus) had come into effect. Drnovšek, formerly from the liberal reforming wing of the old ZKS, as well as Slovene representative to the Yugoslav federal State Council in its last period, was elected as leader of the Liberal Democrats before succeeding as prime minister. Peterle succumbed to a third vote of no-confidence, while Drnovšek was able to form a new coalition with a narrow majority in parliament on 14 May. This coalition brought together the Liberal Democrats with the Democrats, the Social Democrats, the Socialists and the Greens, in addition to which the former communist SDP supported the government while not joining the coalition. This gave the coalition a centre-left character, although a focus on economic and political modernisation was central to its agenda.

The Drnovšek-led coalition could not rely entirely on its support in the Assembly and continued the trend of apparently fragile government set in the Peterle period. The government was inhibited in implementing elements of the reform plan and criticised for this, but it was seen as being successful in macro-economic stabilisation, for which it gained much credit and was relatively popular (although this progress was largely due to the strategy of

---

[34] It was notable that in this period the representatives of the Roman Catholic church did not demonstrate commitment to Peterle, suggesting perhaps that the church itself understood how far out of touch with society the Peterle programme was.

the Bank of Slovenia operating independently of government as a result of the previous government's policy). The main focus for criticism from the opposition was the government's failure to return land nationalised under communism to the Roman Catholic church, rather than its performance in other areas – this was seen as unjust because the church had avoided interference in politics.

The opposition parties sought to form their own coalition to counter the government's, the key parties being the SKD, the Slovene People's Party and the National Democrats. This move was made in preparation for new elections under the new electoral law passed by parliament in September. The emphasis on providing for more effective government in the new system meant that the elections, which had to be held before 23 December, would pave the way to a period of more stable government and political consolidation.

The political significance in this was not so much the different policy programmes which might be pursued, since nearly all parties across the political spectrum continued to be broadly part of a national consensus on key policy directions. Rather, the parties were separated by the past. Support for the Drnovšek government came primarily from those associated with the former communists, with only a few exceptions – among them Jože Pučnik, leader of the Social Democrats. The real arguments seemed to be about aspects of the communist period, or even more about the Second World War.[35] In terms of electoral prospects, although this agenda was mainly driven by opposition politics, it did little to help those pushing those issues.

The outcome of the elections favoured the former communist elements generally and the government in particular. Milan Kučan was again elected President, receiving an overwhelming 63.9 per cent of the vote, thus confirming his personal authority. In the National Assembly Drnovšek's Liberals gained the largest single block of seats, twenty-two, based on 23.3 per cent of the vote.

---

[35] On the impact of the Second World War in political discourse in the 1990s, see the useful chapter 'The Second World War in Slovenia, 1991-1995' in Doroteja Lešnik and Gregor Tomc, *Rdeče in Črno*, Ljubljana: Forum/Znanstveno in Publicistično Središče, 1995, pp.187-205. Lešnik and Tomc account for this phenomenon in terms of the end of communism and the opening of democratic discussion, both of which provided the opportunity for those non-communists forced to remain largely silent for over fifty years finally to have their say.

The next largest representation was that of the SKD with fifteen
seats derived from 14.5 per cent of the vote. Not far behind the
SKD, the former communist association of the SDP and a number
of minor parties – the Združena Lista Socialnih Demokratov (ZL)
– gained 13.6 per cent in the poll and took thirteen seats in
parliament. Two other parties gained significant support. The
SNS took 9.9 per cent of the vote and eleven seats under the
leadership of Zmago Jelinčič, who openly advocated a policy of
expulsion of non-Slovenes from the country, and the SLS with
8.8 per cent of the vote managed to gain ten seats in the Assembly.
The remaining seats went to the DS (six), the Greens (five), the
SDSS (four), with the two national community representatives
making up the complement (although the category of 'others'
which did not translate into seats in the assembly accounted for
as much as 17.9 per cent of the vote).

By 25 January Drnovšek, buoyed by the clear sense of a desire
for stability and continuity in the electorate, was able to form a
government which was approved by 60 out of 90 votes in the
National Assembly, with 26 votes against. In large part this was
because the SKD, recognising the political trend and its own
poor performance in the election, joined the coalition, in return
for Peterle's being made foreign minister. This gave the coalition
government a broad base but also built in a degree of fragility,
given the different perspectives of the Liberals and the SKD, not
to mention the other coalition partners, the ZL and the SDSS
– which, in spite of its demise in the elections, kept its major
figure, Janez Janša, in the post of defence minster.

Nonetheless, Slovenia stabilised politically and economically in
1993. In spite of a poorer overall economic performance than in
the previous year, the obvious ideological divisions within the
coalition, and a series of scandals, the coalition reached the end
of the year in a relatively secure position. But there were signs
of a cultural and political stagnation that would impact on both
the economy and the political scene. In spite of a series of political
intrigues, the coalition government remained secure. However,
the war in Bosnia continued to be felt in the former Yugoslav
country in the healthiest position.

In many ways 1993 represented the beginning of a return to
normal. *Mladina*, the weekly Slovenian publication which, more
than any other, had played a crucial role in the demise of the

old Yugoslav federation through its duels with the Yugoslav People's Army and the old communist authorities in the late 1980s, returned to form. This time, however, there was an irony: Janez Janša who, as a journalist for the publication, had pilloried the former Yugoslav defence secretaries Admiral Branko Mamula and General Veljko Kadijević, was now the target. In the style of its finest moments, *Mladina* carried an advertisement for subscriptions with a picture of Janša looking in a mirror and seeing a JNA general, with the caption 'Imagine that in four years you would be defence minister'.[36]

Janša became the focal point of criticism for a number of reasons. The first was the impression that Prime Minster Drnovšek and the cabinet were all afraid of the defence secretary and the authority he wielded – another analogy with the old Yugoslav federation, where everyone acted under the shadow of what the military might do. Other reasons included his perceived feud with President Milan Kučan, his radically altered, somewhat grandiose thinking on Slovenian defence and security matters, and his alleged association with arms smuggling to Bosnia and Hercegovina.

Despite working closely together on the independence project, Janša and Kučan never quite became allies. Observers put this down to Janša's continuing belief that Kučan had a role in his arrest by the army in 1988 and the fact that Kučan had been a communist (curiously overlooking Janša's own former role as a leading figure in the communist youth movement). While Kučan, at least openly, ignored this in a dignified way, Janša demonstrated his resentment in a series of curious public moves.[37]

---

[36] *Mladina*, 14 September 1993.

[37] The most notable was his refusal to allow the Slovenian army's Guard of Honour to take part in September's celebration of the 50th anniversary of the 9th Corps (of the Partisan army) – although this was reversed on the eve of the celebration and the guard participated. The celebrations in Nova Gorica, where the Corps was formed and both Partisans and communists had been traditionally strong because they had led resistance to Italian anti-Slav policies, including massacres, included a speech from President Kučan. Although the official reason offered for the initial refusal to provide the guard was that the unit's involvement in public ceremonies should be limited to those concerned with Slovenia's independence, it seemed clear that Janša had wanted to spoil the occasion for Kučan.

Apart from going through a radical shift in his personal views in the space of four years – from favouring pacifist demilitarisation, through armed neutrality and territorial defence, to the creation of a Slovenian army and the standard Central and East European aspiration to join NATO, all this being reflected in policy positions – Janša was also prominent because of his alleged role in transferring arms to Bosnia and Hercegovina. In July a consignment of 120 tonnes of matériel was discovered to have been stored at Maribor airport. The documentation associated with the shipment – published inevitably, in *Mladina* – indicated the involvement of Slovenian military intelligence and the highest levels of the Ministry of Defence. The affair engaged the defence minister in a tortuous *pas de deux* with the Slovenian judiciary, as the two wrangled over legal and security issues.

A crucial source of information concerning the Maribor arms shipment was the VIS (Varnostno-Informativna Služba), the internal security service, controlled by the Interior Ministry. For most of the year a running battle had been conducted through the press between the Defence and Interior Ministries intelligence services. This was also seen as Janša's 'new guard' against one-time communists associated with the old regime (it was also of course linked to the defence minster's resentment of Kučan). The Maribor scandal was exposed in return for revelations in the spring that the internal security service had been funded both in the old days and since independence by proceeds from casinos in Slovenia, effectively run by security service chiefs. It was known as the 'HIT affair' (after the tourist concern HIT), and there were implications that Kučan and others who had been part of the leadership under communism were, at least marginally, involved. A parliamentary inquiry was established to investigate the matter.

While the government and the various personalities associated with the sets of scandals survived the year, one positive outcome of a year of leaks and exposés was the demise of the fascist right. This followed the publication of old secret police files in which Zmago Jelinčič, leader of the fascist Slovene National Party, was identified as an agent of KOS, the Yugoslav military counter-intelligence service. With its leader thus discredited, the party fell apart into a series of splinter groups, although it was by no means completely destroyed.

These internal political scuffles indicated that, in spite of its relative political and especially democratic maturity when compared with all other post-communist countries, Slovenia was not entirely free of the problems faced in Central and East European politics. However, thanks to the relative openness of the old communist regime and the early development of pluralist modes in the mid-1980s, it was probably the closest to West European standards. Despite positive developments in the country's relations with Western Europe, the shadow of the war to the south continued to loom, notably in the autumn when heavy skirmishes between Krajina Serbs and the Croatian army had Serb surface-to-surface missiles landing 5-8 km. from the Slovenian border – a stark physical reminder that Slovenia was still implicated in the Yugoslav war of dissolution. This was felt in economy and psychologically, the latter having certain social ramifications.

In part, social and psychological factors would determine how Slovenia would develop. Some of these, such as 14 per cent unemployment, were largely local, whereas others, such as the presence of refugees from Bosnia and Hercegovina, were of wider significance. A few refugees became involved in theft and prostitution, and as a consequence all of them were kept in effective confinement, with former military barracks serving as hostels and written permission being required for them to go out for strictly limited periods. The presence of refugees meshed with continuing psychological phantoms from Bosnia, the absence of someone else to blame for Slovenia's problems and a general lack of direction. These problems had to be weighed against political and economic consolidation.

For the remainder of the parliament elected in 1992, the character of Slovenian politics remained broadly the same. There was underlying political stability, based on Drnovšek as prime minister and on coalition government, while surface issues primarily concerned personalities and individual actions, appearing to suggest a more delicate political complexion than actually was the case. There were some suggestions that the government was susceptible to pressure group activity, as in the concessions it made when 5,000 students demonstrated against cuts in the subsidy for student meals in January 1996. However, other protests were apparently ineffectual, such as those organised by Janša's SDSS in the spring of 1994 against alleged corruption, including the self-enrichment of

well-placed former communists through the privatisation programme.

Despite a series of changes in ministerial appointments which
might have created major problems for the government, it faced
only three serious challenges: two of these involved parties withdrawing from the coalition, and the third, the linked questions
of property rights and relations with Italy and the European Union,
was the only issue on which serious policy differences emerged
in Slovene politics throughout this period. However, Drnovšek's
government finally withstood all of these with relative ease.

The first withdrawal from the coalition, in March 1994, was
connected with the rivalry between Janša and Kučan noted above.
The SDSS left the coalition government after Drnovšek sacked
Janša as defence minister, following the discovery that Ministry
of Defence security personnel had beaten up a civilian who had
been found secretly investigating Janša's work as minister of defence.
The servicemen had acted illegally because the man in question
was not a defence employee, and they therefore had no authority
over him. However, the fact that the man in question was an
operative of the internal security service (disbanded later that year),
working on orders from the interior minister (it was believed
but not proved that he was acting on behalf of the President),
added political spice to the issue.

By May the minister of the interior, Ivo Bižjak had resigned
following a string of allegations regarding the behaviour of his
'secret police'. It was discovered that the service had been involved
in illegal break-ins, not only in Slovenia but also in Austria.
However, although embarrassing the Bižjak resignation was no
more than an awkward irritant to the government, as were other
resignations that year: of Miha Jazbinšek as minister for the environment, Miha Kozinc as minister of justice, and Jožica Puhar
as minister of labour, family and social affairs (none of these was
connected with the Janša and Bižjak departures, the Jazbinšek
case was asso-ciated with accusations of corruption and incom-
petence). While Janša was keen to stress that this string of ministerial
losses, as well as the removal of several senior officials, reflected
on the prime minister, Drnovšek was relatively untouched. His
personal position continued to be strong and the coalition remained
dominant, with the three remaining partners together possessing
fifty-nine of the ninety seats in the National Assembly. New

ministerial appointments were made and little difference in government could be perceived.[38] The second exit from the coalition came in January 1996. This involved the ZL and followed the dismissal of one of its members, Maks Tajnikar, as minister for the economy. Tajnikar had been accused of arranging government assistance for the TAM factory in Maribor in order to help his own friends and political supporters in that city. Because assistance to TAM had been a government-backed policy, this was a surprising move which seems to have been a part of Drnovšek's calculation to move towards the political centre-ground for the elections to be held at the end of 1996. The move away from interventionist policies was also reinforced by a government decision to cut pensions. This ensured that the ZL's position in the coalition would be untenable.

However, with precisely half the members of the Assembly still supporting the coalition and the strong probability that the two national minority votes would always favour the government, as well as a sense that many not in the coalition, such as the ZL, would be unlikely to go against it in a confidence vote, the Drnovšek government continued towards the elections with the prime minister seemingly unassailable. Drnovšek himself was still enormously popular as an individual, as was Kučan and, to a lesser degree, Janša. Drnovšek's performance as prime minister was approved by 60 per cent of the electorate in mid-1996, while the LDS, at 20 per cent, was the only party registering support in double figures in opinion polls.[39]

The one partner that remained in coalition with the LDS throughout the term of the parliament was the SKD. Ironically the only salient policy difference to emerge in Slovene politics focused on the SKD leader and foreign minister, Peterle. Property rights in Slovenia had become a major issue in connection with the country's relations with neighbouring Italy and the EU (see Chapter 6). On 10 October 1994 Peterle arranged a compromise deal on some of Italy's demands regarding expropriated property. However, his concessions, though relatively minor, were not backed

---

[38] The new appointments were: Jelko Kacin, defence; Andrej Šter, interior; Pavel Gantar, environment; Meta Župančič, justice; and Rina Klimar, labour, family and social affairs.

[39] *Dnevnik*, 22 July 1996.

by the government and led to his being accused of treason and assertions from the LDS that the SKD was not patriotic. By the end of the month he had left office, alleging in turn that both Drnovšek and Kučan, as former communists, were anti-European. This was no more than the final moment in a decision which dated back to the appointment of Jožef Skolc as Speaker of the National Assembly in September, against Peterle's wishes.

The Peterle resignation could have rocked the government, involving as it did one of the few serious political differences to affect it, but instead the SKD remained a partner in the coalition, with its other three holders of ministerial portfolios continuing in office. This was even the case after the failure of Peterle's bid to be selected as chair of the Foreign Affairs Committee in the National Assembly (to replace Zoran Thaler of the LDS, who had replaced him as foreign minister). Peterle's bid failed because, despite promises of government support by Drnovšek, not enough LDS deputies supported him, resulting in a defeat by thirty-two votes to twenty-seven. There were further linked problems in May 1996, when the SKD supported a vote of no-confidence in Thaler over his approach to the Italian question, prompting Drnovšek to announce the end of the coalition – an act of dissolution revoked the next day, as the electorally vulnerable SKD reaffirmed its support for the months remaining till the elections scheduled for 10 November. The SKD, though always under some internal strain as well as external pressure from other right-of-centre parties to leave an essentially centre-left coalition, retained a higher profile and more influence than it would have done in opposition by being associated with a generally successful and popular government.

Overall, the SKD's position regarding influence on government was contingent on other developments. When other parties left the coalition, its strength grew. The same was true following its surprise success in local elections in December 1994 – a key factor in persuading the party to remain in the governing coalition despite the Peterle resignation. With over 18 per cent of the overall vote, the SKD had support around one percentage point higher than the LDS. Yet overall the coalition was most harmonious when the SKD was weakest, as the SKD rightly felt unable to rock the boat without the risk that it would end up drowning, thereby losing the benefits it gained from coalition, such as the LDS's compromise on matters relating to the church and religion.

It was clear that success in local elections was not likely to be translated into success at the national level in 1996. Polls again began to register strong support for both Drnovšek and Kučan, leaving the SKD and the other parties subject to the reality of roles as extras. Slovenia had a political system that offered underlying stability and progress, but at the price of superficial fragility and latent problems of stagnation – either in the event of continuous rule of one kind or in a situation where it was not possible to form a coalition and policy drift would follow.

Hiatus: Drnovšek and Kučan forever?

The political system designed to ensure consensus and stability served to consolidate the political leadership of Drnovšek and Kučan. Both were returned in elections held in 1996 and 1997 respectively, and it began to seem as though there could be no political life in the country without them. The fortunes of other figures such as Janša and Peterle waxed and waned but they never moved far enough into the confidence of the people. This was a mixed fortune for Slovenia. On the one hand, stability and continuity in policy was ensured, but on the other, it meant too great a reliance on one set of actors for the country's long-term benefit as opportunity and access were denied to potential successors.

Neither Kučan nor Drnovšek would actually last forever (leaving aside mortality, Kučan at least was not allowed to stand again at the end of his term in 2002), but it became ever more clear after the 1996 and 1997 elections that it would require politicians of similar calibre, possessing subtlety and self-limitation, to make the system work effectively, avoid stagnation and offer a programme which would ensure progress and prosperity. This was especially true of government, as the situation following the elections to the National Assembly in November 1996 proved. While the LDS was returned again as the largest single party and Drnovšek became candidate for prime minister, there was a considerable hiatus in which policy ran adrift, with important consequences.

Kučan's position was confirmed by the presidential elections on 23 November 1997, when he obtained a further five-year term. His victory saw him take 55.6 per cent of the vote, with the next most successful candidate, the rising young leader of the National Assembly, Janez Podobnik of the SLS, gaining only 18 per cent. None of the other six candidates gained more than 10 per cent of the vote. The relatively strong performance of Podobnik, whose brother Marjan had been a founding member and first leader of the modern SLS in 1988, was a positive sign for the political future of the country. He was a respected and popular figure, in some ways sharing the qualities associated generally with Kučan and Drnovšek. On the political level his popularity was clear in the Assembly vote for Speaker, which saw him gain eighty-two of the ninety votes available. Here, Janez Podobnik, was a figure about whom serious discussion could begin regarding future contests for President or prime minister. For the time being, however, Kučan one of the most astute, competent and durable political leaders in Central and Eastern Europe remained unassailable in office, despite recurrent accusations from Janša harking back to the past.

Similarly, Drnovšek seemed irreplaceable as prime minister, even if the situation following the 10 November 1996 election was less than straightforward. The results again saw the LDS emerge as the largest single party, with twenty-five seats. This put the onus on Drnovšek to form another coalition government with himself at its heart, although this was not as straightforward as it had been four years earlier. It took until 9 January before he was elected as prime minister by the narrowest margin, with just forty-six of the ninety Assembly votes.

However, this was not the end of delay. The relative dominance of the LDS was not so great as four years earlier. The SLS gained nineteen seats, the SDSS sixteen and the substantially diminished SKD ten. The remaining seats were shared by the ZL (nine), the DSUS (five), the SNS (four) and the national communities (two). This partly explains the delays in forming a government. Although the initiative lay with Drnovšek as leader of the largest party in the Assembly, there were potential alternative coalitions which might be formed – including around just three parties – the SLS, the SDSS and the SKD, using the label 'Slovene spring' – which held precisely half the seats in the Assembly. It required only one vote, or bloc of votes, to command a majority, and was in a position to block any proposal from Drnovšek, so long as its component parts remained together.

Having squeezed in as prime minister because one member of the SKD broke ranks with his party to support him, Drnovšek first tried to form a government comprising four left-of-centre parties, including his own LDS, the ZL, DSUS and the SNS. However, the total number of votes available to this coalition without a defection from at least one member of the 'Slovene spring' group and including the two representatives of the national communities, was only 45, precisely half the Assembly. On 6 February the proposed government was rejected by one vote – meaning that one individual from the coalition parties had defected. With this the process of coalition formation had to begin again.

Because the electoral system favoured a centrist party such as the LDS led by an able politician such as Drnovšek, this ensured that there was scope for another attempt. Drnovšek could exhaust all options until the point where the President would be forced to call fresh elections in accordance with the constitution. This meant that the prime minister had until the end of February to have two-thirds of his ministerial nominations confirmed, thereby permitting the government to take office. Thus there was a disciplining deadline.

After a further three weeks, having once more demonstrated his political and diplomatic skills forming and leading coalitions, Drnovšek was able to form a government on 27 February which was favoured by fifty-two votes to thirty-seven. The key to this outcome was the prime minister's wooing of the SLS. The notion of Slovenia's national interest and the realisation that problems could be caused by unresolved questions in government were important in persuading SLS leader Marjan Podobnik to take his party into the government coalition, as was the offer to him of the deputy prime ministership and the allocation of other ministerial appointments.

At once this took the sting out of potential opposition and shored up the LDS, in that only two more votes would be required for a majority in the Assembly. In the end it was the five votes of the DSUS which were added, creating a curious coalition of a small leftist party, with essentially the characteristics of a pressure group, and the two parties laying claim to the traditions of the two largest – and opposing – forces in Slovenian politics. As the vote for the government showed, support for this curious coalition even gained an errant vote from the opposition in addition to

the fifty-one available from the three parties in government combined with the two seats for the national communities.

This aberration was the tip of an iceberg: the two major right-
of-centre parties, the SDSS and the SKD, found difficulty in
maintaining a common front. For example, Janša, leader of the
SDSS, seemed interested in nothing more than trying to sully
the reputation of the prime minister and the government in order
to provoke early elections. In May 1998 he was heavily defeated
in an Assembly vote he had prompted on impeaching Drnovšek
for alleged illegal dealings between the government intelligence
service SOVA (Slovenska Obveščevalno-Varnostna Agencija)[40] and
Mossad, the Israeli secret service. However, Janša's proposal was
conclusively defeated, and the long-term effect was to damage
his political profile and ambition.

After several years of aspiring to replace Kučan as President,
Janša appeared to have realised not only that he was unlikely to
achieve this but that the key office was that of prime minister.
However, his chances of becoming prime minister and having
the opportunity to prove his credentials as a leader and statesman
were damaged each time he appeared to focus on personalities
and on trying to settle scores; public opinion and the leaders of
the SKD tended to respect Drnovšek as prime minister and to
be more concerned with policy matters. However great the friction
between the SDSS and the SKD may have been, there was little
chance that both of them and the ZL would vote in the same
way on any issue other than that of trying to oust Drnovšek and
his government.

The delay in forming a government had consequences in more
than one way. The interregnum meant that, although formally
membership of NATO remained a popular option, Slovenia was
omitted from the list of three Central and East European countries
invited to apply to join the Alliance. This was a blow to Drnovšek,

---

[40] SOVA had replaced VIS on 17 June 1993. It was different from VIS in
two ways. First, it answered to the government, not to the interior minister.
Secondly, its remit was broader than the essentially internal role of VIS, taking
on the role not only of internal security but also of intelligence gathering. The
Ministry of Defence continued to have its own service, VOMO (Varnostno
Obveščevalna Služba Ministerstva za Obramba), while the Interior Ministry had
the UKS (Uprava Kriminalistične Službe).

to the government and to the psychological confidence of Slovenes for whom prospective membership would have meant better conditions for external investment and trade, given that admission could only signify peaceful and stable conditions. The failure to be invited to join the Alliance, though resulting from a number of factors (see Chapter 6), could only properly be explained by a certain drift in the national approach to this question and the consequent lack of focus on maintaining the policy. Despite the confident belief of the outgoing defence minister Jelko Kacin early in the year that Slovenia would be invited to join the Alliance in the summer, there was a degree of complacency whereas all in fact was not well. This was despite the spirit of NATO's Partnership for Peace programme (as well as the vital work of Ambassador Mirko Cigler) having led to the first-ever NATO political meeting being held outside a NATO country, in Ljubljana. By the time this took place in March, it was clear that the prospect of membership was diminishing.

However, accession to the EU looked hopeful following the recommendation of the European Commission to include Slovenia in the ranks of likely early entrants and the substantial parliamentary vote in July to ratify the EU Association Agreement. However, the failure to make the NATO invitation list prompted the resignation of the foreign minister, Zoran Thaler, after he failed a confidence vote in July. Thaler continued in office until his successor, Boris Frelc of the LDS, was appointed in September.

Regardless of being rocked by the NATO decision, Drnovšek's government continued to be popular. The local elections of 22 November 1998 showed that in party terms this favoured the LDS which increased its share of the vote by 7 per cent as SLS support fell from 13 per cent in the national elections to 10 per cent, leading to rumours that it might break with the coalition so as not to suffer as the SKD had done in the previous government. Through 1997 and 1998, the government continued in office, in spite of other minor reverses. These included the loss of the defence minister twice in 1998, the first time because of further evidence of defence intelligence personnel acting illegally (this time setting up a listening post inside Croatia). After his in resignation February, Tit Turnšek was replaced by Alojz Krapež. However, no one could have expected that in this turbulent period he too would be gone by the end of the year. Krapež was replaced by Lojze Marinček, already minister of science and technology, who would undertake both responsibilities temporarily.

Other issues causing irritation to the government included recurring strains over matters such as property rights, especially when the Roman Catholic Church made a potentially damaging entry on to the political scene after the appointment in 1997 of a new hardline Archbishop, Franc Rode. He created a schism in public opinion which threatened to have an impact on the governing coalition when he wholly unrealistically threatened to take the case of Church land to the European Court of Justice – something that would only enter the realm of possibility if Slovenia were to accede to the EU.

In response Drnovšek promised that there would be a deal acceptable to the church. The deal, struck after much discussion, especially within the ruling coalition, excluded the church from the clauses in the denationalisation legislation which blocked the return of land owned on a feudal basis before the Second World War. This vote was only passed in the Assembly because almost one-third of the deputies, essentially former communists opposed to the amendment, abstained in order to help the prime minister.

However, the former communist influence continued to be felt as a new dimension in politics emerged. The National Council began for the first time to play a significant role. Unable actually to overturn legislation, it exercised its capacities to the limit. Having already worked to delay pension and taxation reform legislation, it frustrated Drnovšek, who had worked hard to resolve the church property question, by rejecting the amendment passed by 41 to 21 in the National Assembly in July 1998. While this was irksome to the government, as were delays in other areas, rejection by the National Council would always be overcome provided that a majority in the National Assembly could be arranged.

Church property was just one of the factors creating tension between the different strands within the coalition, yet the essential stability of government was maintained and, on the whole unchallenged. The inability of the opposition to dent Drnovšek's commanding position was reinforced not only by the prime minister's popularity but also by that of Marjan Podobnik as deputy prime minister and by the comfortable re-election of Kučan as President. While this result could be attributed largely to Kučan's own reputation and record, it is probable that the effective performance and essential stability of Drnovšek's government were also important conditions for the President's victory.

Drnovšek's prowess was proved again, as was his apparent indispensability. Thus it was quite likely that for the foreseeable future Slovenia would be governed by a Drnovšek-led coalition and, even more certainly, by an LDS-dominated government. The outcome of the 1996 election showed that even where the clear potential for an opposition majority existed, the combination of electoral system and political culture favoured stability and continuity meant that the LDS, with Drnovšek as its leader, was likely to retain its key position in the formation of governments.

The constitutional and electoral systems favoured stable coalition government, based on the significant strength of one centrist party, and it was hard to imagine that even a fragile but fragmented coalition such as that formed by anti-communist parties after the first elections in 1990 could form an effective government under the post-1992 system. Until some other political leader could orient his party to the significant central area of the political spectrum successfully covered by the LDS, it was likely, but not absolutely certain, that Drnovšek's LDS would be the stable pivot of governance. This was little more than a continuation into the democratic era of the essentially consensual politics, only marred by minor questions regarding individuals, which had already developed under the communist system.

The stagnation induced by complacency was noted earlier, but in the period after the elections it took a different form, leading to policy drift and provoking a change in the electoral mechanism in time for the elections in 2000. In the three-and-a-half months between the election and the eventual formation of a government Slovenia was effectively rudderless. As will be seen in the following chapter, this had important consequences for the country's ability to deal with one crucial international issue – NATO.

6

SECURITY

Political stagnation, induced by the combination of the electoral system and political differences, had a significant impact on Slovenia's dealings with NATO and the European Union. These were the two pillars of European security upon which Ljubljana sought to build its own security. While the idea of joining processes of European integration had been prominent at the time of independence, it was only subsequently that it began to have real meaning and purpose. The idea of forging links with the Atlantic Alliance, on the other hand, was an aspiration that emerged during the early 1990s. In both cases the approach to prospective membership was made problematic not only by international circumstances and decisions but ultimately by factors within Slovenia itself. Among these were attachment to traditions and to aspects of sovereignty that made adaptation slower than it needed to be, and might actually hamper relations with international organisations.

As will be seen, the armed forces had been successful in the short conflict that paved the way to Slovenian independence, but their restructuring was not begun soon enough. Compounded by the political stagnation at the end of 1996, this proved fatal where Slovenia's approach to NATO was concerned. On the other hand, although there were also notable difficulties over association with the EU, Slovenia eventually managed to overcome outstanding issues and internal preoccupations. This and changes in the defence sphere left the country in a transformed security situation.

The 'Ten Day War' and independence

On 18 July 1991 the Yugoslav government announced that all units of the JNA would begin their withdrawal from Slovenia. This followed the army's humiliation in combat with the Slovene

Territorial Defence Force (TO – Slovenska Teritorialna Obramba) and Interior Ministry Special Forces – essentially police units – in a 'Ten Day War' which began with Slovenia's declaration of independence on 25 June.[1] The country had thus secured its independence partly through the use of armed force. The price of independence was relatively low. According to official figures, only thirteen Slovenes lost their lives (four each from the TO and the Interior Ministry Special Forces, plus five civilians) while a total of 112 were wounded. On the JNA side, thirty-nine soldiers were killed and 163 wounded. In addition, ten non-Slovene civilians were wounded.[2] The conflict was so

---

[1] The war engendered a variety of books, ranging from the mainly pictorial to the solid and detailed. The former was represented by a glossy volume produced by *Mladina, Deset Dni Vojne za Slovenijo: Izbor Fotografij in Tekstov iz Odboja med 26 VI in 5 VII 1991* (Ten Days of War for Slovenia: Photographs and Texts From the Period of June 26 to July 5 1991), Ljubljana: Mladina Monolit, 1991. The best representative of the latter is Janez J. Švajncer, *Obranili Domovino: Teritoralna Obramba Republike Slovenije v Vojni za Svobodno in Samostojno Slovenijo, 1991*, Ljubljana: Viharnik, 1993, which uses operational records to give a relatively detailed account of the conflict throughout the country. A similarly useful detailed account, in both a Slovene and an English version, is the defence minister's memoirs, covering the years before independence as well as the war and independence: Janez Janša, *Premiki. Nastajanje in Obramba Slovenske Države 1988-1992*, Ljubljana: Založba Mladinska Knjiga, 1992; and, from the same publisher, *The Making of the Slovenian State 1988-1992: The Collapse of Yugoslavia*, 1994. Silva Križman *et al., Dan Prej*, Koper: Primorske Novice, 1994, takes Janša's book and an interview with him and sets out to demonstrate that the conflict started in the coastal Primorska region a day earlier than Janša says in his book and confirms in the interview from June 1992 (the title means 'The Day Before'), through reproduction of interviews and reports, primarily in the regional newspaper *Primorske Novice* for which the authors worked as journalists. On the role played by the Interior Ministry 'militia' see Pavle Celik, *Izza Barikad*, Ljubljana: Založba Slovenske Novice, 1992. Despite this material, which is mostly based on contemporary reporting or practical involvement, independent study and analysis of the conflict remains to be done: even where a major analysis of all aspects of it was planned by a team of experts at the University of Ljubljana, it was found to be too ambitious, producing only preliminary and summary findings – in themselves, valuable enough. See Marjan Malešič, 'Fragmenti iz Analize Vojne v Sloveniji' in Anton Grizold (ed.), *Perspektive Sodobne Varnosti. Iz Obramboslovnih Raziskav II*, Ljubljana: Knjižna Zbirka Teorija in Praksa, 1998, pp. 201-26.

[2] *Slovenija. Geografska, Zgodovinska, Pravna Politična, Ekonomska in Kulturna Podoba Slovenije*, Ljubljana: Založba Mladinska Knjiga, 1998, p.134.

brief and limited in scope at least in part because of the way in which the TO performed.

The TO was based on the old two-tier defence system which characterised the Yugoslav doctrine of 'General People's Defence'.[3] In that system the JNA was intended to be the better-equipped, better-trained forefront of defence which was meant to repel or slow down an aggressor while the second line of defence, the territorials, was mobilised. Whereas the JNA was run by the Federal Secretariat for Defence, the TO forces were organised by republican defence secretariats. Following the first democratic elections in 1990, the first minister of defence was Janez Janša, former scourge of the JNA as a journalist. He and three others were the leading architects of Slovenian strategy – his deputy (later information minister) Jelko Kacin, the chief of staff Janez Slapar, and the interior minister Igor Bavčar.[4]

Immediately after the first multi-party elections in Slovenia the JNA began attempts to disable its territorial defence capability. The first round of elections took place on 8 April 1990, and between 17 April and 15 May the JNA tried to prescribe without consultation a new defence doctrine in which the republics would lose their role. At the same time it began attempts to disarm TOs in some areas. In Croatia, with obvious later consequences, it succeeded in seizing virtually the whole TO arsenal. In Slovenia, however, it managed only to expropriate 40 per cent of equipment, which left the country with a base from which to build, with the addition of imports of light anti-tank and anti-aircraft rocket systems, a force to match the JNA.

The JNA's attempt to impose a new doctrine also carried with it the full subordination of TOs in all the republics to JNA headquarters in Belgrade. To counter this move Slovenia officially placed its TO under the sole command of the Slovenian government. At the same time a set of national protection units known as 'Manoeuvre Structures of National Protection (MSNZ – Manevrski Strukturi Narodne Zaščite) were set up. These were

---

[3] See James Gow, *Legitimacy and the Military: the Yugoslav Crisis*, London: Pinter/New York: St.Martin's, 1992, pp.46–50.

[4] Other figures were important as well, notably Anton Bebler. He was Professor of Defence Studies at Ljubljana University, from which programme Janša and Kacin, among others, graduated.

established with the greatest secrecy. Only seven people at the top level, including Kučan, Peterle, Janša and Bavčar, knew of the whole set-up at the republican level, and all communications were delivered personally.

The aim in creating the MNSZ was its very secrecy: it duplicated the normal command structure of the TO but adapted it for special needs without anyone knowing. Altogether 21,000 TO and police personnel were mobilised into these units between May, when the JNA disarmed the TO, and October. A full development plan was agreed at Kočevska Reka in August[5] by secret committees, containing members of the TO command structure. While their loyalty was to Slovenia, for a transitional phase they also had to deal with the JNA and were formally part of its command structure. Thus for a period of crucial planning and re-organisation the federal army was duped into believing that it had control of the TO. When Slovenia moved to full control of the TO, the JNA tried to change its top echelon, imposing its own nominees, but the move failed because the key structure, the MSNZ, was beyond the influence of the federal command, which did not even know of its existence.[6]

The JNA leadership appears to have undertaken operations in Slovenia after 25 June 1991 on the basis of two miscalculations. The first was that, in spite of the evidence that Slovenia's TO had been prepared to resist any JNA moves after the declaration of independence, a show of force would be enough to prevent Slovenian independence. The second was that, if the first assumption proved wrong, the JNA could resort to escalation – something which would essentially be backed by the outside world, given the public pronouncements of key figures on the international diplomatic scene.

Both assumptions were ill-founded. The TO proved effective against the limited and half-hearted JNA force deployed in Slovenia. The JNA was confused because it had not expected any military

[5] Švajncer, *Domovino*, pp.11–12.

[6] The secret locations at Kočevje were associated with the post-Second World War massacres of wartime foes by the communists, and only a small number of approved Slovenes knew of them. Thus, strengthened by their linguistic distinctiveness, the Slovenes were able to prepare their independence campaign in clandestine circumstances.

engagements. Its units were deployed on the basis of plans to resist external invasion, and merely made a show of force. It saw its Slovenian deployment as a policing operation.

When the JNA found itself engaged in battle, the second assumption, that escalation would resolve matters, was also found to be false. There seems to have been a belief that superior forces would gain an easy victory, a 'Balkan Storm' similar to the 'Desert Storm' operation by a US-led coalition against Iraq. It was further assumed that it would receive some international backing.

However, at the outset of armed hostilities, the international community, in the shape of the EC's presidential troika, took an active interest, with an offer to mediate. As a result, although the JNA hesitantly began an escalation, including fifteen bombing or strafing missions in Slovenia, primarily against civilian targets, it was confused and constrained. Humiliated, and diffident about using its firepower in an attempt to crush the weaker Slovenian forces, the JNA seems to have written off Slovenia to concentrate on Croatia.

The poor intelligence involved in the JNA campaign, typified by the calamitous wrong assessment that despite the signs and preparations Slovenes would not fight,[7] cost the JNA dearly. So, possibly, did the failure to judge that, despite its success, the TO could only have held out at the same level for a few more days.[8] However, the Slovene campaign had been well planned by Janša's ministry and its armed forces since well before the referendum on independence at the end of 1990,[9] and was well executed. Essentially the war had effectively been lost by this stage because, in the Clausewitzian sense of war being a continuation of politics by other means, the essential political question regarding Slovene independence had been *de facto* settled. By this stage, there was no way that military success by the JNA could reverse Belgrade's political defeat.

---

[7] Gen. Milan Aksentijević, interview, *Death of Yugoslavia*, programme 3.

[8] This was confirmed to one of the authors by a senior diplomatic and defence figure.

[9] One defence official privately showed one of the authors an operational and tactical blueprint, dated November 1990, which the TO had been able to use for its planning.

Where analysis was weak on the JNA side, Slovenia had extremely good intelligence throughout the period leading up to the conflict, as well as during and beyond it. This was exemplified in the republican defence ministry's removal to new premises on the eve of a JNA attempt to seize its headquarters. As conflict broke out, the TO was able to anticipate JNA moves because it had an intelligence network throughout the army. According to one well placed source, they even had non-Slovenes in the army command supplying information.

Good Slovene intelligence added to poor federal intelligence enabled Slovenia to use the element of surprise to its advantage. The JNA's belief that there would be no resistance in Slovenia meant that it was immediately confused once it found itself being met with force. Not knowing which way to go – retreat or escalation – the JNA was pulled in two directions at once. Surprise played an essential part, given not only the JNA's potentially superior forces but its presumed familiarity with Slovenian strategy. This required, first and foremost, the avoidance of frontal war and reliance instead on guerrilla tactics and on initiating armed clashes in situations to Slovenia's military advantage. This asymmetric action required publicity to give it full effect; thus integrated media management was an essential part of the Slovene strategy.

In operational terms the emphasis was on attacking tanks and armoured vehicles in ambushes. Vehicles would be trapped with a combination of wholly local troops and mobile units, for example, on a mountain road. Short-to-medium-range anti-armour weapons – notably Singaporean copies of German Armbrust rockets – could then be used to destroy tanks within a range of 2,500 metres. Utilities were cut to JNA facilities. With regard to JNA air power, Soviet-made Strela-7 anti-aircraft rockets were used against both helicopters and fixed-wing aircraft.[10]

It was attacks of this kind on helicopters which appear to have provided the first incidents of hostile fire in the ten-day campaign. Slovenian forces, needing armed clashes to demonstrate that the country was defending itself, shot down two helicopters over Ljubljana – both unarmed and the first of which had a Slovene

[10] In addition Slovenia made limited use of Gazelle, Augusta and Hirondelle police helicopters, although essentially for medical and reconnaissance purposes only, but with a few instances of ground attack.

pilot and was carrying bread to resupply JNA units trapped in their barracks. Slovene officials, on the basis of information that the second phase of JNA operations was to transport special detachments of federal police to be installed at border posts and reinforcements for its special forces,[11] had warned the JNA 5th Military District Command in Zagreb that if helicopters continued to be flown they would be shot down.[12] This incident appears to have been the first real engagement of the war,[13] after a policy not to be the first to use force and reluctance on the part of TO personnel to open fire when the time came.[14] It also defined the whole conflict. The helicopters were shot down at the moment when, without any chance for investigation and checking, the images of destroyed helicopters could be beamed across Europe in main evening news broadcasts.

The purpose of Slovenian strategy was twofold. The first requirement was to harry the JNA, and the crucial second intention was to tell the world that the Slovene people were bravely defending themselves. To this end, Slovenia established an international media management centre in advance of the conflict itself and used Jelko Kacin as information minister to give regular briefings to the international press which would then carry Slovenia's message to the world, based on its armed action – or indeed on the perception of it.

Although Kacin did not lie in his press briefings, he was not averse to letting editors draw their own conclusions where this served the strategy. In one case he informed his audience that

---

[11] Janša, *Premiki*, pp.168-71.

[12] Igor Bavčar, Interview, *Death of Yugoslavia*, programme 3. Bavčar reports how the JNA officer in charge of the operation, General Andrija Rašeta, broke down in tears, asking how the Slovenes could do such a thing after the helicopters had been shot down.

[13] The only evidence of earlier action appears to be the possibility of incidents earlier on 27 June, reported in a log of events published as an annex to Janša's book, although this does not seem to be corroborated elsewhere. See Janša, *Premiki*, p.317.

[14] On the no-first-use understanding (the interpretation taken by commanders in the field, though not entirely consistent with the order issued), see Švajncer, *Domovino*, p.29. On the reluctance actually to open fire, note should be taken of Bavčar and Janša – see Bavčar, Interview, *Death of Yugoslavia*, programme 3, and Janša, *Premiki*, p.170.

there was a burned-out armoured personnel carrier at a given point, and the press duly reported another successful use of anti-armour weaponry by the TO. In reality the vehicle had been trapped by a TO unit, abandoned by its crew and only later set alight by children. Kacin had done no more than announce the location of the destroyed vehicle, but the message had been received that destruction was the result of armed action.[15] This integrated strategy of armed clashes and media management worked effectively.

This integrated military-media strategy was complemented by a significant consensual diplomatic offensive. Demonstrating cross-party solidarity, political groups and informal representative visits were arranged to numerous countries, quietly to prepare the way for the message that Slovenia was a well-run country of democratic orientation which could not preserve these qualities within the Yugoslav federation. While it was important to spread the word everywhere and anywhere, it was quickly realised that an independent Slovenia would be in no position to establish links with all the eighty-four states with which the Yugoslav federation had diplomatic relations, let alone the eighty or so with which it had no link. Efforts were therefore concentrated on the shaping of foreign policy. This meant, among other things, secretly contacting as many of the small number of Slovenes in the Yugoslav diplomatic service as could be trusted, forging links with the larger Slovene émigré communities, and building links with neighbouring countries and especially with those capitals judged to be the most 'interesting' for Slovenia in its current situation – most notably Washington, Bonn and Prague.[16]

By May 1991 Foreign Minister Dimitrij Rupel's operational plan was ready for the final weeks before independence. As a result of earlier activity and research, a more or less clear view had been established on relations with a wide range of countries.

---

[15] Kacin in discussion with James Gow. His key role in the war is reflected in the title 'The Great Victor' of the collection of articles by and about him published under his name: Kacin, *Veliki Zmagovalec*, Maribor: Založba za Alternativno Teorijo, 1991.

[16] Dimitrij Rupel, *Slovenskega Pot do Samostojnosti in Priznanja*, Ljubljana: KRES, 1992, pp.84-7. On links with émigrés, in 1990 the Slovenski Svetovni Kongres (Slovene World Congress) was set up to establish contacts between Slovenes in different parts of the world.

The primary relationship was clearly to be with Austria, the one country on which Slovenia could rely – reflecting a decision in the Austrian Foreign Ministry in mid-1990 to create a sphere of influence in Central and Eastern Europe in the lands that were once part of the Habsburg Empire. Although no written agreements had been signed, there was hope on the Slovenian side that Vienna would recognise a declaration of independence by Ljubljana and give its assurance of, at the very least, diplomatic and political support regarding 'third' countries, and the continuation of business with Austrian banks.[17] When independence was declared, Austria and its Foreign Minister Alois Mock did indeed take the lead in promoting Slovenia's interest although, to the disappointment of the Slovenes, there was no formal recognition – a reflection of Austria's preparations for joining the European Union within a few years.

Good relations and friendly support were also anticipated with Germany because of excellent relations with two of the Länder – Baden-Württemberg and Bavaria – and on a personal level between foreign ministers.[18] There was also the hope that Belgium and especially Luxembourg (then about to take the presidency of the European Community) would be helpful, but less confidence in the Netherlands, despite positive contacts with the Dutch ambassador in Belgrade. Support was expected from some of the (still) Soviet republics, including Russia and, more for their symbolic value, Estonia, Latvia and Lithuania.

While interest was shown by Cyprus and understanding was expected from Switzerland and the Scandinavian countries, there was little confidence in gaining support and sympathy from any other countries. France and Spain were clearly opposed, while relations with Italy were mixed, relying on personal and political contacts that did not necessarily translate into policy. Britain was judged to be hostile on the grounds that Slovenian and especially

---

[17] The present and following paragraphs are based on Dimitrij Rupel, *Skrivnost Države: Spomini na Domače in Zunanje Zadeve, 1989-1992*, Ljubljana: Založba Delo-Novice, 1992, pp.120-2.

[18] Rupel, *Skrivnost Države*, contains a foreword, produced as a letter in German in the book and in Slovene on the back cover, as well as a somewhat gratuitous photograph of the former Slovenian foreign minister with Hans Dietrich-Genscher, the German foreign minister through this period.

Croatian independence would lead to the rehabilitation of those who had associated with the Nazis during the Second World War. Most important of all, the United States was judged not to understand the Slovenian position and the 'realities' of the Yugoslav break-up – a view based on Austrian information passed to the government, as well as on the meetings between the Slovenes and the Americans on the eve of independence. This convinced the Slovenes that the United States was hostile to their aspirations.[19]

Mostly these judgements proved well founded. In the months following the declaration of independence, Slovenia continued its diplomatic activity, with negotiations, held on the Croatian island of Brioni (a former residence of Tito), involving all the Yugoslav parties and mediated by the European Community at the end of armed hostilities in Slovenia. The Slovene delegation comprised Kučan, Peterle, Bavčar, Rupel and Drnovšek and, despite much tension, the talks worked well for Slovenia and were judged by Drnovšek to have been chaired with skill by the Dutch foreign minister Hans van den Broek.[20] While the initial ceasefire agreement was not without problems, as Kučan certainly realised,[21] it served Ljubljana's needs. Slovenia, along with Croatia, agreed to suspend its declaration of independence for a period of three months to allow negotiations to take place, and, during that period it was agreed that the JNA would withdraw completely from Slovenia. In effect this meant Slovenia's independence.

On 8 October, when that moratorium expired, the declaration was re-affirmed. By December, Germany, working to an agreement among EC members dating from 6 October but against the views of many other EC members, forced the pace. First it put pressure on reluctant countries to honour the commitments they had made in October. This resulted in the production of a set of guidelines

[19] *Ibid.*, pp.133-4. While the United States was in fact opposed to independence – its main opposition was to unilateral actions – this was offset with the comment that it would never stand in the way of democracy. See Warren Zimmermann, 'The Last Ambassador: a Memoir of the Collapse of Yugoslavia', *Foreign Affairs*, vol.74, no.2, Mar.-Apr. 1995.

[20] Janez Drnovšek, *Moja Resnica*, Ljubljana: Založba Mladinska Knjiga, 1996, p.251.

[21] James D.D. Smith, *Stopping Wars*, Boulder, CO: Westview Press, 1995, p.221.

for recognition by the EC, in those former Yugoslav countries being invited to seek recognition of independent international status, and lastly in a commitment to announce a decision on 15 January 1992. But by the time that date arrived, Germany's independent indication of its intentions (at some cost to EC harmony) had created a situation in which there could be no other outcome than recognition of Slovenia.[22]

Slovenia's independence was gained through a mixture of diplomacy, armed force and propaganda, and perhaps the last of these was the biggest weapon in its armoury. The use of television and print media, as well as political and diplomatic representation, paved the way: through good use of the country's already well-developed communications and news media facilities, the Slovenes were able to get their small conflict featured on front pages and television screens around the world. As a result, enough international opinion was quickly persuaded that the JNA's actions in Slovenia had to be stopped, and thus pressure was brought to bear on the federal forces. These were tactically outmanoeuvred – on the ground, as JNA units were either captured or destroyed in combat with the TO, and in the international arena.

After only ten days' fighting the *de facto* independence of Slovenia had been acknowledged and it would only be a matter of time before full recognition followed. As an admission that this was the case, the JNA began withdrawing its 22-24,000 personnel from Slovenia after another ten days. With that withdrawal completed at the end of October 1991 and Slovenia officially recognised by the EC member states on 15 January 1992, its security concerns changed drastically. The emphasis in both the armed forces and foreign policy moved from preparation for war to participation in international life.

From territorial defence to the Slovenian Army

In the years after independence the Slovenian defence community was required to establish the armed forces for everyday service in more normal circumstances than those of war and preparation

---

[22] See James Gow, *Triumph of the Lack of Will: International Diplomacy and the Yugoslav War* (London: Hurst/New York: Columbia University Press, 1997, pp.59-64 *passim*.

for war. However, it was not wholly clear what this peacetime profile should be: a new version of that which had existed earlier, or an armed force of a different type altogether? Indeed, might it be more appropriate for the country to have no armed force at all? These were the questions that confronted the Slovenes as they tried to convert pride in success against the JNA into a longer-term purpose. Eventually, an emerging sense that international cooperation was a more realistic and important function for the Slovenian armed forces than defence of the homeland without allies against a much stronger opponent began a move away from their traditional territorial character towards a more volunteer-based force.

This process of change began before there could be any clear sense of where it would lead. On 11 April 1992 the first regular contingent of 2,300 conscripts was sworn into the TO. Although this force had evolved from the old Yugoslav defence doctrine, it was significantly different in three ways. First, territorial defence was now to be the only instrument of defence, whereas in Yugoslavia the federal army had provided a better-equipped and supposedly more sophisticated mechanism; these two tiers had been supposed to act together, with the regular army providing the lead. The second difference concerned the formation of the officer corps. Whereas previously all officers were trained in military secondary schools and academies, future Slovene officers would be university-educated with the addition of courses in officer training. It was expected that this would produce a more 'civilianised' military élite, who would also be technologically adept. A contingency of this was the third difference: officers would not necessarily or normally be signing up for a lifelong military career. It was anticipated that the training system would leave them suitably placed to pursue civilian careers at almost any stage and with relative ease. In its essence, the idea of territorial defence envisaged the officers of the new armed force as civilians who happened to be in uniform.

There were also big differences for conscripts. Whereas in Yugoslavia they had served fifteen and then twelve months, often far from their homes, life for conscripts in Slovenia was destined to be much more agreeable. In such a small country they could rarely be more than two hours from home while they undertook three months' basic training and a further four in active units –

although there was normally a reprieve for the final month, making the total period of service in reality only six months. This meant that at any one time the Slovenian armed forces would have around 15,000 troops in their ranks each year, but that the actual number in uniform at any moment would be 7-8,000 and never normally exceed 10,000. In addition to the conscript component, these totals also included up to 2,000 regulars, some 300 of whom would be involved in training newly-joined conscripts.

After service all conscripts would enter the territorial defence reserve, in theory ready for rapid mobilisation if needed. Either as conscripts or as reservists they would always perform duties close to home (with the exception of some larger mobile brigades with specific anti-armour and air defence roles) in one of the twenty-six military regions, grouped into seven military districts.[23] This structure had only minimal permanent organisation, with potential battle units to be composed of conscripts and reservists in time of need. However, it still had a permanent command structure, subordinated to the general staff in Ljubljana, headed by the chief of staff who in turn was answerable to the defence minister. The division into regions and districts reflected the fact that the armed forces had their roots not only in the action of 1991 but also in the OF (Liberation Front) and Partisan period of the Second World War. But it was assumed that the forces could provide resistance in the event of an attack on the country and was otherwise a cheap option for maintaining an armed force in peacetime. It maintained some defensive capability and gave the country a symbol of statehood.

However, there were clear problems with maintaining this approach to defence. The first was that no matter how far it was consistent with tradition, it assumed either defence in depth by means of small engagements over the long term in the event of occupation, or that an attack would be deterred. On the question of actually having to defend the country, it was clear that Slovenia had now moved into an era where it was virtually unthinkable

---

[23] The seven district headquarters (*Pokrajnski Štab*) are located as follows: Kranj (Gorenjska district), Nova Gorica (Northern Primorska district), Postojna (Southern Primorska district), Novo Mesto (Dolenjska district), Maribor (Eastern Štajerska district), Celje (Western Štajerska district) and Ljubljana (Ljubljana district) –also the site of the national command.

that it would be invaded and have to rely on the territorial defence concept. In addition, there was the question of credibility for the armed forces, should such an unthinkable event occur: with only six months training for conscripts and such a small number of personnel under arms at any one time, a potential aggressor was most unlikely to be deterred after a close look. While this did not greatly matter because there was no serious prospect of invasion, it made all expenditure on defence seem pointless and wasteful beyond symbolising statehood and keeping those who enjoyed being involved in the territorial system happy.

Slovenia could continue with this arrangement provided it was content to accept that defence did not really matter and that the defence concept was not questioned within the country. However, as the Slovenian authorities began to reassess their position during the 1990s, they began to see ever more clearly (even if supporters of the traditional approach were sometimes slow to do so) that things had to change. Slovenia's new position in the world required new armed forces. These were needed for two practical reasons. The first requirement was a force capable of rapid reaction to, and repulsion of, a cross-border incursion by one of its neighbours and implicitly deterring such an attack (not a full-scale occupation to be resisted over the long term). This was an almost unthinkable scenario, but it was one which could not wholly be excluded; for example, there were concerns about occasional intrusion into Slovenian air space by Croatian military planes. The second reason for change was to be able to use the armed forces as part of a broader security policy for the country – in particular, by demonstrating that Slovenia was a responsible member of the international community of states and in forging a partnership with – the transatlantic military-political alliance created by Western countries at the start of the Cold War – NATO.[24]

Establishing consensus on moving in these directions was not straightforward. This was very much a matter of personalities, with the antipathy between the titular supreme commander, President Kučan, and the defence minister between 1990 and 1994, Janša, dominating the defence agenda.[25] As the minister who took

---

[24] The North Atlantic Treaty Organisation, based on the North Atlantic Treaty signed in Washington, DC in April 1949.

[25] Anton Grizold, 'Civil-Military Relations in Slovenia' in Anton Bebler (ed),

credit for masterminding the campaign for independence using the territorial system, Janša was clearly reluctant to abandon something which had worked and in addition had made his reputation.

What seemed to be a desire to maintain the defence system as his own personal empire became entangled with 'suspected unlawfulness, violations of regulations, indiscipline, criminal offences and various forms of corruption'.[26] Janša, in the words of one expert (and aspirant for his job), had 'allowed, if not encouraged, his "cult of personality" to develop in the military establishment'.[27] His hold on the defence ministry, in effect, was impeding Slovenia's transition to civilian control of the military and the transformation of its armed forces that the new circumstances seemed to require. Eventually he was dismissed as defence minister in March 1994 after almost four years in the post, when a majority of the National Assembly voted to remove him at the request of Prime Minister Drnovšek.

One of the first acts of Janša's successor – his one-time deputy and former information minister, Kacin – was to publish a letter castigating his predecessor for promoting incompetent officers on political grounds and for abnormalities in the procuring of equipment.[28] However, Kacin's period of office was also problematic. While he was in a position, crucially, to begin the re-orientation of Slovenia's security policy, his period as defence minister was weakened by personality clashes with subordinates loyal to Janša among others. By February 1995, less than a year into his term of office, there was a parliamentary interpellation to remove him,[29] although he was later reappointed and served as defence minister until the crucial period of hiatus at the end of 1996 and beginning of 1997. Despite these problems of civil-military relations (which continued[30]), the direction of Slovenia's defence had begun to

---

Civil-Military Relations in Post-Communist States: Central and Eastern Europe in Transition, Westport, CT: Praeger, 1997, p.108.

[26] Anton Bebler, 'Civil-Military Relations in Slovenia' in Constantine P. Danopoulos and Daniel Zirker (eds), *Civil-Military Relations in the Soviet and Yugoslav Successor States*, Boulder, CO: Westview Press, 1996, p.205. This is the best analysis to date of civil-military relations in post-independence Slovenia.

[27] *Ibid.*, p.207.

[28] *Delo*, 17 June 1994, cited in Bebler, 'Civil-Military', p.207.

[29] Grizold, 'Civil-Military', p.108.

change and was then consolidated under successive defence ministers.

The framework was set for a twelve-year transformation of the renamed Slovenian Army (Slovenska Vojska), between 1998 and 2010. Broadly, this restructuring would see reduced reliance on traditional territorial forces and the development of lighter, more flexible and mobile units which would be both more relevant to military affairs in the new century and better suited to cooperation and interoperability with NATO forces. The inevitability of professionalisation was recognised formally in projections which envisaged a decisive increase in the professional contingent and a gradual decrease in the number of compulsory conscripts by the end of the period. At the end of 1998, there were already 4,150 personnel on regular contracts, of whom 13 per cent were women (a notable development) and 40 per cent were in positions which required specific military education.[31]

The change in approach did not mean completely abandoning the traditional territorial element, but it did lead to reduced emphasis on it and to significant reductions in the overall reserve force. The reserve component was envisaged as the lowest level of a three-tier army. Its size would drop from 60,000 to 33,000 over the period, with conscription being maintained but the numbers obliged to perform service curtailed. In line with the territorial tradition, these forces would be non-standardised, and mobilised in defence support roles with or without integration with existing structures, depending on circumstances.

[30] At the beginning of 1998 Defence Minister Tit Turnšek was forced to resign after two VOMO operatives were arrested in Croatia and the vehicle surveillance equipment that they were using was impounded. In the summer of 1998 it was still possible to find indications that personal connections were 'more important politically' than qualifications: the defence minister Alojz Krapež was criticised for giving the rank of second-lieutenant to Niki Romšek, wife of the director of government services and general secretary in the defence ministry during the Janša era, who was appointed head of personnel issues in the general staff (*Delo*, 6 July 1998). At around the same time, an army officer, Major Ladislav Troha, conducted a personal protest outside parliament over irregularities in the military which he wanted to draw to the attention of both the public and legislators (*Delo*, 6 July and 5 August, 1998).

[31] Ministry of Defence of the Republic of Slovenia, 'The Structure of the Slovenian Armed Forces' at http://www.mo-rs.si/mors/eng/kadrsvan.htm, 27 November 1998.

The second tier to be developed over the period of transition was the main defence force. This would be the largest element of the standing force, performing the full range of military activities, including training and particularly provision of logistical support. Those accepting voluntary conscription would be inducted into this tier which would be the mainstay of Slovenia's defence capability.

The plan's first tier of defence would be the key instrument in security policy and the most significant aspect of the restructuring: the decision to create a modern rapid reaction force, trained and equipped to operate in any role in Slovenia. The primary purpose of this element was to facilitate international cooperation and Slovenia's international role. The key was to have forces which could 'participate in humanitarian activities and peace support operations' and 'participate in exercises, training programmes and operations within PfP'.[32] [Partnership for Peace, the NATO programme for cooperation with non-NATO members]. PfP was important as it provided a stepping stone to possible NATO membership (albeit, late in the day – see below). Thus the 10th Battalion for international cooperation, the first professional battalion to be developed, was the spearhead of the country's efforts to become a part of the Euro-Atlantic military-political family.

The desire to forge closer links with the North Atlantic alliance also, it must be assumed, produced one of the more curious features of the restructuring. Slovenian defence planners copied the command structure of the 700,000-strong US military for an armed force which would have a standing strength of no more than 10,000. This created a top-heavy structure in which hierarchy was diminished and command and control viability reduced because of the number of direct links in the chain of command that this would require. One of the new generation of perceptive defence commentators, Blaž Zgaga, pointed out that whereas US and European NATO chiefs of staff had three or four direct links to other parts of the defence structure, the chief of staff in Slovenia would have seven. One level down, the number of direct links increased: as against three to six in the average Western military set-up, there were twenty-one in the Slovenian army.[33] While

---

[32] Ministry of Defence of the Republic of Slovenia, 'Reorganisation of the Slovenian Armed Forces' at http://www.mo-rs.si/mors/eng/reorgan.htm, 1 February 1999.

this would ultimately be survived or amended (and was certainly not wholly inappropriate for identifying roles and tasks), it was an indication of the problems of adjustment Slovenia faced. It was also a signal that the country was moving towards modern, flexible armed forces that would allow it to play a role in the world rather than espousing isolationist, neutral territorial defence.

Eight years after independence, Slovenia's defence requirements had been transformed and its armed forces were in the process of being restructured. Discussion of the country's position and the role of its armed forces had resulted in a move away from the successful traditional model of territorial defence to strategically more useful modern, flexible forces. The central element in the decision to restructure was the sense that international cooperation and moves towards partnership with and possibly membership of NATO would only be realistic with appropriate armed forces. As will be seen in the next section, a clear understanding of this and of the required restructuring process came too late to prevent the country's being left off the NATO invitation list for new members in 1997. When the three new Central and East European members with which Slovenia had been associated – Poland, Hungary and the Czech Republic – formally joined the Alliance in April 1999 on its fiftieth birthday, Slovenia was not with them.

Jilted by NATO but keeping the faith: Slovenian security policy

In the course of the 1990s, defence and foreign policy concerns were transformed beyond recognition. The dominant discourse on security matters had moved radically from demilitarisation and more pacifist approaches, through reliance on traditional territorial means, to the commitment to shaping a small flexible modern armed force for the new century. Thinking about security matters was no longer concerned with Socialist Yugoslavia, or with independence and the actual need for physical defence focused instead on making Slovenia count in Europe and the world, and in this context the important goal was membership of NATO. However, when at its Madrid Summit NATO decided in July 1997 to invite new members to join, Slovenia was not on the

---

[33] *Delo*, 5 August 1998.

1997 to invite new members to join, Slovenia was not on the list despite the expectations of its defence minister only six months before the invitations were announced. It was merely mentioned as a potential candidate for the future. While the decision not to invite Slovenia was clearly one taken elsewhere, it was factors within Slovenia which permitted it to be taken.

After independence, Slovenia found itself in an environment largely free of threats. There was no prospect at all of armed conflict with Italy, Austria and Hungary, although political and diplomatic problems existed. While it was possible to conceive of a threat from Croatia to the south, this was far outweighed by other factors, most notably the relationship of both countries with the West. Nonetheless, there were some questions regarding Croatia with both maritime and air aspects, as well as the more easily resolved problem of border delineation.

A series of incidents in the early 1990s created tension with the southern neighbour. Overflights by Croatian military aircraft prompted an antagonistic verbal response by Janša, then defence minister; the main source of concern was surely not so much the possible threat from Croatia as the sense that its violation of Slovenian airspace demonstrated how little Slovenia could do to protect it. While defence officials at the time insisted that the hand-held air defence equipment used in the conflict with the JNA would suffice if the necessity arose,[34] this was clearly not the case. Slovenia needed need both medium-range air defence equipment and a small air force to provide limited capability for airspace control – and to assist in training for ground-based air defence forces. Although budgetary constraints made such developments difficult, changes were begun while Kacin was defence minister.

Where maritime affairs were concerned, Slovenia was in a peculiar position. With only a small stretch of coastline, it needed some form of coastal protection, but this was not initially judged to require a navy; the police could perform this function with small coastal patrol-boats. Aside from customs protection, the only question for Slovenia was that of coastal' waters – one that could not be answered with armed force. The country's 42 km. of coastline at the top of the Adriatic Sea had coastal waters that

---

[34] In discussion and interviews with James Gow.

merged with those of Italy and Croatia, but while it was a thorny issue to resolve, it was not one with the potential to generate armed conflict.

Where both airspace and maritime questions were concerned, the answer for Slovenia lay to a large extent in making provision for its security by joining organisations such as NATO and the European Union which could provide frameworks for solving those problems although, as will be seen regarding the European Union, they could themselves pose problems. By 1994 prospective membership of NATO was being discussed, both within and outside Slovenia. The impetus from outside stemmed from the assessment in some NATO countries that Slovenia would be a good candidate politically in any enlargement of the Alliance because it had no previous formal connection with Moscow and had no border with the former Soviet Union. This made it a potential candidate that could be held up to the Russian Federation to demonstrate that enlargement would not necessarily be antagonistic to Moscow, but might actually enhance stability in Europe. Slovenia was not a country that mattered militarily, but it was a politically marketable candidate.

The internal debate was different. Although it embraced the external dimensions of the country's overall security situation and foreign policy, it also involved discussion of the armed forces and the nature of Slovenia's approach to security issues. This was important because advocates of NATO membership and modernisation were dealing with constituencies which favoured neutral or non-aligned positions, involving either demilitarisation or continued reliance on territorial defence.

Interest in demilitarisation and neutrality developed in the late 1980s, alongside criticism of the JNA and rejection of compulsory military service. The concept had theoretical attractions for Slovenes worried about the JNA while they remained within Yugoslavia. As for others, such as the Central and East European countries easing their way out of the Warsaw Pact and the Soviet embrace, then for the Baltic states of Estonia, Latvia and Lithuania in trying to escape from the Soviet Union itself, non-hostile concepts were useful in facilitating a process of separation without giving offence.

Demilitarisation was an idea that needed to be explored and explained,[35] although a majority of people understood it clearly

to mean the complete absence of an army and armaments.[36] In
a time of transition, as much as 38 per cent of the population
supported demilitarisation, with just under 30 per cent favouring
the idea of a Slovenian army in 1990. However, between September
1990 and the beginning of 1991, there was already a perceptible
shift towards the idea of forming a Slovenian army.[37] With the
experience of the Ten Day War, the notion of demilitarisation
did not gain further support, but nor did it immediately disappear.
Moreover, the concept of a Slovenian military which emerged
was one based on territorial defence, with its focus on civilians
taking up arms. This was not demilitarisation, but it reflected
similar attitudes to having a modern armed force.

The idea of an armed force covered by the territorial system
was generally consistent with the mythic Slovene notion of
'defence of the hearth'.[38] However, while defence of the homeland
was clearly the paramout value for those who had served in the
'Ten Day War', the protection of human rights and global peace
also began to emerge as important values in the armed forces.[39]
This was consistent with the overall change that would occur in
security policy. The official agenda was soon characterised by a
desire to join not only the processes of political and economic
integration in Europe but also the evolving security structures
and the humanitarian and international peace support roles. Slovenia,
therefore, entered the NATO Partnership for Peace Programme.

This position did not appear without political difficulty. The
idea of defending Slovenia's newly-acquired sovereignty was one
thing, but committing sovereign power to new collective activity
was completely different – and, where the European Union was

[35] Marjan Malešič, '(De)miltarizacija in Civilna Obramba' in Anton Grizold *et
al.* (eds), *Demilitarizacija Slovenije in Nacionalna Varnost: Zbornik*, Ljubljana:
Znanstveno in Publicistično Središče, 1991, pp.64-74, offers a fine basic introduction to some of the issues.

[36] Mojca Pesec-Vengust, 'Demilitarizacija in Javno Mnenje Slovenije (Rezultati
Raziskave Nacionalna Varnost Slovenije)' in Grizold, *Demilitarizacija*, p.161.

[37] Pesec-Vengust, 'Demilitarizacija', pp.160-1.

[38] Ljubica Jelušič, *Legitimnost Sodobnega Vojaštva*, Ljubljana: Knjižna Zbirka Teorija
in Praksa, 1997, n.7, p.115 compares this with other military traditions.

[39] Ljubica Jelušič, 'Slovenska Javnost o Varnostnih Dilemah Svoje Države' in
Anton Grizold (ed), *Razpotja Nacionalne Varnosti: Obramboslovne Raziskave v
Sloveniji*, Ljubljana: Knjižna Zbirka Teorija in Praksa, 1992, p.108.

concerned, involved the transfer of some of those sovereign rights. Drnovšek and those liberals and former communist reformers who with him made up the centre ground saw no alternative to moving in this direction. Others were sceptical about the sacrifice of 'sovereignty'; these included Janša's Social Democrats, as well as the SNS and especially the SLS, who voiced the strongest opposition. All were exploiting a substantial strand of popular sentiment. Indeed, it was not until early 1997, when the critical point regarding Slovenia's prospects with NATO had been passed, that the SLS agreed to support the Drnovšek government's strategy on European economic and security integration. This was after it had joined the coalition government at the end of a political hiatus which ensured the failure of Slovenia's aspiration to be included in the NATO invitation list at that juncture.

Slovenia's courtship of NATO had begun three years earlier. In January 1994 the National Assembly made the first clear move in that direction by adopting supplementary measures on the existing General Principles of National Security. This paved the way for Ljubljana to be one of the first capitals to sign up for Partnership for Peace (PfP) on 30 March. From there, through the planning and review process, Slovenia's first Individual Partnership Programme was agreed and the following summer its armed forces took part in their first joint exercise in the United States. With Slovenia then joining the North Atlantic Cooperation Council (curiously reversing the pattern of most other countries which were members of the NACC before joining PfP), it was in a position openly to begin work on persuading the Alliance to accept it as a new member, being the first country to open an individual dialogue with it on 17 April 1996. However, in spite of being first on the harbourside at this stage, by the time decisions were being made a little over a year later, and following two more presentations, Slovenia had missed the boat.

In part, the reasons for this failure can be seen in its presentation, which stressed the character of the country rather than the ways in which it could be a strategic asset. Ljubljana was addressing the NATO enlargement list of five fundamental conditions for membership, rather than going further and selling itself as a positive asset. To meet the conditions, Slovenia pointed out that it was stable and democratic, that it had a market economy, that there were high levels of protection for human rights, that there was civilian control of defence, and that the country had no security problems with its neighbours, with whom any problems that might arise could be solved through discussion. While these were indeed fundamental requirements, they were not in themselves persuasive.

In later stages the Slovenes did introduce political arguments to support their candidature. Among these was the influence that Slovene membership would have on security in South-eastern Europe – meaning primarily the former Yugoslav lands. It would send a message to Slovenia's warring South Slav brethren (the South Slav link was not recognised explicitly). Given the major NATO presence in the region, this argument was of limited value, although it chimed with thinking in some Western countries.

There were two further political reasons, verging on the strategic. The first was that Slovenia would be the obvious bridge between Italy, an existing member of the Alliance, and Hungary, one of its prospective members, should Hungary be invited to join. While it was true that Hungary, which was invited to join, would not be contiguous with an Alliance member-state, this was not a precedent: Iceland and (until 1986, when Spain acceded) Portugal, as well as Greece and Turkey (leaving aside their antagonistic relationship with each other), were not territorially linked to other members. This in its own right was not likely to add weight to Slovenia's case. Slovenia did develop trilateral activity with Italy and Hungary in late 1996, but this did not lead to the formation of a joint brigade until early 1998, by which time it was too late to make any difference. Indeed, its formation was catalysed by the failure of Slovenia's approach to NATO. The second quasi-strategic political argument put forward had originally disposed some members of the Alliance to take a favourable view of Slovenia's membership since it could not be found objectionable and threatening by Russia. However, once the time came to make the decisions on inviting new members, this issue had lost most of its prominence (although Russian sensitivities remained) following the signing of the NATO-Russia Founding Act in May 1997.

A further political argument was that Slovenian membership would be practically cost-free for the Alliance. The basis for this was that the Slovene government had already committed funds to modernise the armed forces, and in doing so would only procure equipment that would facilitate compatibility with NATO. Slovenia could thus claim that it was spending more *per capita* on defence than any other potential candidate for NATO membership[40] (this, it has to be said, was a distortion of actual expenditure, given that Slovenia had a much smaller population than the other leading candidates). The claim that 'integration of Slovenia into NATO would involve no expenses – or only negligible ones – for NATO or its members' was questionable (as it was for the other Central and East European countries).[41] In particular, the sense that all was well did not take into account the fact that the delays in adopting and implementing a course of modernisation in the armed forces left the country with much still to do. This was an important consideration in the NATO decision to omit Slovenia from its invitation list.

Until a relatively late stage, Slovenia had clearly been on the short list. As the then foreign minister Davorin Kračun put it, the country was an ideal candidate: he expected to be 'in the first wave of enlarging NATO' because the country fulfilled 'all the conditions for membership'.[42] At the beginning of 1997, as Prime Minister Drnovšek was struggling to form a coalition (see pp. 168-71), the outgoing defence minister Kacin incautiously declared that his country would be on the list in the summer and there would be a major meeting in Ljubljana in the spring[43] – not as it happened, without reason. The meeting indeed took place on 24-27 March, when for the first time, the NATO Political Committee met outside NATO member countries. While this provided a platform for Ljubljana to demonstrate its worth at a decisive moment, the opportunity was not taken. The fears of the Slovenian representative to NATO, Mirko Cigler, that his country's candidacy was slipping away were confirmed, with representatives from NATO countries remaining unimpressed and expressing the judgement that they had heard nothing new.[44] In particular this included the speech by the foreign minister, Zoran

---

[40] Republic of Slovenia, Ministry of Foreign Affairs, 'Slovenia and NATO' at http://www.sigov.si/mzz/ang/nato.htm, 5 February 1999.

[41] *Ibid.*

[42] *The Independent*, 16 October 1996.

[43] Cited in Economist Intelligence Unit, *Country Report*, 1st Quarter 1997, p.11.

[44] Views expressed to James Gow at the meeting.

Thaler, who would be impelled to resign after the announcements at the Madrid summit.[45]

There was other reasonably strong justification for Kacin's optimistic statement. In the summer of 1996 the US Defense Secretary, William Perry, had visited Slovenia for talks with Kučan and Drnovšek, and said at the time that Slovenia was a good candidate for NATO membership and in many ways (he did not include the defence sphere) a model for other Central and East European coutries in transition.[46] This strong indication seemed to be confirmed in other ways. The US State Department, in its report on allocations for foreign policy commitments to the US Congress, placed Slovenia in the same category as the three countries which would in fact receive invitations in the summer; and the chairman of the House International Relations Committee, Benjamin A. Gilman, while proposing legislation in 1997 to assist additional countries with links to the Alliance, noted that the previous year's enlargement legislation had focused on 'the frontrunners for selection' – the three countries invited and Slovenia.[47]

Given such positive signs, it is necessary to explain why Slovenia missed out on NATO. The Slovenes tended to look outside the country for explanations, which was not unreasonable, given that it was the NATO members and not the applicants that had made the decision on which countries to invite. However, this approach does not provide a thorough understanding of the issue, and plays down Slovenia's own responsibility for its fate.

Some observers reacted to the rejection by suggesting that despite the political and diplomatic commitment by government and parliament since 1994, it was wholly unimportant – even that the moves towards NATO had been an abuse of power by the government, against the will of the people.[48] This was clearly

[45] This speech was still posted on the Slovenian Foreign Ministry web site at the beginning of 1999: http://www.sigov.si/mzz/ang/go-apag.htm.

[46] Economist Intelligence Unit, *Country Report*, 3rd Quarter 1996, p.27.

[47] Press Release News from the House International Relations Committee, 'House Adopts Gilman Bill Providing for Further NATO Expansion', 11 June 1997. We are grateful to Anton Bebler who brought the appropriations information to our attention.

[48] Rastko Močnik, *Dnevnik*, 30 May 1998, cited by Anton Bebler, 'Močnik Neresno o resni temi', *Dnevnik*, 4 July 1998.

inaccurate. However, other more reliable analysts still did not wholly explain the outcome. Their weakness was to avoid confronting Slovenia's own share of responsibility.

A few Slovenes abroad placed some responsibility on their own country, comparing the strongly mobilised support of ethnic Polish communities in the West, notably in the United States, and the lack of effective support from ethnic Slovenes. In part, this support from the Polish diaspora was obtained by diplomats working to ensure Poland's candidacy;[49] hence Slovenian diplomats were to blame for not being able to mobilise support in the same way as their Polish counterparts.

A further explanation locating what happened beyond Slovenian control focuses on the fact that is was NATO members that made the decision. In particular, the role of the United States was taken as central. According to one senior figure, a former ambassador, the outcome, whatever the explanation, was 'nothing to do with Slovenia'.[50] While there are elements of denial in this position, it also contains elements of reason.

The NATO decision only to invite three countries was largely influenced by two main factors. The first was the decision of the Administration of President Bill Clinton that three was the number of new members that it would be able to persuade the US Congress to endorse. From that point on, it was going to be difficult for other Allies hoping to admit more than three new members to persuade Washington to do so. Arguments might have been found to support adding Slovenia alone, which could just have carried the day – above all because it is clear that until a late stage the Administration was contemplating an invitation to Slovenia. However, any possibility of this happening was trounced by the second factor: the emergence of Romania as a well-supported potential candidate.

Romania had been slow to implement real reform and transition after communist rule, but following elections in the autumn of 1996 produced a strongly reformist government for the first time, a good deal of support gathered for including Romania on the invitation

[49] Anton Bebler, 'Poljska diaspora svoji domovini pomaga, Slovenska...', *Delo*, 6 June 1998.

[50] In discussion with James Gow, July 1998.

list. This was led with characterstic zeal by France, attaching itself in the name of 'Latin' solidarity. This was decidedly disadvantageous for Slovenia. There was no way that most NATO countries could contemplate inviting Romania: its reforms, while vigorous, were only recent and not yet reliable, and the Romanian military would have a long and expensive road to travel before it could meet NATO standards. It was feared that Romania's admission at that stage would be detrimental to the Alliance.

However, there were concerns among those who rejected the idea of an invitation to Romania that complete rejection would set back the prospects for reform there. Countries such as the United States and Britain did not want to send a message to Bucharest that reform would not be rewarded. Therefore, Slovenia's omission from the list became the solution to a difficult situation. There was a desire both to secure NATO enlargement – which would have been seriously damaged, if not destroyed, by including Romania on the invitation list in 1997, given existing scepticism in the US Congress – and to send Romania positive signals. It was judged that leaving such an obvious candidate as Slovenia outside the process would convey to Romania, as well as to others, the message that the process would continue and, in the language of the Madrid summit, the door would remain open.

The Madrid summit statement clearly named Slovenia and Romania as countries which would be worthy of consideration in 1999 at the Alliance's Washington summit, and both were given a sop to encourage optimism. They were put into this category because they were judged to have further to go in terms of reform. This was true for Romania in all areas, but was only true for Slovenia where defence restructuring was concerned. It was this area, which made no real difference while only four countries were seriously being considered for membership, which provided the pretext for Slovenia to be put into the second rank of candidates.

Defence restructuring was one of three areas in which Slovenia, through its own efforts, when there was still time, might have prevented this outcome – or, at least, made the dismissal of its case more difficult. The fact that in NATO terms the country had no real armed forces provided the US Administration with the excuse it needed to limit the number of candidates to three: Slovenia still had a task to be done before it would be ready.

Taking note of this, it urgently began, in 1998, its twelve-year restructuring plan.

The second way in which Slovenia might have tried to alter its destiny concerned Austria. A potentially compelling strategic reason for NATO to consider Slovenia for membership had been its own relationship with Russia, but when this effectively disappeared as a question relating to Slovenia, another political and strategic argument, this time regarding Austria, remained. As a neutral country Austria had internal political divisions to resolve over whether it should become a member of the Alliance, with which it had good relations. Officials from Austria and from NATO and its member states held out some hope that Austria might be a candidate for NATO membership if these divisions could indeed be overcome. Slovenia could have deployed the argument that its accession to the Alliance, along with that of Hungary, would create pressures for Austria's making an application and facilitate its progress. While this might not have been decisive, it was potentially a much more persuasive argument for Slovenia's membership than any put forward in its presentations to the Alliance and would have significantly strengthened the position of the country's diplomats.

The final way in which things might have been different was through political and diplomatic activity. The hiatus following the 1996 elections could not have come at a more crucial time,[51] since it left the Slovenian campaign freewheeling for over three vital months. While diplomats continued with their mission, it was without leadership and without ministers and political figures to make visits, issue public statements and provide strength and dynamism to the cause. In some ways it seemed as if the Slovenes, preoccupied with elections and forming a government, were resting on their laurels in the aftermath of the visit by US Defense Secretary William Perry in 1996 and taking too much for granted. While political and diplomatic action could not have removed the relative weakness of Slovenia's military case for accession, a much more vigorous and insistent approach might have created an atmosphere in which an invitation to Slovenia would have seemed inevitable,

---

[51] This is acknowledged in passing by Anton Bebler, 'Slovenia and the NATO Decisions in Madrid', *Le Monde Atlantique/De Atlantische Wereld*, no.65, December 1997, p.32.

whatever the condition of the armed forces and the situation elsewhere.

So in the end it was not only decisions made outside the country that affected Slovenia's application to join NATO, but internal factors. While Slovenia could not decisively influence the relationship between the US Administration and Congress, or that between Washington and its Allies, it could have made some difference and, above all, removed the obstacles in the way of its being omitted from the invitation list. The relatively slow pace at which Slovenia approached military reform and embraced the prospect of NATO membership, leaving it vulnerable over military restructuring, as well as the great lapse in government and clearly driven policy following the 1996 elections, left Ljubljana's campaign for membership unprotected when the wind suddenly changed in the six months before NATO's Madrid summit.

The blow for Slovenia was considerable, but there was the promise that some form of reconsideration would be offered in 1999 at the Washington summit. Yet by the beginning of that year it was virtually certain that there would be no immediate further enlargement given the need to accommodate the three countries that would join in the spring. However considering the claims of Austria and other Cold War neutrals, it was possible that the process might continue in a way which would see Slovenia invited between 2002 and 2005. For the time being its desire to count in Europe and the world would have to focus on other areas. Here too the final decisions would be made elsewhere, but would depend on Slovenia's house being in appropriate order.

EU courtship: the culmination of 'Europe now' – Europe soon?

The disappointment over NATO in the summer of 1997 was compensated by inclusion, at almost the same time, on the list of countries invited to open accession talks with the European Union. For Slovenia, with its effective but small economy in need of a wider market and already trading significantly with EU countries, this was of greater importance. Yet the path to an invitation had not been straightforward, despite Slovenia's apparent credentials. As will be seen, this involved both problems raised by Italy and attitudes within Slovenia. Indeed the difficulties with

Italy were a significant test for Slovenes of their preparedness to meet the European integration they desired.

From early in the 1990s (and leaving aside the dissolution of the Socialist Federal Republic of Yugoslavia), Slovenia and the European Union were important to each other. The general importance of the EU to Slovenia was self-evident. Slovenia's move towards declaring independence in the late 1980s and early 1990s was largely motivated by the desire to join the processes of integration in Europe (even if that process was sometimes oversimplified). Less obvious was the importance of Slovenia to the EU: Slovenia had clearly emerged as the only one among the countries of Central and Eastern Europe which was already well on the way to being fit for full membership, and if the EU was going to begin to integrate those countries, Slovenia was likely to provide the best early opportunity to show real commitment with the guarantee of successful integration.

Relations with the EU improved in 1993 with the ratification in parliament of a Trade and Cooperation Agreement and, more critically, the opening of discussions on an association agreement, along the lines of those made between the EU and the Višegrad countries. Attitudes to the EU's Commissioner for External Relations, Hans van den Broek, were noticeably more cordial following his initial visit to Ljubljana to discuss the matter in the autumn of 1993 than they had been beforehand in the press and generally.[52] Slovenia's leaping into the front rank of EU candidates was appropriate given the structure of its external trade and its political character.[53]

---

[52] This was because as chair of the European Foreign Affairs Council van den Broek had led the (then) European Community's diplomatic involvement in the Yugoslav break-up.

[53] The PHARE 'Slovenia Indicative Programme 1994-95' agreed between the European Commission and Slovenia (essentially, the EC's view of the country) noted that it 'compared favourably to most other economies of Central and Eastern Europe' and that in terms of 'democratic institutions and the transformations [sic] of its economy' Slovenia had 'achieved considerable success'. (PHARE is the name given to the European Union technical assistance programme for former Communist countries of Central and Eastern Europe; originally specifically for Poland and Hungary in 1989 – the acronym stands for Poland and Hungary Assistance in Restructuring Economies – it was quickly extended to all states in the region.)

From the Slovenian point of view, however, it was significant that comparisons were being made with the Višegrad countries rather than with the former Yugoslav ones. For Slovenia there was now the prospect of a free-trade arrangement with the four – Poland, Hungary, the Czech Republic and Slovakia – extending beyond the trade liberalisation agreements already signed with the latter two.

Coming from behind, Slovenia had overtaken the other Central and East European countries in the eyes of the European Commissioners as the outstanding candidate for accession in the next round of EU enlargement. It was now seen to be in a 'fast lane' along with the Czech Republic – behind the Czechs on privatisation at this stage but ahead by most other criteria. This analysis reflected the country's relative economic health and political stability. The coalition government of Janez Drnovšek faced challenges from some of its members, but this was a minor crisis, with Drnovšek appearing as a confident figure whose course would not be significantly deflected and who still had cards to play in the event of a downturn.

Despite the relatively positive prognosis in the early 1990s, a shadow hung over Slovenia's future: its relationship with Italy. This was probably the single factor that could have destabilised the country internally and thwarted its European ambitions. The problem concerned the area which straddled the border between the two countries and property questions arising from the end of the Second World War. The cross-border area is ethnically mixed on both sides and was the subject of dispute at the end of the war. It became particularly sensitive in the 1990s because of the acts of forcible expulsion, migration and expropriation of property that occurred in the 1940s. The Italian government raised the property issue in negotiations between the EU and Slovenia for an association agreement. Thus, while on its merit Slovenia was regarded as ahead of the Central and East European field, it continued to fall behind in formal terms because of the failure to conclude an association agreement.

As a member of both NATO and the EU, Italy was suspected in Ljubljana of blocking Slovenian moves towards closer relationships with both bodies (although in the end it was actually to be a principal advocate) as a means of inducing Slovenia to revise the Osimo Treaty. This had been signed between Italy and Yugoslavia in the light of the Helsinki Final Act in 1975, and both served to confirm agreement on post-1945 borders. The suggestion was that the Osimo Treaty might be revised, given that it was made between Italy and Yugoslavia and Slovenia had now gained independence, thus changing the situation. In that treaty property questions, including compensation, were considered to have been settled.

From the Slovenian side, therefore, there was no question of tampering with the treaty. Italy's position was taken as aggressive, although the revisions sought did not concern the border but restitution of property to pre-1945 Italian owners who had emigrated from Yugoslavia. Payment of compensation was the most that Slovenia regarded as appropriate for discussion. Italy also showed an interest in the minority Italian population living in the coastal region (and, more especially further down the Istrian coast in Croatia). For its part Slovenia raised the question of the status of the Slovenes in Italy who, following recent changes in Italian electoral law, effectively lost representation in local and national assemblies. Slovenia sought ethnic–regional arrangements equivalent to those afforded to the Austro-Germanic population in the Alto Adige (Südtirol).

There were also tensions over the Italian government's introduction in June 1994 of tougher police and military border controls, supposedly in order to clamp down on arms smuggling and the transit of political terrorists. However, any awkwardness in the Italian–Slovenian relationship remained relatively minor and was assuaged both by the establishment of joint working groups on the Osimo Treaty questions and by a visit to Slovenia in August by the then Italian Foreign Minister, Beniamo Andreotta. At that stage Andreotta gave a strong assurance that Italy would support and promote its neighbour's access to Western organisations.

The issue at stake was commonly reported as Italy's 'blocking' Slovenia's association agreement. More accurately it was a matter of Italy setting a peculiar condition for association: harmonisation of property rights with EU countries. This would enable Italians to purchase property in Slovenia – satisfying the desire of Italians who, for any one of a variety of reasons, left Slovenia at the time of the communist takeover to regain their old family homes, or at least to have the right to buy property.

At first the question of alignment of property rights was seen as an infringement of the Osimo Treaty. However, it quickly became clear that this was a question that Slovenia would have to deal with at some stage anyway, since Italy's condition for association would one day be a condition for becoming a full member of the EU. The sensitivity of the topic, however, meant that a popular opposition figure, such as the former defence minister Janez Janša, could seek to make a nationalist cause out of it, permitting a significant challenge either to the Drnovšek government or, in a presidential election, to President Milan Kučan. Leaving aside the impact on the government itself, this would have a knock-on effect into the economic sphere. The Slovene authorities worked to minimise the inevitable internal impact of the dispute with Italy.

For the EU the problems between Italy and Slovenia were akin to those between Greece and Macedonia, albeit of less prominence and conducted in a more moderate tone. However, it was a challenge to the EU's common foreign and security policy (CFSP), and to its enlargement policy. It was important for the other members of the EU to encourage Italy to be constructive in finding a way around the problem, as well as for them to find ways to enable Slovenia to come to terms with Italy in particular and the Union as a whole. If Slovenia was a star candidate for a phase of enlargement into Central and Eastern Europe, then it was essential for pragmatic reasons that the difficulties over the association agreement should be overcome. The pragmatic dimension was also related to a more spiritual one: if the EU was unable to find a relatively easy way to integrate a country like Slovenia, it would miss an opportunity to restore some of the faith and confidence lost in the bruising involvement in former Yugoslavia, as well as suffering a further loss of image and political energy.

Having dealt with the matter quietly at first Slovenia began to fight back a little. It raised questions about the rights of Slovenes on the Italian side of the border. It was possible that, guided by other members of the EU concerned for the Union's future health, the two countries might be able to reach some kind of agreement giving Slovenia concessions over the rights of Slovenes in Italy, if not corresponding rights for its citizens concerning property in Italy. Agreement on matters of this kind was feasible and likely to enable the Ljubljana government to defuse any dangerous political challenges more easily. However, all developments depended primarily on bilateral negotiations between the countries.

For Slovenia the important thing was to strike a deal with the EU as a whole. This would involve its a notional reinterpretation of the Italian condition for its membership. As the harmonisation of property rights was usually only a condition of full membership, Slovenia could begin to emphasise that which was positive in the situation. Ljubljana could begin to see the property rights' question not as an act of Italian hostility, but as a mark of Slovenia's advanced position as a candidate for full membership: already, in the association agreement, it was dealing with matters usually reserved for accession. Adopting this approach would make possible the immediate opening of negotiations for full membership.

While the negative aspects connected to Slovenia's EU association agreement could be detrimental to both Slovenia and the Union, there were alternatives. Both Slovenia and the EU could emphasise the positive, and with that spirit prevailing, as well as recognition of necessity all round, they were able to reach an association agreement which was initialled in June 1995. This followed Italy's dropping of its veto on such an agreement in March after the Slovenian authorities, taking the positive approach, agreed to make the necessary changes to the constitution and laws regarding the rights of foreign nationals to purchase property – the key demand Italy had been making.

However, this was not the end of the painful story. The association agreement was due to be signed in September 1995, but this did not happen till 1997, when the ratification process began. This was because both Italy and Slovenia continued to have differences over implementation of the agreement: Italy would not sign without guarantees from Slovenia that it would act quickly on the property rights issue. Progress only came after the EU took measures to move the process along.

In December 1995, under the presidency of Spain, the EU had taken two initiatives. The first was to seek a compromise arrangement in which Italian citizens who had lived in Slovenia for three years would be entitled to purchase property as soon as the association agreement was ratified. Other EU citizens would be able to do so three years after ratification. The Slovenian government accepted this proposal, but it still had to be argued internally since it represented a significant climb-down from the

Drnovšek government's previous position that it would only change the country's constitution four years after signing the agreement.

The second initiative was effectively to bully Slovenia into accepting either Italian terms or a compromise proposed by Spain. In a move which shook the Slovenian government, the EU decided to cease negotiations on removing the outstanding problems regarding signature of the agreement. This effectively meant that to get the agreement signed Slovenia would have to begin work on changing its constitution and property laws without delay. As a result Slovenia accepted the EU terms, in an atmosphere made easier by the election of Romano Prodi as Italian prime minister in May, and Rome withdrew its objection to Slovenia's association agreement on 28 May 1996, leading to its signing thirteen days later. Thereafter the priority was to secure the passage of sensitive legislation and constitutional change. This meant amending the 1991 Constitution, under the terms of which, according to Article 68, 'Foreigners may only acquire title to property fixed to lands under such conditions as are determined by statute. Foreigners may not acquire title to land, other than by inheritance, except in circumstances where reciprocity of such rights of acquisition are recognised.' This was done in July 1997.

Because Slovenia's association agreement with the EU was conditional upon its accepting an obligation to change the prohibition on non-Slovenes purchasing property, appropriate changes were made. However, in spite of this the prohibition remained: no non-Slovene other than those excepted under Article 68 of the Constitution had the right to purchase property or land in Slovenia, then or until at least three years afterwards. The constitutional change was dependent on the association agreement entering into effect, and this would only happen when Slovenia and each of the fifteen EU members ratified the agreement. Slovenia did this in July 1997 as well.

Thus everything that had been delayed for years was accomplished on 14 July, when the National Assembly changed the relevant provisions of the constitution, and on the following day when it ratified the association agreement. This paved the way for the most historic step of the three: the announcement by the European Commission of its list of proposed candidates for future accession, in which Slovenia's name was included.[54] Last-minute legislation had paved the way for Slovenia to make an immediate transition from being a country unable to complete an association agreement with the EU to one moving towards full membership. With these proposals agreed by the European Council on 13 December, discussions on accession opened in March 1998 on the basis of the Slovenian government's 'Strategy of the Republic of Slovenia for Accession to the EU'.[55] This offered the prospect of accession around the year 2002.

Thus the setbacks over NATO in the summer of 1997 were offset by success with the EU. This success was not without pain. The difficulties over Italy were a foretaste of what membership of the EU would mean in many ways. Primarily it implied the opening of Slovenia economically and politically. While the problem over Italy was particular, it would acquire the nature of a general problem with Slovenia's accession to the EU.

Having begun the 1990s as part of the disintegrating Yugoslav federation, by the end of the decade Slovenia was well on the road to integrating into Europe. As a country already trading heavily with EU members, accession offered major opportunities, but it also held challenges. Its security environment had been utterly transformed. From the management and manipulation of a territorial defence force intended to support the army against which it was eventually deployed, Slovenia's defence capability was being re-shaped to meet the needs of modern, flexible, cooperative international missions. Transformation in status and security needs only came late in the decade after the failure in 1997, despite seemingly favourable circumstances, to be invited to open talks on joining NATO. While the NATO door was left open (rather, it was promised that it would be opened again some time), the rejection was a jolt to the Slovenes. Although there

---

[54] The European Commission's report on Slovenia contained some reservations about the operation of the judicial system, corruption and the return of property confiscated under communism, as well as the state administration's ability to implement the *acquis communautaire* effectively. However, it found that Slovenia generally met the requirements and, despite the reservations over the *acquis*, already satisfied many of the obligations concerning the internal market. See Economist Intelligence Unit, *Country Profile 1997-98*, p.11.

[55] *Strategija Republike Slovenije za Vključevanje v EU* at http://evropa.gov.si/iso/euf_02.html, October 1998.

was consolation in blaming the outcome on outside factors, the reality was that Slovenia had not put itself in as favourable a position as it could have. The key was not to repeat the same mistake.

Slovenia came dangerously close to suffering the same fate with the EU. After years of indulging in what was, in reality, the politics of pride, it found that combatting Italian demands regarding property rights was less important for the future of the country than securing its accession to the EU as early as possible. Perilous measures had to be taken to ensure Slovenia's place within the EU. This required bullying by the EU first and then a last-minute dash to accomplish legislation only one day before recommendations were to be announced in July 1997.

There was a clear need to ensure that no similar problems emerged as Slovenia developed its relationship with the EU towards full membership. The problem was that sometimes parochial and backward-looking concerns for homeland and old ideas of sovereignty, which obstructed the country's dealings with both NATO and the EU in different ways, had to be overcome. Political stagnation, introspective personalities and old issues, and possessiveness for its own sake would have to be avoided if Slovenia were to pursue a successful security agenda and reap the domestic benefits of involvement in European processes. Internal prosperity and external security both depended on the ability to meet the challenges of internationalisation.

7

CONCLUSION

Slovenia's independence for the first time created a state solely in the name of the Slovenes and placed them in charge of their own fate. After centuries of incorporation in empires, Yugoslavia in the twentieth century provided the opportunity for self-determination. Through those centuries and the experience of two versions of Yugoslavia, the fate of the Slovenes was tied to others. The second Yugoslavia served as an incubator for the emergence of a fully-fledged Slovenian state in 1991 after the collapse of communism.

A decade after independence, having negotiated the sometimes perilous currents that flowed in its wake, Slovenes were required to face the consequences of independence and the long-term challenges that came with it. Whereas in the past cultural preservation and explanations of what made them unhappy could always be found by reference to others in empires or collective states, they would now have to look inwards for answers and, in doing so, find appropriate ways to harmonise with the outside world. It is these two themes that this final chapter explores.

No one left to blame

One of the comforts that Slovenes could find throughout the ages was that, as part of a larger entity, they did not need to be responsible for their own destiny to more than a limited extent. As one small people in one small part of a larger political community, they could get on with life in their own way, and matters other than small local ones were always the charge of someone else, somewhere else. If things went wrong, or if the Slovenes found their self-regarding focus interrupted, then the fault would lie elsewhere. One of the major differences encountered by an independent Slovenia was the need not only to take charge of its own destiny but also to accept responsibility for it.

Slovenia's independence, coming when it did, was largely based on a rejection of socialist and federal Yugoslavia. Yugoslavia was to blame in many ways: at the end it was a constitutional and political construct that no longer worked, a federation in which Serbia attempted to bully and dominate, and in which the Serbo-Croatian-speaking majority sought to squeeze out the use of Slovene (along with other languages) in official life. It was also a federation in which the poorer southern regions were a drain on Slovene wealth and prospects.

As various stages in the past, the thrust of Germanisation, the looming threat of Italian occupation or Napoleonic liberation were all matters which exceeded the Slovene grasp politically – even if culturally there were defensive responses. At no stage was there a situation in which the Slovenes could shape their own future in their own interests. In these historic situations they were never in a position where they had to look to themselves for explanation. This left them with a tendency to be self-regarding and narcissistic (though not arrogant) rather than self-critical and measured.

The test that Slovenia faced and its customary response to problems were both to be seen in the first decade of independence. Where the country's progress was less than expected or desired in a particular area, the reason for this might be found, according to popular opinion, in the fact that it had not yet managed to distance itself sufficiently from the Yugoslav farrago, or that the world simply did not understand, or that Slovenia was too small to count, or that difficult neighbours, especially Italy, were placing pressures on the young country. While, on one level, this type of answer had some justification, it always omitted that crucial dimension: the degree to which Slovenia and the Slovenes were responsible themselves.

This was also the case with EU and, especially, NATO membership. The Slovenes managed to be carried along by EU moves towards enlargement, having taken responsibility for their own future and accepted late in the day that their greater interest lay in following determinedly the route to EU accession. The answer lay not with Italy or the EU, nor in Slovenia arguing that the question they were posing over property rights in the association agreement was unfair or mistaken. In the end it was a matter of internally weighing the benefits of prospective EU membership against those of ethnic and political pride in clinging to a nationalistic interpretation of land and sovereignty that would no longer have a place if the country were to accede to the EU.

In contrast, the assertion that, whatever the explanation for Slovenia's absence from the list of invitees to join NATO, 'it was not because of Slovenia' was wholly in accordance with the traditional pattern. While it was evident that it was a NATO decision not to invite Slovenia, as well as there being factors involving the United States and the Alliance as a whole which shaped that decision, there was also a need to assess what could have been done differently by Slovenia itself.

An explanation of the failure regarding NATO which focuses on Slovenia would include the slow pace at which the country had embarked on appropriate military restructuring because of attachment to traditional homeland notions. It would also have to take into account the deadening impact on the political and diplomatic front of governmental impotence and inertia after the 1996 elections – itself induced by the political system. This had meant that a new government could not be formed for over three months at the vital moment when the external tide turned against Slovenia. Lastly, there was a failure to deploy suitable strategic arguments to persuade the Alliance of Slovenia's virtues.

The outcome over NATO and the experience of dealing with entry to the EU both brought shocks to Slovenia. While these were survivable, given that Slovenia was flagged as a potential future candidate for NATO membership and made the EU list, they were also indicative of the relative complacency that characterised Slovenia's approach. Content with themselves, basking in international praise for their transition in general, and only unhappy with the temporary difficulties inflicted by outsiders and external circumstances, Slovenes might understandably think that NATO and EU membership were all but foregone conclusions. Chastened by the experience, they would have to confront themselves.

In many ways Slovenia's independence was a prize, but in others it was a trial. The new state was in a rather similar situation to spoiled individuals who had grown up in wealthy circumstances and large houses with everything done for them, who because of this had always enjoyed opportunities through life and who had married in a way that satisfied all their cares: However, when after divorce these individuals were faced with the need to adjust to living in their own small house without the services and companionship they had known, they were lost and in need of some serious lessons about life. So too Slovenia, despite the appearance of adulthood, had to begin learning the truth about itself and how to find its way in life. The country had arrived at a point where there was no one left to blame for things apart from itself.

The challenge of internationalisation

The need to look inside rather than outside itself for answers is critical to the way Slovenia will deal with the challenge of internationalisation which it inevitably has to face. As a small advanced economy, it needs trade to prosper and so cannot afford to be isolated. The arrangements that go with such trade inevitably require openness both economically and politically to external influences. This is a major problem for a country and people who have been historically concerned with parochial insulation against such influences in broader political communities. Having gained the exercise of sovereign rights, Slovenia and the Slovenes must learn how to reinterpret and redistribute those rights if they are to prosper.

Despite the political and diplomatic difficulties faced in its dealings with NATO and the EU, Slovenia showed that there were areas in which it could take its place in the world with relative comfort. One of these was the United Nations where, having become a member on 22 May 1992, it was elected as a non-permanent member of the Security Council, on 14 October 1997, and in August 1998 took the presidency of that body. Slovenia used its position in the UN to stress its commitment to international peace and security.

Slovenia's role at the UN, aside from statements and initiatives by its permanent representative, had developed through contributions to various UN peace missions around the world, albeit in the modest way a small country could afford. By the end of 1998 there were two Slovenes serving with the long-standing UNTSO operation in the Middle East, while a platoon was committed to another of its oldest operations, UNFICYP, in Cyprus, as part of a multi-national battalion in which Austrians and Hungarians also served. This platoon included members of the 10th Battalion of the Slovenian Army, the vanguard unit for modernisation and international co-operation. Finally, despite its recent historical association with Bosnia and Hercegovina and the other former Yugoslav lands, Slovenia contributed with transport and medical support to the UN-authorised NATO-led SFOR operation.[1]

Slovenia was elected to the presidency of the Security Council at what might have been expected to be a relatively quiet moment. However, the Slovenian presidency was immediately involved in major international crises, including the Democratic Republic of the Congo (formerly Zaïre), Iraq and Kosovo. The last of these showed the awkwardness of Slovenia's international commitment: in an interview with the *International Herald Tribune* to mark his country's taking the presidency,[2] Prime Minister Janez Drnovšek rejected the idea of its playing a particular role over Kosovo, which had been a factor in Slovene politics before independence. This province in southern Serbia with an overwhelmingly ethnic-Albanian population became engulfed by armed conflict in 1998. Drnovšek said that Slovenia might be well placed to advise others, but had to play a cautious role because of recent history. Although there was wisdom in this comment, it also showed that, however far Slovenia had advanced beyond the old Yugoslavia, it could not leave it behind entirely even when playing a full international role. Communist Yugoslavia had given the Slovenes the legal and institutional apparatus of full statehood, but had insulated that state within the bounds of the federation – only they were subject to the pressures of dealing with other South Slavs rather than those of living in international society. These pressures alone posed questions for Slovenia and the Slovenes, questions that, despite their progress following independence, could not be left behind completely. But, there were other, greater challenges.

At the threshhold of the twenty-first century no state, let alone a small fledgling one, could be an island. The meaning of sovereignty in international life was different from that in communist Yugoslavia

---

[1] Slovenia's contribution was three helicopters and one transport aeroplane, as well as offering the use of military medical facilities and the airbase at Cerklje.

[2] *International Herald Tribune*, 5 August 1998.

and different again from simplistic nineteenth-century Germanic notions of ethnically-defined sovereignty. Sovereignty was something that might be respected by other states, but a small state could not actually defend it in terms either of territory or of exercising sovereign rights.[3]

Integration into European and international life poses dilemmas for Slovenia and the Slovenes because in international terms sovereignty implies a process of opening up, whereas internal sovereignty has largely been built through language and culture, the hallmarks of national particularity.[4] General integration into the European and international processes – politics, economics, communications – has language needs and concomitant value demands that run counter to the preservation of much that is traditionally Slovene. In particular, much in Slovene culture is antithetical to the 'Americanisation' that accompanies international integration.

Slovenes, as consumers and as a cultural community, are schizophrenic. On the one hand, many embrace new goods and attitudes, but on the other there is considerable loyalty to known 'national' products and values, curiously limiting the ability of international goods, from food and drink to manufactures, to penetrate Slovenia as comprehensively as they do in other transition countries. Similarly, while the wealth and opportunity exist for many Slovenes to travel the world, there is an old-fashioned predilection to take vacations on 'our coast' (by which is curiously meant the Croatian islands and the Istrian and Dalmatian coastline – one of the few immovable legacies of the Yugoslav period).

Not only this, but the newness of full statehood has in some ways enhanced attachment to old values. There is an unavoidable absence of state and democratic traditions which might have enabled the new state to feel comfortable with the changes it faced, but instead coping with the realities of being a real state in the 1990s

---

[3] This point is made in a commanding discussion by Peter Kovočič Peršin of Slovenia's burden following independence and the challenges it faced (although the discussion at times seems clouded with anti-Americanism and the perspective is one that a 'modern' Slovene nationalist might find sympathetic). The present analysis concurs in many respects with Peršin's, demonstrating the continuing relevance of an analysis written in the early years of independence. Peter Kovočič Peršin, *Zaveza Slovenstvu*, Ljubljana: Znanstveno in Publicistično Središče, 1993, n.25, p.65.

[4] See Kovočič Peršin, *Zaveza*, p.65.

was a complicated matter. Those realities make the preservation of cultural and social peculiarities increasingly hard. The Slovenes are thus caught between tradition and contemporary existence.

On the other side of this equation, the problem for Slovenia is not only the impact of transnational processes upon it, but also its impact on processes of integration. For example, it is not inconceivable that it will be embraced by the EU but then find itself causing trouble and disruption as it seeks to protect its sovereignty and its cultural specificity in face of the *acquis communautaire*, or future, fresh directives from the European Commission. If Slovenes resented impositions from the Yugoslav federation and others, it is not imposible that they will feel and respond in the same way in an integrated Europe.

Likewise, the reality of the country's size and the concerns of Slovenes about their preservation as a nation are an issue. If the tenets of communism regarding the status and preservation of peoples and ethnic communities in Yugoslavia could not satisfy the Slovenes, then they were unlikely to find their experience in the wider world more reassuring. Both ideologically and practically, communist Yugoslavia·was a greenhouse for Slovenia and the Slovenes. Inside an integrating Europe they will have to battle far harder than they did in Yugoslavia to ensure 'national survival' in traditional terms.[5]

Yet this battle could not be one for preservation of the political and cultural achievements of 'emancipation' as such. Nor could it seek protectionist national control of industries in the way that even some of those who have been most perceptive in appreciating the need for accommodation with the modern world have advocated.[6] While Slovenia will survive in the wider world, whatever happens, this can only be through adaptation, not conservation. Yet conservation often seems to preoccupy Slovenes. If there is no adjustment and accomodation the Slovenes will in many senses have no future.[7]

In some ways a Slovenia approaching integration in a modern and flexible way might offer something to its people as an ethnic community beyond the trappings and symbolism of being allowed

---

[5] Kovočič Peršin, *Zaveza*, p.83.

[6] These included Kovočič Peršin in *Zaveza*, pp.107-9.

[7] Kovočič Peršin, *Zaveza*, p.79.

to run their own affairs and use the primary international currency that is sovereignty. By joining a European Union in which much is made of regional development at the same time as development of the Union as a whole and its member states, Slovenia could serve as a catalyst over time for the regional association of ethnic Slovenes residing in existing EU countries, Italy and Austria, while at the same time embracing a concept of cross-border regionalism which would permit other communities in those areas to flourish. If it took such an approach, Ljubljana would be linked again in some way with Klagenfurt and Trieste, the other two feet of the tripod upon which Slovene culture developed before separation from them created the conditions in which the Slovenian state was eventually formed.

Slovenia looks set to meet the challenges of integration in European and international life at the start of the twenty-first century, but it may not do so without some difficulties as traditional and modern international cultures meet. Some kind of compromise will have to be found that allows for cultural peculiarity yet incorporates the country's need for prosperity and a secure existence. Union with Europe might even add to the avenues for cultural development. For Slovenia this perhaps offers the best route to the necessary fusion of openness and being culturally immured. The only way to preserve culture is to open it and permit adaptation. There is every sign that this will be accomplished successfully. The record of the 1980s and '90s is clear. Despite both the presence of history in political debates and the attachment to tradition, Slovenia has consistently transcended the politics of the past through self-restraint.

When Slovenia acquired an independent international personality, the idea that the new state was in some sense the embodiment of *Slovenstvo* was undeniable. The dream of nationalists since the beginning of the nineteenth century had been achieved. However, it was also a modern phenomenon. Statehood had come not only as the result of the dreams and campaigns of nationalists but also as a function of democratisation, economic liberalisation and the promotion of individual human rights. While these two phenomena were not mutually exclusive, there was a clear tension between them.

The Slovenian state gained independence in perhaps the most propitious circumstances possible, with relatively little conflict and pain. It did so on the basis of a strong degree of internal consensus and with both political stability and an advanced economy with potential for development. While there were inevitable problems of adjustment, these were mostly minor compared to those of the other communist states undergoing transition or becoming independent for the first time – to say nothing of the countries that gained independence from colonial rulers since 1945.

Yet the new state also has the problem of reconciling its modern outlook and direction with its role as the embodiment of all that is peculiarly Slovene. To continue positive development and make the most of the favourable circumstances in which it finds itself, Slovenia needs to find ways to reconcile actual and latent tensions between the old and the new. This will mean finding an equilibrium between the Slovenes' need both to preserve traditional values and to live a prosperous and comfortable life in the contemporary world. In a sense this is also a need to balance the possibly divergent desires of the Slovenes, and differences between the Slovenes as an ethnic community that has preserved its characteristics and Slovenia the country.

Ten years on from independence, Slovenia has extricated itself from the Yugoslav morass and moved on to the edge of European integration, a point at which it must accept and deal with the challenges independence has brought for the country's future. Cultural conservation can no longer outweigh other factors in Slovene consciousness. Nor can others be blamed, as in the past, for Slovenia's misfortunes and failings. There is no longer an empire, a kingdom or a communist federation to which responsibility can be shifted. The Slovenes will have to turn inwards for ways to reconcile their dilemmas and create an equilibrium with the wider world.

The indications at the time of writing are that this will be done. Both on the path to EU membership and in preparation for a later stage in the process of NATO enlargement, they have looked at themselves and begun to produce answers from within. Qualities that are peculiary Slovene are capable of embracing change. The challenge is to make cosmopolitan openness a part of *Slovenstvo* and so preserve it.

INDEX

Index